THE COLD WARRIORS

THE COLD WARRIORS
A POLICY-MAKING ELITE

JOHN C. DONOVAN

Bowdoin College

D. C. HEATH AND COMPANY

Lexington, Massachusetts   Toronto   London

When he shall die,
Take him and cut him out in little stars,
And he will make the face of heaven so fine
That all the world will be in love with night
And pay no worship to the garish sun.

William Shakespeare

CONTENTS

ACKNOWLEDGEMENTS

My sincere thanks go to the following friends and colleagues for reading substantial portions of the manuscript and for letting me have the benefit of their thinking: Judge Frank M. Coffin, Preston Abbott, Kenneth M. Dolbeare, Elizabeth Donahue, Douglas M. Fox, Everett C. Ladd, Jr., Daniel Levine, Richard E. Morgan, and John Romanyshyn.

The impact of their individual and collective criticism has saved me from countless errors and—more than most of them will suspect—has affected the interpretation.

Timothy Parsons and Edwin Lee, in the midst of their busy undergraduate careers, eased the task of writing by locating many of the materials drawn upon in this study. Carey Donovan, assisted by Christine Donovan, helped enormously in putting the notes in good order. An unusual measure of deep gratitude goes to Mrs. Gladys McKnight who typed, retyped, and then added words of encouragement at every stage in the long process of preparing the manuscript. The fact that she has worked closely with me now on three books in recent years indicates how indispensable she has been to the effort.

Finally, my love and special thanks to Beatrice and the kids for their patience in the face of this continuous process so much of which takes place in the midst of family life.

J.C.D.

. . . a political science which is faithful to its moral commitment of telling the truth about the political world cannot help telling society things it does not want to hear. The truth of political science is the truth about power, its manifestations, its configurations, its limitations, its implications, its laws. Yet one of the main purposes of society is to conceal these truths from its members. That concealment, that elaborate and subtle and purposeful misunderstanding of the nature of political man and of political society, is one of the cornerstones upon which all societies are founded.

Hans J. Morgenthau

INTRODUCTION

It may be helpful if this current study is located in the body of my own work. My original interest in national security policy is shown in a study completed in 1949, based upon a detailed examination of the role Congress played in writing the neutrality laws of the 1930s.[1] There one sees a Chief Executive and Congress engaged in a long and frequently bitter struggle over the nature of United States responsibility in world affairs. American isolationism in the 1930s was, of course, largely a reaction to Wilsonian idealism, a reflection of certain stereotyped notions about why we went to war in 1917: the "dupes" of "wily European power politicians," and so forth. The neutrality laws were shaped by men who were determined to keep this country out of another *European* war. The isolationism of the 1930s was not directed against Asia. Indeed, one important group of Congressional isolationists, led by Hiram Johnson, was, as one might say today, rather "hawkish" where our Far Eastern interests were concerned.

This is perhaps the point to note that typical American attitudes relating to the Far East have historically differed from our common attitudes toward Europe. Columbus discovered America while seeking a new route to Asia. Generations of immigrants migrated to these shores with their backs deliberately set to Europe, from which they were escaping. The Pacific Ocean early became an American sea. It was an admiral of the United States Navy who opened Japan to the Western world. In the nineteenth century we acquired the Hawaiian Islands, the Philippines, and Alaska, whose outermost Aleutian Islands almost touch the Siberian land mass. On the coast of Maine, where I live, one knows old Yankee families in which a few individuals survive today who were born on ships sailing the China seas. We were never "isolated" from the Far East, but have been strangely attracted toward its mysteries for generations. Americans have been sailing the Pacific Ocean, asserting American power, influence, and ideas in Asia for two centuries.

This Asian interest is often slighted in studies of American foreign policy with all its contemporary, Western, industrial, and "democratic" tendencies. What has not been forgotten—indeed we may have learned the lesson too well—is our experience with aggression in the 1930s and with the failure of collective security mechanisms. Besides my living through the period, my study of Congressional isolationism has provided me with an appreciation of the policy climate of the 1930s. This is vital in understanding the mentality of influential American policymakers during the Cold War period, and their easy vulnerability to the "Munich syndrome." The official views of Dean Rusk, for example, first as an Assistant Secretary in the Truman years and then as Secretary of State throughout the Kennedy-Johnson era, show how deeply he was influenced by a psychological imperative to view the events in Southeast Asia these past twenty years as being analogous to the situation during the age of Hitler's aggression in Europe a generation earlier.

American Cold War attitudes become clearer when they are seen in contrast to the dominant isolationist mood of the 1930s. In the face of Stalinist "expansion" (as they regarded it), men like Rusk and Acheson were determined *not* to repeat the mistakes that had been made in the common Western failure of not resisting the Nazi aggressions. Collective security arrangements would work this time, if for no other reason than the official American determination to make them work *unilaterally,* as it were. The United States was the active, "responsible" leader of the anti-aggressive (the so-called "free world") forces. The United States would lead the way in military preparedness, especially in nuclear weapons, and, hence, would deter aggression. This is the *Munich syndrome.*

My next effort in policy analysis came years later (in 1967) following a decade of active involvement in politics and government that included a stint as state chairman of a political party, as campaign manager to Edmund S. Muskie in his first Senatorial campaign, as his administrative assistant in the Senate, as an unsuccessful Congressional candidate, as executive assistant to Secretary of Labor W. Willard Wirtz, and finally, for a year, as the administrator of a large federal domestic program, the manpower training program. My book *The Politics of Poverty,* drawing in part on this background of experience, examined the forces that produced the Economic Opportunity Act of 1964, center-piece of the controversial Johnson war on poverty; the study placed these forces in the context of Presidential-Congressional-bureaucratic policy-making. In the course of my research, I became very much interested in the role that bureaucratic tech-nicians play in shaping public policy, a subject neglected in the literature of political science. Their policy-influencing role, even in the field of social reform, appears to be an important one.[2]

This book was followed three years later (1970) by *The Policy Makers*,[3] which views the policy-making process more broadly and over a longer period of time. Based on an analysis of the war against poverty and the Americanization of the war in Vietnam, this study attempts to get "inside" the policy-making process, as, for example, within the agencies of the institutionalized Presi-dency and the Congressional power structure. Although the pic-ture one gains is of a process in which policy changes occur incrementally, the substantive results indicate the disproportion-ate influence exerted by men who are located at certain strategic positions in the process. At this point, I found myself as a political scientist confronting the most persistent policy bias I have en-countered in all my work these past twenty-five years: the anti-Soviet containment dogma that has been such an integral feature of the whole Cold War era. I learned that George Kennan, whom I had regarded as a principal architect of containment, had actu-ally entertained serious doubts about the doctrine from the very beginning. Kennan seems sincerely mystified by the manner in which his famous Mr. X article enunciated a doctrine that soon became installed as national dogma. Containment, as Kennan views it, was a technical concept aimed at restraining the ex-pansion of Soviet power in Europe; it was never intended for application in Asia, nor was it intended as a military doctrine. Yet the doctrine-turned-dogma persisted at least through the admin-istration of Lyndon Johnson and was applied with great military force in Asia, as we all know, with tragic results. Kennan has since explained how his opposition to *military* containment led to his exclusion from Dean Acheson's inner circle.

Although my earlier studies and my own experience had made me familiar with many of the difficulties that inhibit the effecting of fundamental change in public policy, the preliminary examination of the containment doctrine that I undertook in preparing *The Policy Makers* led to the study upon which this book is based. I was struck by the apparently inexorable manner in which United States national security policy for a period of more than two decades clung to a set of assumptions that were seldom questioned—so far as I could discover—in official analyses of the nation's security position, even when the position had been altered, possibly in fundamental ways, by changing circumstances: for example, by the development of the new Europe and by the growing schism in Sino-Soviet relations, to mention only two of the more profound changes. Of course, I was aware of the tendency in huge bureaucratic structures for the organization to continue doing what it has been doing. The very nature of group decision-making, which characterizes the administration of these organizations, tends to produce *incremental* policy development. One knows this from domestic policy-making.

But incrementalism is, after all, merely a *tendency* within the policy-making processes of large bureaucracies; furthermore, even incremental policy-making produces change, over time. How, then, is the remarkable persistence of the containment dogma to be accounted for? Why was our anti-Soviet reflex, which was exerted first in the Eastern Mediterranean in 1947, elevated to a kind of universal dogma within which all American national security decision-making was constructed for a quarter of a century? Who provided the initiative in formulating the doctrine of containment in the first instance? Who were people who controlled our national security machinery between 1945 and 1968? What was their view of the world? Were there no alternatives to containment? Why was the containment dogma accepted so uncritically for almost a quarter of a century? Why was it extended to Asia? Whose interests were served? There has been precious little analysis in political science of these questions that hardly seem trivial.

Hamilton Fish Armstrong, on the eve of his retirement as editor of *Foreign Affairs*, not exactly an anti-establishment journal, stated the problem to which the analysis in this book is directed:

Unless we evaluate and not merely enumerate the elements in our society as they condition the quality of our foreign policy we shall not make progress in changing what we feel is wrong with it. And wrong it must have been. Not, in the experience of the present writer, since the Harding era when we denied our enlightened self-interest and retreated from responsibility in our foreign relations, while confessing to scandal and tawdry commercialism at home, has the world had such a poor opinion of us. American principles, which sometimes were characterized as naïve but in general were respected as sincere and humane, now are freely called hypocritical and self-serving; the weight of American material and military power, looked to in the past as a mainstay of world stability, is now mistrusted and feared.

Armstrong poses a vital question: "What are the characteristics of our society which account for our having been left in such a pitiable situation?" [3]

Who is responsible for creating the strategic doctrine that so transformed the American position in world affairs? Where were the countervailing forces that would serve to correct the situation long before it became "pitiable"? The elite spokesmen whose essays have been featured in *Foreign Affairs* during the first quarter-century of the Cold War must bear some responsibility for the isolated America Amstrong now sees.

Curiously enough, the issue of *Foreign Affairs* that carried Armstrong's essay also presented Zbigniew Brzezinski examining "How the Cold War Was Played." [4] Brzezinski's purpose in this effort was "neither to seek the cause of the cold war nor to assign moral or historical responsibility for it." Instead, Professor Brzezinski sees the Cold War "as more the product of lengthy and probably ineluctable historical forces and less as the result of human error and evil." "Probably ineluctable" is a notion one might wish to ponder further. In the meantime, the analysis in this book assumes that humanity—human error and evil—is part of the historical process and that it is appropriate to seek an understanding of the nature of American responsibility in the Cold War, which was *not* a game being played. Who provided the intellectual and political leadership in the Cold War?

Introduction Notes

1. See John C. Donovan, "Congress and the Making of Neutrality Legislation, 1935–1939" (Ph.D. dissertation, Harvard University, 1949). This study was ably summarized by James A. Robinson as part of his *Congress and Foreign Policy* (Homewood, Ill.: Dorsey Press, 1967).

2. *The Politics of Poverty*, 2nd ed. (Indianapolis: Pegasus, 1973), has since been revised to include the 1967–72 experience.

3. *The Policy Makers* (Indianapolis: Pegasus, 1970).

4. Hamilton Fish Armstrong, "Isolated America," *Foreign Affairs*, Vol. 51, No. 1 (October 1972), 3–4.

5. Zbiginiew Brzezinski, "How the Cold War Was Played," *Foreign Affairs*, Vol. 51, No. 1 (October 1972), 181–209.

1 BEYOND PLURALISM: ELITE ACTIVITY

... the more serious and pertinent question is how qualified our eminent men are for the task of policymaking in a revolutionary age.

Henry Kissinger (1962)

This book, I wish to make clear at the beginning, is not a history of the Cold War. Cold War histories, ranging from the semiofficially apologetic to the avowedly revisionist, have appeared in rich profusion. Nor does this book offer an examination in depth of every major Cold War national security decision. Rather, what is attempted here is a study of a number of key decisions, widely spaced in time, each of such obvious importance to us as a nation that no one is likely to argue that any of these decisions lacks significance. One of my original purposes was to see whether there might be a common pattern of decision-making running throughout the course of the past quarter-century. This, in turn, led to an inquiry about the kinds of people who have been influential policy-makers at crucial moments of national security decision-making since the hardening of the Cold War in the late 1940s.

Are there common patterns in the decisions to drop the atomic bombs on two Japanese cities in 1945, in the hasty construction of the Truman Doctrine in 1947, in the American effort to underwrite anachronistic French colonialism in Indochina in 1950, in the attempts to bring about a major American rearmament program during the Eisenhower years, and in the more recent and traumatic decisions that led to the Americanization of the war in Vietnam? Is this latter experience an aberration, or is it a logical extension of global interventionism growing out of an earlier period in the Cold War?

As my research progressed, I found that the study would inevitably focus on why the United States went so deeply into

Vietnam and that this would necessitate an examination of the ideological framework within which decisions were made. More than I had originally imagined, it became increasingly clear that the tragic American experience in Vietnam had its origins in what should properly be called "intellectual" commitments made earlier. Who was responsible for making these commitments? Who provided the leadership and by what process was Ho Chi Minh transformed into an Asian Hitler menacing the fate of Western civilization?

From the outset of my examination of Cold War decision-making I was aware, of course, that I should have a choice in structuring the hypothetical framework within which this study would take place. I might, for example, assume that the making of policy proceeds much as conventional political science suggests that it does, with President, Congress, State Department, Defense Department, the "public," parties, and interest groups—all functioning in a natural "balance of interests" setting to produce national security policies conceived and dedicated to protect and promote the vital interests of the American nation here, there, and everywhere. Or, at another extreme, I might assume that policy is made in a complex hierarchical system that moves in essentially mindless fashion its peculiar wonders to wrought.

This approach has recently been described by Graham T. Allison as follows:

> To be responsive to a wide spectrum of problems, governments consist of large organizations, among which primary responsibility for particular tasks is divided. Each organization attends to a special set of problems and acts in quasi-independence on these problems.... Government leaders can substantially disturb, but not substantially control, the behavior of these organizations.[1]

I will not deny that this latter approach has occasionally seemed tempting, as a starting hypothesis. After much reflection, and influenced by the publication of the Pentagon Papers when this manuscript was in its first draft, I found myself returning to the writings of C. Wright Mills.

MILLS'S POWER ELITE

Mills found that there was no longer an economy, on the one hand, and a political order, on the other, containing a military establishment. Rather, he saw the political economy "numerously linked" with the military order. As the domains have tended to coincide, the leading men—the high military, the corporation executives, the political directors—have tended to come together in the form of a power elite. Mills wrote in 1956:

> What I am asserting is that in this particular epoch a conjunction of historical circumstances has led to the rise of an elite of power; that the men of the circles composing this elite, severally and collectively, now make such key decisions as are made; and that, given the enlargement and the centralization of the means of power now available, the decisions that they make and fail to make carry more consequences for more people than has ever been the case in the world history of mankind.[2]

Mills was fascinated by the structure of power in American society. His theory of power elite domination is closely tied to his perception that modern technology transforms political, military, and economic institutions in fundamental ways. Most important to political analysis is the tendency for these basic institutions to link. "The push and drive of a fabulous technology," in Mills's view, has created a triangle of power. This is not merely a structural fact; it holds the key to understanding the role of the power elite. The political order, once a decentralized system with a weak federal center, has been transformed into a powerful centralized executive apparatus extending into all parts of the social structure. The economy, at the same time, has come under the domination of a few hundred corporations, administratively and politically interrelated. This is where "the keys to economic decisions" are held; and, what is more to the point, this economy is "at once a permanent war economy and a private-corporation economy."

Finally, there is the military establishment, no longer simply "a slim establishment" limited by an atmosphere of "civilian distrust." Lately it has become "the largest and most expensive feature of government," managed with "all the grim and clumsy efficiency of a great and sprawling bureaucracy." The high military now have "decisive political and economic relevance" in the American technocratic society. Mills views the transition to this new structure of power as the result in part of a shift in the "attention" of the elite from domestic problems in the 1930s to international problems in the 1940s and 1950s. This change created a kind of vacuum in which Mills's power elite grew. Since the government of the United States had been shaped historically by "domestic clash and balance," the government had neither suitable agencies nor the traditions for "the democratic handling of international affairs."

If we are to understand "the unity" of this new power elite, Mills insists that we shall have to pay close attention to the "psychology" of its members. "Insofar as the power elite is composed of men of similar origin and education, of similar career and style of life, their unity may be said to rest upon the fact that they are of similar social type, and to lead to their easy intermixing." But there is also "the interchangeability of positions" between the three dominant institutional orders, a phenomenon marked, of course, by the easy movement of high-level personnel within and between the political, military, and economic structures.

One cannot overemphasize how important the structure and the mechanics of these institutional hierarchies are to Mills's conception of a power elite. The psychological and social unity of the elite (and I would want to add the ideological unity) are reinforced by those particular hierarchical institutional "structures" that are the products of the new corporate-military-industrial-educational-Cold War-"system." Mills's interpretation deserves consideration in terms of recent national security decision-making precisely because it assumes that there is a vital relationship between a powerful elite, the creature of the Cold War system, and the basic institutions that tend to dominate our new Cold War society. Mills's theory is not simplistic. He very clearly states alternatives that seem eminently sensible:

(a) if these hierarchies were "scattered and disjointed," then their respective elites might tend to be "scattered and disjointed"; but,

(b) if they have many interconnections and points of coinciding interest, then the elites may tend to form a coherent kind of grouping.

The relationship between elite groupings and the institutional matrix of the new Cold War society remains largely unexplored, a decade and a half after Mills's death. Mills's theory has received astonishingly little attention in relation to national security policy. Although there is a large body of empirical data concerning several major Cold War decisions and how they were made, academic political scientists have displayed a curious lack of curiosity about the possible emergence of a national security policy elite during the past three decades. G. William Domhoff, who has written extensively following a neo-Millsian approach, has put together one chapter entitled, "How the Power Elite Makes Foreign Policy."[3] Although Domhoff promises to show *who* makes United States foreign policy and *how* it is made, his initial effort fails, for the most part, to connect a power elite with actual decisions, as he himself notes. Domhoff's chapter does provide a service in calling attention to the role that the Council on Foreign Relations has played as a talent pool for the overwhelming majority of civilians who have figured prominently in national security policy-making since the end of World War II. Except for an article by Joseph Kraft appearing in *Harper's Magazine* in 1958, it was virtually impossible to find a study of the CFR prior to the appearance of Domhoff's book. Recently, J. Anthony Lukas reexamined the council as an agency of the establishment in a *New York Times Magazine* article.[4]

In the meantime, "respectable" academic political science, especially as practiced by specialists who write about national security matters, has failed to give adequate attention to some of the more obvious questions that immediately spring to mind when one reads the impressive work of C. Wright Mills. Is there not, by this time, a body of empirical data about Cold War decision-making that would test the relationship between policy elites and the new concentration of power found in the center of military, economic, and political national policy-making? Who are the men most responsible for the initiative in the fundamental shaping of Cold War policy over a period of more than twenty-five years? Is there any basis for viewing these men as members of a policy elite? Do they display evidence of being influenced by factors tending to produce psychological, social, and ideological unity? How much competition is there between elite groups over the objectives of national security policy? Do the members of policy elite groups reflect the biases of an upper social class, as Domhoff suggests?

THE ALMOND-SCHILLING MODEL

Unquestionably, the most influential model of foreign policy-making is the one constructed by Gabriel Almond more than two decades ago.[5] Almond views the policy-making process in terms of an elite structure characterized by a number of autonomous and competing groups astride a largely apathetic and indifferent mass. Some of the best work done by political scientists in the field of national security decision-making follows the Almond model. An excellent example of a study explicitly based on Almond's model is found in Warner R. Schilling, Paul Y. Hammond, and Glenn H. Snyder's *Strategy, Politics, and Defense Budgets.* The key components of the foreign policy process, following closely the terminology and concepts of Almond, have been broadly described by Schilling:

> an elite structure characterized by a large number of autonomous and competing groups; and a mass structure characterized by a small, informed stratum, attentive to elite discussion and conflict, and a much larger base normally ignorant of and indifferent to policy and policy-making.

Schilling feels that the condition responsible for the "competitive" character of the elite structure is "obvious"; that "members of the policy elite normally differ significantly about the ends and means of foreign policy." [6]

I will say immediately that I see nothing "obvious" about the nature of elite structure, one way or the other. As a starting hypothesis, however, I think it quite possible that we may have evolved by this time a national security policy elite whose members characteristically do *not* differ significantly about the *ends* of Cold War policy, however much they may disagree over ways and means of carrying on the struggle. There are, it seems to

me, similar difficulties with Schilling's explanation of the "auton-
omy" of diverse policy elite groups. The "fact," as he sees it, is
"that power is both widely dispersed among the participants in
the process and drawn from a variety of sources independent
one from the other." This conclusion was based on one case study
that examined the struggle between the military services over
shares of the defense budget in the early stages of the Cold War.
We have had more than two decades of Cold War experience
since Almond constructed his model and since men fought over
the fiscal 1950 defense dollar. Surely a case can be made for the
argument that structural factors surrounding the foreign policy–
defense decision cluster make that area much more susceptible
to elite domination than most strictly domestic decisions. The
elaborate "checks and balances" that we assume apply in major
segments of national decision-making all too often appear to
stop at the water's edge.

Since Schilling sees a "diffusion of power," it follows logically
that his model must provide a basis for collaboration *at the elite
level*. Thus, he finds that the various members of a policy elite
"must group together on the basis of some amalgam of interest
if they are to have any prospect of seeing their individual preferences compete successfully against the goals and programs advanced by others." The Almond-Schilling school assumes "the
absence of a single locus of power" as a plurality of elite groups
works together on the basis of "voluntary coordination." The
theory further assumes a conflict of goals that may not always be
present in reality, and it slides over the crucial question: what
"amalgam of interest" would be likely to hold a Cold War policy
elite together over a long period of time?

Schilling was writing, of course, before the Americanization
of the war in Vietnam. Indeed, he was drawing upon a series of
studies of defense decision-making in the late 1940s and early
1950s. The time has come to move closer to the world in which
we are now living; that is to say, to the United States that has
been shaped and conditioned by twenty-five years of the Cold
War. For this purpose we need an approach that recognizes the
convergence of economic, military, and political power in the
postindustrial society, that understands the decision-making processes of huge bureaucratic structures, and that examines the re-

lationships between the new Cold War institutions and the kinds of men who reach the higher levels of technocratic policy-making. If we assume that the initiative in the preliminary shaping of national security policy is an elite preserve, it would seem to be a necessary task in political analysis to examine the manner in which elite leaders link the objectives of the nation's foreign policy with the larger goals and purposes *they have in view.*

HILSMAN—A PLURALIST INSIDER

One of the liveliest accounts of how national security policy was made in the early 1960s appears in *To Move a Nation,* by Roger Hilsman, who was himself a "crisis manager," a "civilian militant," a "cold war technocrat." The book is jammed with insights drawn from Hilsman's experience in 1961–64, first as Director of the State Department's Bureau for Research and Intelligence and later as Assistant Secretary for Far Eastern Affairs. Hilsman, a political scientist, follows the Almond-Schilling approach to national security policy-making; that is, policy-making is a political process, a process that is viewed as being essentially pluralistic. Hilsman's model, borrowed from Almond, postulates a series of concentric circles. The "innermost circle" includes:

> the President and the men in the different departments and agencies who must carry out the decision—staff men in the White House, the Secretaries of State and Defense, the Director of the CIA, and the Assistant Secretaries of State and Defense who bear responsibility for whatever the particular problem may be.[7]

Although Hilsman notes that some matters never go beyond this small circle, he insists that "even here the process is political." The kind of politics that informs the decisions of a small circle within the higher echelons of the national security decision-making apparatus Hilsman labels the "closed politics of highly secret decision-making."

The second circle includes "other departments of the Executive branch and other layers within the agencies and departments already involved, including Presidential commissions, scientific advisory panels and so on." Faithful to the assumptions of pluralism, Hilsman finds that this second layer soon becomes involved in the process of making national security policy even though the debate may still remain secret from the press, the Congress, and the public. He further notes: "The longer a policy debate goes on, no matter how delicate the issue is, the more people will become involved, until eventually the debate spills over into the public domain." [8]

The third circle involves Congress, the press, interest groups, and "the attentive public." Hilsman lumps them all into something he calls "the public arena": "In this arena a decision on policy may be made in one of several ways."

Hilsman mentions the Cuban missile crisis in October 1962 as a decision that became "public, but it never did enter the public arena for decision. The decision was made in the arena of closed politics."

Hilsman follows Schilling in believing that there is a "strain toward agreement" built into the process as various competing actors struggle to reach a consensus. Hilsman also suggests that issues play an important part in the process:

> [T]here are rival policies for dealing with them; and the rival policies are sponsored by different groups of advocates competing for the approval or support of a variety of different constituencies.

Going still further, Hilsman insists: "On every major issue of foreign policy there has been disagreement and usually the differences have cut across institutional lines." [9]

There are a number of difficulties inherent in the model Hilsman offers. In the first place, he has little to say about the outermost circle of participants, the general public, or, as some would have it, the mass public, as distinct from Almond's "attentive" public. The mass public has recently been described by a leading student of national security policy-making as "a group normally ignorant of and indifferent to foreign policy matters, unless aroused about some highly visible issue." [10] Secondly, Hilsman tends to blur the distinction between the "attentive public" and the Congress, which has been thought, traditionally, to have both a political and a constitutional role in national security policy-making. Finally, there would seem to be reason for distinguishing between Almond's "policy and opinion elites" and "the official policy leadership," a distinction Hilsman fails to draw.

Satisfied that there is no ruling elite, in the C. Wright Mills sense, Hilsman finds "a wide variety of people" involved in the making of United States foreign policy. These include:

> the President, the members of the Cabinet, other members of an administration, civilian and military officials in all the great departments, ambassadors and their staffs overseas, members of the Congress, the press, members of the attentive publics, interest groups, specialists and experts in universities and research organizations, and on occasion, the mass public.[11]

Obviously Hilsman has portrayed a spectrum too wide to constitute a ruling elite. At the same time, he has so "loaded" the process with pluralist elements (are they of equal weight?) that his approach provides no clear basis for examining the functioning of elite groups in the policy-making process.

The study of policy-making has been dominated for at least twenty-five years by political scientists who have accepted uncritically pluralism's happy assumption that all groups share approximately equally in shaping the policy consensus and its unstated corollary that those left out are probably best left silent. The examination of elites in policy-making has often lacked rigor. Little attention has been given to the possibility that the making of Cold War policy might become the special responsibility of a relatively compact and coherent elite group whose members hold a view of the world that they believe coincides with the public interest.[12]

At the same time, leading pluralists have been diligent in rejecting outright the power elite interpretation that C. Wright Mills brought forth nearly two decades ago. At the highest levels, Mills saw a unified elite sharing a common social background and moving from command post to command post through an easy interchangeability of positions. In the middle levels where political parties, interest groups, and the working bureaucracies predominate, Mills found "a drifting set of stalemated forces." He also suggested that the middle does not link the bottom with the top, while the bottom of the structure seemed "politically fragmented" and "even as a passive fact, increasingly power-less." In the middle of the 1950s Mills saw a mass society emerg-ing at the bottom of the social structure. Despite the apparent similarity between at least two-thirds of the reality Mills saw and the model Gabriel Almond created, the pluralist grip on political science is such that Hilsman was able to say recently that "Mills can be dismissed as little more than a pamphleteer."

DAHL'S CRITIQUE

Clearly there is a problem here, and it did not originate with Roger Hilsman. The basic pluralist critique of Mills's power elite was written by Robert Dahl of Yale. Dahl, finding Mills's theory "quasi-metaphysical," argued that the existence of a ruling elite can be strictly tested only if (a) the hypothetical ruling elite is a well-defined group; (b) there is a fair sampling of cases in-volving key political decisions in which the preferences of the ruling elite run counter to those of any other likely group that might be suggested; and (c) in such cases, the preferences of the elite regularly prevail.[13]

Dahl astutely warned about the danger of confusing a ruling elite with a group having a high potential for control: "The actual political effectiveness of a group is a function of its potential for control and its potential for unity." Another "bad test," Dahl sug-gested, would be to confuse a ruling elite with a group of in-dividuals who have more influence than others. It would be equally erroneous, he continued, to generalize from a single scope of influence; after all, bankers influence fiscal policy, and farmers influence agricultural policy, and so on. A ruling elite would have predominant influence on the full range of policy.

Assuming that the pluralist interpretation were correct, how should we account for the persistence of the containment dogma for more than two decades? Is contemporary pluralist analysis prepared to accept the possibility that an elite grouping with a high potential for control may have moved close to exercising effective control over a broad range of national security policy? If a well-defined elite group were found to be involved in a number of key political decisions vital to our national security and if the group's preferences regularly prevailed, it should be noted that such a group would come close to meeting the exacting tests Robert Dahl proposed, at least in the national security area. At the same time, the presence of such a group would not necessarily carry any special meaning for the making of domestic policy where the pluralist political and social forces and the constitutional checks and balances are presumed to operate with some effectiveness. It is conceivable that national security policy-making may constitute a special case in recent American experience. It is also possible, of course, that elite penetration in other policy areas has been neglected in pluralist-biased political analysis.

"FRONT MEN" AND "IN-AND-OUTERS"

Hilsman identifies two groups as having unusual influence in the shaping of national security policy: career professionals and Presidential appointees. The technical expertise of the career professionals in the foreign, civil, and military services is bound to be a factor in policy-making. Some of the career professionals rise to command posts in the bureaucratic structures of the decision-making apparatus, where they inevitably exert special influence on the substance of policy. Secondly, there are those men Hilsman refers to as "the front men" or alternatively, following Neustadt and Yarmolinsky, as "the in-and-outers," a peculiar American phenomenon.[14] The front men function as *advocates* of policy, according to Hilsman: They "represent the President to the career specialists and the career specialists to the President" as well as building "a consensus for policy within the Executive branch, on Capitol Hill, and with the press and public." The front men, it appears, are the advocates of a policy created elsewhere. But where? Since they are Presidential appointees, one assumes that it is Presidential policy they are advocating; but it is not clear what the relationship is between President, front men, careerists, and the bureaucratic structures in *formulating* the policy. At this point, Hilsman proves to be a less than satisfactory guide. Who are the front men? Where do they come from? What do they think? Hilsman reports that many of them come from Wall Street, but he remains uncurious about Domhoff's thesis that an upper-class elite, centering in the Council on Foreign Relations, dominates this circle of front men. Hilsman, always the good pluralist, perceives the front men as coming from "diverse" sources; that is, Wall Street, prestigious law firms, foundations, and leading universities.

Hilsman fails to make the point that the distinction between careerist and front man may not be meaningful once one reaches the inner circle of closed politics. There are men who have made a career, a professional career, of the Cold War; they are specialists in an unusual kind of crisis-managing; they are not necessarily very different from the front men in temperament, style, and social position; and they may move from one category to the other: a technocrat may become a front man.

For purposes of introduction, only three front men-technocrats will be mentioned briefly here; there are scores of others. William Bundy has served at the higher levels of the CIA, the Pentagon, and the State Department, and is now the editor of *Foreign Affairs*. Bundy has been a Cold War professional most of the time since he graduated from Harvard Law School over a quarter of a century ago. Dean Rusk has been a Cold War professional since his early career as an Army officer in Asia during World War II. Paul Nitze is a civilian militant of extraordinary persistence and resilience whose policy preferences are reflected in NSC–68, in the Gaither report, and in numerous other aspects of Cold War decision-making between 1950 and 1968. Hilsman, of course, does not view these men as members of a power elite; indeed, he does not refer to them as being members of a *policy* elite. The ease with which they move from the centers of power in one institution to another fits "the interchangeability of positions" aspect, an intrinsic feature of Mills's "power elite," but Hilsman passes this by. No attempt is made to discuss the common ideology that these men share, nor is any effort made to locate them in terms of social class. Hilsman sees national security policy-making in terms of a consensus-building process taking place in the struggle of competing groups and interests. This is the way his front men operate:

They are the ones who kick and push and shove to get the government to recognize a problem and face up to policy choices rather than drift in indecision. They are the ones who sponsor policy alternatives, who do the work of enlisting support, arguing, selling, persuading, and building a consensus around a particular course of action. It is their leadership or lack of it that determines whether a decision will be vigorously or indifferently carried out.[15]

The only thing wrong with this picture is that it appears to bear slight resemblance to the manner in which a key group of national security "front men" made policy in the 1960s. Consequently, Hilsman's prescription for the future seems less than adequate:

The effectiveness of foreign policy depends peculiarly on the front men. If their quality, training and progressive experience can be improved, so will foreign policy. The nation should pay careful attention to their upbringing, care and feeding.[16]

Hilsman, like Almond and Schilling before him, remains content with the assertion that the innermost circle of national security decision-making encloses a political process. Bureaucratic politics, in this view, is pluralistic in nature. The arena of closed politics encloses a struggle between competing elements that are in disagreement over the ends, as well as the means, of United States policy toward the external world. Hilsman's view of how this process works often seems fuzzy. More troublesome is the expanding body of empirical data—as found, for example, in the Pentagon Papers—indicating that the struggle within the innermost circle, the arena of closed politics, did *not* involve significant disagreement over the *ends* of United States national security policy during the 1960s.

If elite circles contain a kind of pluralism-in-miniature in which competing forces struggle over the objectives of national security policy and in which sharp policy alternatives are posed, how is the remarkable persistence of the containment dogma over a long period of time to be accounted for? How are we to explain the manner in which official opposition to Soviet expansion in the 1940s was rapidly elevated to universal dogma, a dogma within which virtually all official American national security thinking and activity were constricted for a quarter of a century? Who were the people in charge of the "command posts" during the long years of the Cold War? Did they accept the containment dogma uncritically? Did they place an extraordinarily heavy reliance on our military strength? Were policy alternatives posed and, if so, by whom? Was Vietnam an aberration, or was it the logical extension of United States Cold War policy? Does it make any sense to explore such questions as these in a context which makes room for the possibility that a policy elite may have exercised disproportionate influence in the making of Cold War policy?

The "in-and-outers" are real; this much we know. They move easily and gracefully from private positions of power and affluence to the command posts of the new militarism and then on again to prestigious offices in the higher circles of the established order. McGeorge Bundy moved from provost of Harvard to Presidential Special Assistant for National Security Affairs to the presidency of the Ford Foundation. Robert McNamara's managerial talents carried him to the top of the Ford Motor Company and to serve two Presidents as Secretary of Defense before being elevated to the World Bank. Dean Acheson used a prestigious law firm as his base while moving back and forth over the decades as Assistant Secretary, Undersecretary, Secretary, and ubiquitous Presidential adviser in key moments of Cold War crisis. These will stand for the time being as recognizable examples of "in-and-outers" who played major roles as civilian militants in the recent past.

There were also crisis managers who were less visible to the public. Charles Hitch left the RAND Corporation, prime Air Force think-tank, to help Robert McNamara install PPBS (a new management system) in the Pentagon and then moved on to the presidency of the University of California, our largest multiversity. Jerome Wiesner, president of MIT, the nation's most important educational branch of the military-industrial complex, served as President Kennedy's Science Adviser. This followed earlier service as Executive Director of the Gaither committee in 1957, whose secret report helped provide the rationale for rebuilding the military during the 1960s. Roger Hilsman offers another example of a professional civilian militant who was little known to the public until the appearance of his book *To Move a Nation.*

Although both the front men in-and-outers and the professional Cold War technocrats appear to be logical candidates for membership in a coherent elite (or a set of circulating elites), neither has been examined carefully in terms of their possible influence in the making of national security policy during the past quarter-century. Almond and Schilling's work in this area is based upon material drawn from the late 1940s and early 1950s. Hilsman's study, personalized and impressionistic, may be the best account by a member of the inner circle of the Kennedy experience in national security matters. It is a fascinating book offering an idealized and subjective account of Kennedy foreign policy-making by a Kennedy admirer-partisan-participant-observer. All these studies openly accent pluralist assumptions, while displaying little interest in establishing the precise influence a policy elite may exert in the process. Pluralist-oriented political science rests content with the unproved assertion that there is effective competition among diverse "groups" within the arena of closed politics at the highest level of executive branch decision-making: that is, within the innermost circle of Presidential advisers. This being the case, where is one to turn for a model that will provide a conceptual framework for an examination of Cold War decision-making that is more likely to conform to a quite different view of "reality"?

THE ESTABLISHMENT ORCHESTRATION MODEL

After a great deal of searching, I have concluded that the so-called *establishment orchestration* model, as presented by Kenneth M. Dolbeare and Murray Edelman, offers the most promise for the analysis to be undertaken in this book. Dolbeare and Edelman believe that pluralism, which they label the "competitive-pressures" model, has validity only for minor decisions. Even here, they draw less optimistic conclusions than most pluralists about government's effectiveness in refereeing group conflicts in the public interest; at the same time, they place a greater emphasis on the success that special interests often achieve in shaping public policy. As Dolbeare and Edelman see it:

> Various units and holders of power coalesce to form a coherent and nearly singleminded force capable of managing major sources of private power, the government, and the general public alike.[17]

Although the pluralist view may offer a reasonably accurate interpretation of policy-making at Mills's "middle level," where essentially minor decisions are taken, a more unified and homogeneous power structure controls the major policy decisions at the higher levels, so Dolbeare and Edelman hypothesize.

Two powerful cohesive elements tend to hold this structure together; they supply the "glue" in a society that the establishment orchestrates. First, the men at the top share a common set of values, interests, and political inclinations; and, regardless of the means by which they acquired an upper-class status, these elite members have developed a deep respect, naturally enough, for the system in which they have been successful. Their very presence in positions of power suggests their values; moreover, they see these values not as self-serving, but as in the public interest. The other element undergirding the security of the establishment is the apparent support of major policy decisions by a substantial portion of the public. The majority of the "visible, audible and active" members of the general public appear to endorse and support the actions of the major officials of government because they have "faith in the institutions established by the Constitution." This widespread public acquiescence based upon the effective inculcation of "the familiar American political values and ideology" is one of "the major achievements of the establishment," as Dolbeare and Edelman see it. They also suggest that under ordinary circumstances few major issues arise:

> Most public policies and private practices fit snugly within the approved contours of the established economic, social and political systems, and special interests are free to seek their narrow ends within this context.[18]

Having postulated a system featuring a unified power structure "ready and determined to defend the status quo in dramatic and effective ways on all fundamental questions," Dolbeare and Edelman are not prepared to accept the pure "power elite" theory in which economic resources are the paramount sources of power and "those relatively few persons who own or control the uses of them" hold the command posts in a "virtually unchallengeable" fashion. A power elite, pure and simple, would "set the operative values and priorities in their own private interest"; the structure of power would contain "a more or less definable and self-conscious group of people sometimes labelled, 'the ruling class.'" The establishment orchestration model assumes a multicausal process rather than one based exclusively on economic dominance. While the results may appear similar, the process is different:

> The establishment orchestration model envisions a somewhat more open process, with interchangeable roles for a larger number of top figures, greater mutual dependence between individuals in and out of government, and a greater reliance upon more or less "voluntary" popular support.[19]

Dolbeare and Edelman suggest that a basic "belief system" may be a more potent force than sheer economic interest. This belief system, once influenced quite strongly by the nature of the economic system, is perceived as being self-perpetuating.

In what respects does this differ from a neo-Millsian power elite conception? First, decisive power at any given time may rest with an ad hoc coalition of establishment members. Secondly, elites will be found functioning in a distinctly more complex process than someone like Domhoff assumes. Thirdly, nonelites may succeed in penetrating the process to the point where they occasionally may short-circuit accepted practices or even introduce new priorities.

A few years ago I wrote:

> Policy-making does appear to be an endless process peculiarly subject to marginal changes. But policy also persists because men in key positions persist at it. These men have views of the world, their own images of society, views of themselves and of their special roles in the process which produces policy.[20]

Believing as I do that the way in which public policy is made profoundly influences the substance of policy, I now wish to extend my analysis of policy-making to certain major Cold War decisions. I assume that policies persist, in part, "because men in positions to influence the making of policy find themselves committed to certain policy positions, some of which have become enormously bureaucratized positions." Having said this, I should also add that I am no longer content to work within the "bureaucratic politics" model as presented by Allison, Neustadt, et al. While it seems to be a highly useful model when applied to any particular episode involving bureaucratic politics at a high level, it may also reveal very little about the policy assumptions on which elite behavior is based. The model appears useful in telling us how selected actors behave once we are "in" the situation; for example, the Cuban missile crisis. It is of less assistance in clarifying how we got there in the first place. The bureaucratic politics model tends to accept the bureaucratic setting as a given. A preoccupation with bureaucracy as a policy-shaper may impede the search for the locus of power.

CONCLUSION

The analysis in this book attempts to focus on the inner circle of closed politics just below the level of the President. The study centers on several crucial moments in the Cold War. It examines the activities of a key group of civilian leaders—civilian militants—who are determined that United States military strength shall be the predominant factor in world politics following World War II. It argues that these civilian militants constitute an effective policy elite (which is not to say, a *ruling* elite) and that the members of the policy elite function in a system very much like the establishment orchestration model that Dolbeare and Edelman have created.

It should not be assumed at this point that this analysis will show an upper class functioning as a monolithic force in American society; nor is there any a priori reason to imagine that upper-class influence, exerted through the policy elite, will appear as the sole force affecting national security decisions. This study examines the manner in which elite figures have exercised a disproportionate influence on crucial issues of foreign and military policy so that their policy preferences have prevailed for more than two decades.

The domination of Cold War strategic policy by a distinct policy elite, a select group of civilian militants who assert the needs and purposes of the established order sometimes against the temporary opposition of Presidents and career people and certainly without regard for whichever political party is in office, carries important implications for the functioning of the total political system.[21] In this sense, the study of this elite during a particular time period appears to have a more general applicability. At a bare minimum, the study sheds light on the recruitment of elite members and on certain features of their ideology and perceptions. Although it is too much to expect one study to "prove" or "disprove" a particular model, it provides in this instance an opportunity for testing alternatives to the predominant pluralist conceptions. Unless political science, taken as a whole, becomes much more curious than it has been about questions of elite responsibility, we are probably destined to wallow around in a large soggy body of empirical analysis that tends to justify whatever has been done.

It is this book's modest objective to stimulate a livelier interest in the role elite members play in linking the larger interests and purposes of the established order with the long-range objectives of United States foreign policy. Our study, then, should be viewed as a preliminary examination of elite behavior in the national security field, calling for further analysis of the relationship between elite ideology and elite action in the United States today.

Reference has been made earlier in this chapter to the effect the publication of the Pentagon Papers in 1971 had in shaping the conceptual framework of this study. The publication of the classified documents and the accompanying analysis brought to general public attention a view of the national security decision-making process that had previously been limited to relatively few specialists. In the case of the American involvement in Vietnam, even the specialists who study decision-making had previously been working with extremely limited data. Earlier phases of the Cold War, on the other hand, have been examined rather thoroughly by a series of academic authorities. In addition, there has been no lack of memoir-writing by several key participants, including volumes written by President Truman, Dean Acheson, and George Kennan, each of whom had a special vantage point for viewing the events leading to the Truman Doctrine and the Marshall Plan. The U.S. decision to fight following the North Korean attack in 1950 has been reconstructed with infinite skill so that we have an almost hour-by-hour account of that episode. There is a full account of the way in which NSC–68 was formulated early in 1950, building a case for a greatly increased American military effort. Likewise, the Gaither report of 1957, making a similar case for the expansion of American military power, has since been examined in detail, even though the report has never been released as a public document.[22]

What was lacking until the *New York Times* courageously broke the security barrier was the detailed documentation showing the manner in which the Kennedy and Johnson administrations altered the nature of the U.S. involvement in Indochina by assuming an ever-increasing and direct American military participation in Vietnam's civil war. While there had been ingenious attempts by academic scholars to discover the pattern of decision-making in the 1960–68 period, especially in relation to Vietnam, the most impressive efforts either relied upon information gained through interviews with some of the key participants (who often wished to remain anonymous) or upon analyses prepared by men who had themselves been participants (not infrequently in positions located at some distance from the center of executive decision-making). Especially in the latter case, we were being asked, in effect, to take the analysts' word for what they had to say about the way decisions were made, since their essays were often based on classified documents that could not be cited. It is obvious that either of these two methods is likely to leave the serious student of decision-making unsatisfied.[23]

The *Times* and the several other newspapers that followed the lead of the *Times* in publishing excerpts from the Pentagon Papers performed an invaluable service to scholars in this field (to say nothing of any broader contribution to public understanding) because the documents—limited though they may be in the absence of Presidential papers and other sources—reveal a pattern of decision-making that may be compared with earlier Cold War decisions. We may have a chance to gauge the extent to which "the persistence of policy" proved to be a factor in the experience of the Kennedy and Johnson administrations. We have an excellent opportunity to seek evidence concerning the activity of any policy elite that may have been active in making these decisions. We are offered a glimpse of the kind of thinking that Cold War technocrats employ in making decisions vital to the nation's foreign and military power interests. In the broadest sense, the Pentagon Papers provide suggestive data about the fateful decisions leading to the Americanization of the war in Vietnam, inviting comparisons with a number of major Cold War decisions going back to a time when the United States' role in the world was different from what it is today. At the very least, a comparison of these decisions may help us to understand better the nature of group decision-making within the higher levels of the national security bureaucracy. With a bit of luck, we may also shed some light on where power is located in our society and who wields it and for what purposes.

Chapter One Notes

1. Graham T. Allison, *Essence of Decision* (Boston: Little, Brown, 1971), p. 67.

2. C. Wright Mills, *The Power Elite* (New York: Oxford University Press, 1956), p. 28. All the material on C. Wright Mills in this chapter is drawn from this book.

3. G. William Domhoff, *The Higher Circles* (New York: Vintage–Random House, 1971). Domhoff views the upper class as the ruling class, a thesis he explored first in *Who Rules America?* (Englewood Cliffs, N.J.: Prentice-Hall, 1967).

4. See Joseph Kraft, "School for Statesmen," *Harper's Magazine*, July 1958; and J. Anthony Lukas, "The Council on Foreign Relations—Is It a Club? Seminar? Presidium? 'Invisible Government'?" *New York Times Magazine*, November 21, 1971.

5. Gabriel A. Almond, *The American People and Foreign Policy* (New York: Harcourt, Brace, 1950).

6. See p. 19 of this book, which was published by Columbia University Press, New York, in 1962. Schilling authored one of the case studies, "The Politics of National Defense: Fiscal 1950," pp. 1–266. All references to Schilling in this chapter are drawn from this study.

7. Roger Hilsman, *To Move a Nation* (New York: Delta Book, Dell Publishing, 1964), p. 542. Hilsman has also written *The Politics of Policy Making in Defense and Foreign Affairs* (New York: Harper & Row, 1971). The latter book, while containing some new material, appears to be based largely on the first book.

8. Ibid., p. 543.

9. Ibid., p. 544.

10. Allison, *Essence of Decision*, p. 153.

11. Hilsman, *Politics of Policy Making*, p. 147.

12. See Gaddis Smith's remarkable biography, *Dean Acheson* (New York: Coopers' Union, 1972); and David Halberstam, "The Very Expensive Education of McGeorge Bundy," *Harper's Magazine*, July 1969, for penetrating insights into the mentality of upper-class representatives who sincerely feel that what they want for an American world role must be in the public interest.

13. A useful summary of Dahl's critique of Mills's power elite appears in Hilsman, *The Politics of Policy Making*, chapter 8. For a full statement of Dahl's position, see his *Pluralist Democracy in the United States* (Chicago: Rand, McNally, 1967).

14. See Richard Neustadt, "White House and Whitehall," and Adam Yarmolinsky, "Ideas Into Programs," both of which appeared in *The Public Interest*, 2 (Winter 1966), 55–79.

15. Hilsman, *To Move a Nation*, p. 573.

16. Ibid.

17. Kenneth M. Dolbeare and Murray J. Edelman, *American Politics: Policies, Power and Change*, 2d ed. (Lexington, Mass.: D. C. Heath, 1973), p. 472. In addition to the establishment orchestration model that they prefer, Dolbeare and Edelman also offer clear statements of pluralism that they refer to as the competitive pressures model and the power elite, which they label the economic dominants model. Their book begins with four areas of public policy (national security, poverty and racism, economic growth, and the Third World) and then works back to an analysis of the "system" that produces these policies. All the references to Dolbeare and Edelman in this chapter are drawn from this book.

18. Ibid., p. 472. It is not only the inculcation of the belief system that leads to public acquiescence in elite domination, Dolbeare and Edelman argue; other factors include "lack of alternatives, apathy, political party loyalties, hopelessness, fear of coercion."

19. Ibid., p. 474.

20. The quotations in this paragraph are taken from my book *The Policy Makers* (New York: Pegasus, 1970), p. 101.

21. In fact, both political parties are "in office" together most of the time under the workings of bipartisan coalitional politics. See my *The Policy Makers* for a more detailed analysis.

22. See Glenn D. Paige, *The Korea Decision* (New York: Free Press, 1968); Paul Y. Hammond, "NSC–68: Prologue to Rearmament," in Schilling, Hammond, and Snyder, *Strategy, Politics, and Defense Budgets* (New York, Columbia University Press, 1962); and Morton Halperin, "The Gaither Committee and the Policy Process," *World Politics* (April 1961), 360–384.

23. Eugene Eidenberg, "The Presidency: Americanizing the War in Vietnam," in *American Political Institutions and Public Policy*, ed. Allan Sindler (Boston: Little, Brown, 1969). On the basis

of interviews with a number of key figures (several of whom preferred remaining anonymous), Eidenberg—prior to the publication of the Pentagon Papers—was able to report: "The escalation of American policy on Viet Nam was supported by virtually every senior national security officer to the president." For an example of an essay in which the reader was asked to accept the author's use of classified documents, see Daniel Ellsberg's "The Quagmire Myth and the Stalemate Machine," *Public Policy* (Spring 1971). Among the services Ellsberg performed subsequently in releasing copies of the Pentagon Papers for publication was to provide access to much of the documentation on which this article had been based.

2 CIVILIAN MILITANTS, THE BOMB, AND THE SOVIETS, 1945

There cannot be a well-grounded dissent from the conclusion reached as early as 1945 by members of the U.S. Strategic Bombing Survey "... that certainly prior to December 31, 1945 and in all probability prior to November 1, 1945, Japan would have surrendered even if the atomic bombs had not been dropped, even if Russia had not entered the war, and even if no invasion had been planned or contemplated."

Herbert Feis

The Atomic Bomb and the End of World War II (1966)

This chapter represents what V. O. Key, Jr., once referred to in a different context as a "test boring." The decision to drop atomic bombs on two Japanese cities in 1945 will be examined principally through the eyes of the man who may have been more directly responsible for the decision than was the President of the United States, although the President obviously bore the ultimate, formal responsibility as commander-in-chief. The analysis is based principally on an examination of the record exactly as this man wished to have it presented in an authorized biography. The decision to drop the bombs on the Japanese cities toward the close of a hot war ushered in a new era in international politics that was to be called the Cold War. Historians still debate the origins of the Cold War. My assumption is that the Cold War is closely tied to the development of nuclear weapons, and that the United States' version of the Cold War was adumbrated in the thinking of the men chiefly responsible for shaping the decision to drop the bombs in August 1945.[1] This chapter hopes to learn more about who these men were and to understand how they thought about atomic weapons in relation to the objectives of United States foreign policy. It has been established beyond reasonable doubt that the decision to drop atomic bombs on Japanese cities was related in official thinking to considerations affecting the postwar role of the Soviet Union. Our purpose is not to write revisionist history, but to gain an understanding of elite behavior within the inner circle of closed politics during the first hours of the nuclear age.

The decision to drop the bomb was prepared in the office of Secretary of War Henry L. Stimson, a wealthy, elderly New York lawyer and a gentleman of high character and rectitude. A one-time protégé of Theodore Roosevelt and of Elihu Root, Stimson was an "enlightened" Republican with a long and distinguished career in the public service going back to the administrations of T.R. and Taft and including the office of Secretary of State in the cabinet of Herbert Hoover. When Franklin Roosevelt appointed Colonel Stimson—as he was fondly known among his closest associates—to serve as Secretary of War in his wartime cabinet, a tradition was born in which the stewardship of national security policy in the nuclear age became the special responsibility of men who were members of the higher circles of the established order. FDR's precedent has been followed in subsequent administrations, including those of Presidents Truman, Kennedy, and Johnson.

Stimson's role in the decision and his thinking about the question of using atomic bombs against cities with large civilian populations are set forth in an authorized biography, largely based on Stimson's words, prepared with Stimson's blessing and active participation, by McGeorge Bundy.[2] McGeorge Bundy, who was later to become a national security policy-maker in his own right, wrote the book while serving as a Junior Fellow in Harvard, an institution he later served as provost. McGeorge Bundy is the younger son of Harvey Bundy, a wealthy, patrician Boston lawyer, who served as Assistant Secretary of State under Mr. Stimson in the Hoover administration and as Stimson's Special Assistant in the War Department during World War II. William Bundy, McGeorge's older brother, also became an influential shaper of Cold War policy, as noted in chapter 1.[3]

STIMSON AND THE INTERIM COMMITTEE

On June 1, 1945, before anyone was sure that we had a workable bomb, the so-called Interim Committee recommended to

Secretary Stimson that the bomb be used against Japan, without specific warning, as soon as possible, and against such a target as to make clear its frightful strength. The recommendation, surely without precedent in all history, was made by a committee composed entirely of civilians, including the presidents of Harvard and MIT, because it was the opinion of the committee that any other course involved serious danger to the major objectives of obtaining a prompt surrender from the Japanese. An advisory panel of atomic physicists had reported that they were unable to propose a "technical demonstration" likely to bring an end to the war. There was, as the panel saw it, "no acceptable alternative to direct military use." [4]

"The committee's function was, of course, entirely advisory,' Stimson later wrote. "The ultimate responsibility for the recommendation ... rested upon me, and I have no desire to veil it. The conclusions of the committee were similar to my own, although I reached mine independently." Karl Compton, president of MIT, a member of the Interim Committee that made the recommendation, explained: "it was not one atomic bomb, or two, which brought surrender; it was the experience of what an atomic bomb will actually do to a community, *plus the dread of many more,* that was effective."

This was essentially the view of Stimson, who added:

> In order to end the war in the shortest possible time and to avoid the enormous losses of human life which otherwise confronted us, I felt that we must use the Emperor as our instrument to command and compel his people to cease fighting and subject themselves to our authority through him, and that to accomplish this we must give him and his controlling advisers a compelling reason to accede to our demands. This reason furthermore must be of such a nature that his people could understand his decision. The bomb seemed to me to furnish a unique instrument for that purpose.[5]

No one today would be likely to argue that the bomb was not a unique instrument; there is, however, reason to question the rather astonishing assumption that *only* this unique instrument could have effected a Japanese will to surrender. By the time the two bombs were dropped in early August 1945, the Japanese navy had virtually disappeared as an effective fighting force, as had most of its air force. Tokyo and Yokohama had been gutted by B-29 fire-bomb raids. Our massive Third Fleet was subjecting the Japanese home islands to a continuous air and sea bombardment and blockade that went on for more than seventy days while receiving less than token resistance. As the quotation at the head of this chapter indicates, even Herbert Feis, a long-time associate of Henry L. Stimson, who wrote the quasi-official version of this experience, concluded that the use of the A-bombs against Japanese cities was not a military necessity. Gar Alperovitz has shown that Admiral Leahy, General Eisenhower, and General LeMay were among those who regarded the use of the weapon against Japan as being militarily unnecessary.[6] Yet Stimson did not flinch from the awesome and tragic responsibility thrust upon him by the new technological imperative. "The decision to use the atomic bomb was a decision that brought death to over a hundred thousand Japanese. No explanation can change that fact and I do not wish to gloss over it," he later wrote.[7]

> But this deliberate, premeditated destruction of Hiroshima and Nagasaki put an end to the Japanese war. It stopped the fire raids, and the strangling blockade; it ended the ghastly specter of a clash of great land armies.[8]

The Secretary of War found this meaning in the event:

> In this last great action of the Second World War we were given final proof that war is death. War in the twentieth century has grown steadily more barbarous, more destructive, more debased in all its aspects. Now, with the release of atomic energy, man's ability to destroy himself is very nearly complete. The bombs dropped on Hiroshima and Nagasaki ended a war. They also made it wholly clear that we must never have another war.[9]

Stimson, a profoundly moral man, evidently did not see the moral issue involved in dropping the bomb on heavily populated cities, without advance warning. Bundy explains:

> The true question, as he saw it, was not whether surrender could have been achieved without the use of the bomb but whether a different diplomatic and military course would have led to an earlier surrender. . . . The second error made by critics after the war, in Stimson's view, was their assumption that American policy was, or should have been, controlled or at least influenced by

a desire to avoid the use of the atomic bomb. In Stimson's view this would have been as irresponsible as the contrary course of guiding policy by a desire to insure the use of the bomb.[10]

The way Stimson viewed the objective reveals the instrumental character of the thinking that marked the decision to use the bomb:

the dominant fact of 1945 was war, and . . . therefore, necessarily, the dominant objective was victory. If victory could be speeded up using the bomb, it should be used; if victory must be delayed in order to use the bomb, it should *not* be used.[11]

This latter point is misleading inasmuch as the Manhattan Project team was under severe pressure to have the bomb ready for military use by August, and the first stages of the planned invasion of the Japanese home islands had a target date of November 1. The timing involved bears close examination. Alperovitz explains:

The atomic bombs were used on August 6 and August 9, 1945. As Feis admits, the full invasion of Japan, which might have cost between 500,000 and a million casualties, was not scheduled until the spring of 1946. What was scheduled for November 1945 was a landing on the island of Kyushu, with an estimate of 31,000 initial casualties. Planning for the contingency of a full invasion had to go forward, of course, and statements to the press, both for reasons of morale and to keep pressure on Japan, led the public to expect a long struggle lasting a year and a half. But as we now know, and as Feis affirms, within the United States Government it seemed apparent by July 1945 that other courses of action could have ended the war before the spring of 1946. Thus, at most, the atomic bomb can be credited with having made a landing on Kyushu unnecessary.[12]

Nevertheless, Bundy continues:

The bomb was thus not treated as a separate subject, except to determine whether it should be used at all; once that decision had been made, the timing and method of the use of the bomb were wholly subordinated to the objective of victory; *no effort was made, and none was seriously considered, to achieve surrender merely in order not to have to use the bomb.* Surrender was a goal sufficient in itself, wholly transcending the use or nonuse of the bomb. [Italics mine. This is the understatement of the century.][13]

ALTERNATIVES TO THE DECISION

One of the haunting aspects of the decision is the way in which the alternatives were *not* posed, as is so often the case in group decision-making within large bureaucratic organizations. At no time did Stimson and his committee give extended discussion to the possibility of not using the bomb against targets in Japan. It was simply *assumed* that the bomb would be used. Professor Walter S. Schoenberger,[14] who has probed this decision with meticulous care and who had access to the records of the Interim Committee, has shown that the Interim Committee was appointed to consider the postwar implications of atomic energy and not to advise on the possible military use of the bomb in the war. Stimson, by his own admission, came to the decision to use the bomb against Japan, *independently* of the Interim Committee's recommendation. Although his motives are far from clear, the Secretary may have involved the Interim Committee in the decision in the hope that the three prestigious scientists, Conant, Compton, and Bush, who were members of the committee, might help in mollifying criticism that was already building up among some leading scientists. In any event, as Schoenberger demonstrates, the use of the bomb was simply *presumed* from an early stage in the decision-making process. As early as February 13, Harvey Bundy had drafted a possible statement which began: "On —— 1945, the United States Armed Forces used against the enemy an entirely new weapon."

By May 28—three days before the Interim Committee met to discuss the question—the original draft of the statement had been completed and sent to Harrison, another key civilian aide to Stimson. It now began: "Two hours ago an American airplane dropped a bomb on Nagasaki Naval Base, and the Naval Base ceased to exist."

Schoenberger summarizes what took place in the May 31 and June 1 meetings of the Interim Committee:

At no time was the question of use widely discussed. The important questions, if there were such were *where* it was to be used, *how* it was to be used, and *when* it was to be used rather than *whether* it should be used.[15]

The committee accepted the suggestion already formulated by Stimson and his staff that the bomb be used against Japan on a war plant surrounded by civilian homes and without prior warning.

Professor Elting Morrison, who has written a perceptive biography of Stimson, offers an interesting interpretation of what the Interim Committee represented:

They did not go into the meetings of the Interim Committee on May 31 cold. They had attitudes already developed—independently and by informal collaboration on a common task. The Interim Committee was appointed to give their opinions ordered form, some corporate structure, as the need for a defined decision was presented. The effort to give the decision this kind of support, to invest it with the sanction of a formal judgment reached by orderly procedures, a canvass and resolution of all considerations at some given moment in time, was the expression of the natural desire to make all human acts and decisions appear not only wise but the product of system and right reason. The Interim Committee, insofar as the special matter of using the bomb was concerned, was, in a sense, a symbolic act to demonstrate with what care this enormous conclusion had been considered.[16]

This may be the perfect psychological explanation for the behavior of Stimson, Bundy, Harrison, et al.; but the symbolism, as one reviews the record with Schoenberger, seems highly misleading, to say the least.

ROLE OF BOMB IN POLICY TOWARD SOVIETS

The use of the atomic bomb in August 1945 was related directly to an official view of Soviet Russia's role in the postwar world, a view rapidly taking shape within the higher echelons of the national security apparatus of the United States government. The messianic anti-Soviet views of James Forrestal, Secretary of the Navy at the end of World War II and the nation's first Secretary of Defense, and of James Byrnes, President Truman's Secretary of State, are well known. Relatively little attention has been paid to the views developed by Secretary Stimson and his coterie of civilian advisers, some of whom served as influential Cold War policy-makers long after Forrestal came to his tragic end and Byrnes had retired from public service.[17] These official views were hardening by the summer of 1945 with the end of the war against Japan in view. Stimson, with a powerful assist from his Assistant Secretary, John J. McCloy—who was later to serve as High Commissioner in Germany—played a strong hand in urging FDR to abandon the Morgenthau Plan after Roosevelt and Churchill had initialed an agreement at the Quebec conference proposing a postwar Germany reduced to "an agricultural and pastoral" land. Stimson and his civilian staff in the War Department held distinct views about the kind of political and economic society they wanted to see in Europe. The postwar planning section of the War Department under the direction of McCloy also played a major role in bringing about the reconstruction of Japan. In all this, fear of Soviet expansionist tendencies was a significant force.

The point is not that Stimson and McCloy were "wrong" in resisting the Morgenthau Plan, which was patently absurd, but that civilian leaders in the War Department, where nuclear weapons were being created in secret, played a potent policy hand in shaping United States foreign policy objectives in both Europe and Asia, and that an anti-Soviet reflex increasingly governed thinking in the inner circle of closed politics during the closing months of World War II.

Stimson's personal apprehensions concerning the appropriate posture of the United States toward the USSR following the end of war in the Pacific reached a point of sharp focus at the Potsdam Conference in July. The recommendation to use the atomic bomb had been made early in July. The bomb was successfully tested in the New Mexico desert on July 15. Immediately the American attitude changed in the discussions with Stalin at Potsdam. Previously every effort was being made to bring the Russians into the Pacific struggle at the earliest possible moment. Suddenly the pressure eased. McGeorge Bundy, relying on Stimson's files and recollections, describes the change that took place once the American delegation knew that they had the "unique instrument." The key advisers knew that the bomb would be used against the Japanese.

> The news from Alamogordo, arriving at Potsdam on July 18, made it clear to the Americans that further diplomatic efforts to bring the Russians into the Pacific war were largely pointless. The bomb as a merely probable weapon had seemed a weak reed on which to rely, but the bomb as a colossal reality was very different. The Russians may well have been disturbed to find that President Truman was rather losing his interest in knowing the exact date on which they would come into the war.[18]

The bomb proved to be, in Bundy's words, a "colossal reality," and not only during the Potsdam negotiations. The bomb became the key instrument in the evolving pattern of postwar United States–USSR relationships.

The following item appeared in Stimson's diary and was written at Potsdam after the President received a report describing the successful atomic test:

> [The Prime Minister] told me . . . "Now I know what happened to Truman yesterday. I couldn't understand it. When he got to the meeting after having read this report he was a changed man. He told the Russians just where they got on and off, and generally bossed the whole meeting." [19]

Stalin, morbidly suspicious by nature, was not likely to have found comfort in the fact that the Americans had developed this unique instrument. Henceforth, American air power armed with atomic weapons would remain the principal force of resistance to Soviet aims in both Europe and Asia, at least until the American atomic monopoly was broken. Alperovitz observes: "Stimson and the President counted on the new power to help in forcing Russia to accept American terms throughout Central and Eastern Europe." [20]

BEGINNINGS OF CONTAINMENT

The policy of containment, which appears to have been improvised in the harsh climate of 1947, was actually taking shape as early as the Potsdam conference. Stimson, deeply concerned about the possibility that the United States might later become associated with the Soviet Union in a system of supranational control of atomic weapons, pondered whether the Soviet leaders might be approached on the basis of an American demand that the Soviet system be altered to provide "real freedom" for its citizenry.

"Could atomic energy be controlled," Stimson asked himself, "if one of the partners in control was a state dictatorially and repressively governed by a single inscrutable character? Could there be *any* settlement of lasting value with the Soviet Russia of Stalin?"

The questions troubling Stimson during the Potsdam conference, July 1945, are revealed in a paper he prepared for the President, headed, "Reflections on the Basic Problems Which Confront Us."

The paper needs to be read at some length:

1. With each international conference that passes and, in fact, with each month that passes between conferences, it becomes clearer that the great basic problem of the future is the stability of the relations of Western democracies with Russia.

2. With each such time that passes it also becomes clear that that problem arises out of the fundamental differences between a nation of free thought, free speech, free elections, in fact a really free people, [and] a nation which is not basically free but which is systematically controlled from above by secret police and in which free speech is not permitted.

3. It also becomes clear that no permanently safe international relations can be established between two such fundamentally different national systems. With the best of efforts we cannot understand each other. . . .

4. Daily we find our best efforts for co-ordination and sympathetic understanding with Russia thwarted by the suspicion which basically and necessarily must exist in any controlled organization of men.

5. Thus, every effort we make at permanent organization of such a world composed of two such radically different systems is subject to frustration by misunderstandings arising out of mutual suspicion.

6. The great problem ahead is how to deal with this basic differ-

ence which exists as a flaw in our desired accord. I believe we must not accept the present situation as permanent for the result will then almost inevitably be a new war and the destruction of our civilization.[21]

Bundy advises that Stimson found "some hope" in the Soviet constitution of 1936. Apparently Stalin knew what freedom *ought* to mean, and Stimson thought there might be an American obligation to teach Stalin how to make freedom "real" in Soviet society. Still, Stimson was uncertain how to proceed, how the issue should be posed. He did say, however: "At the start it may be possible to effect only some amelioration of the local results of Russia's secret police state."

In the final paragraph of the Potsdam memo, the Secretary of War indicated that the projected use of atomic weapons against Japan was ultimately related, in his mind, to the manner in which the United States should confront the Stalinist regime:

7. The foregoing has a vital bearing upon the control of the vast and revolutionary discovery of X [atomic energy] which is now confronting us. Upon the successful control of that energy depends the future successful development or destruction of the modern civilized world. The committee appointed by the War Department which has been considering that control has pointed this out in no uncertain terms and has called for an international organization for that purpose. After careful reflection I am of the belief that *no* world organization containing as one of its dominant members a nation whose people are not possessed of free speech, but whose governmental action is controlled by the autocratic machinery of a secret political police, can give effective control of this new agency with its devastating possibilities.

I therefore believe that before we share our new discovery with Russia we should consider carefully whether we can do so safely under any system of control until Russia puts into effective action the proposed constitution which I have mentioned. If this is a necessary condition, we must go slowly in any disclosures or in agreeing to any Russian participation whatsoever and constantly explore the question how our headstart in X and the Russian desire to participate can be used to bring us nearer to the removal of the basic difficulties which I have emphasized.[22]

Following the Potsdam conference, during the period when the atomic attacks were being readied and then launched, Stimson and his civilian assistants, most notably McCloy, Harrison, and Bundy, were thinking "long and painful thoughts" about atomic weapons and the postwar world. Stimson was worried. He had a long talk with Ambassador Harriman, who persuaded the Secretary that any hope he may have entertained that Stalin might bargain about the nature of "freedom" in the Soviet Union was unfounded; the Soviet leader would regard any such effort as a plainly hostile move.

STIMSON'S SHIFTING ATTITUDES

McGeorge Bundy describes the change that took place in Stimson's thinking early in September 1945, just before the Secretary of War retired to private life:

> Might it not then be better to reverse the process, to meet Russian suspicion with American candor, to discuss the bomb directly with them and try to reach an agreement on control? Might not trust beget trust; as Russiar confidence was earned, might not the repressive—and aggressive—tendencies of Stalinism be abated? [23]

Stimson forwarded another memo to President Truman on September 11, urging immediate and direct negotiations with the Russians, looking toward a "covenant" for the control of the atom.

Two paragraphs excerpted from Stimson's lengthy memo will illustrate the extent to which his thinking had been modified. Stimson noted that American relations with Russia were not merely connected with the atomic bomb, but were virtually dominated by it:

> Those relations may perhaps be irretrievably embittered by the way in which we approach the solution of the bomb with Russia. For if we fail to approach them now and merely continue to negotiate with them, having this weapon rather ostentatiously on our hip, their suspicions and their distrust of our purposes and motives will increase.

And later in the same memo:

> I emphasize perhaps beyond all other considerations the impor-
> tance of taking this action with Russia as a proposal of the
> United States—backed by Great Britain but peculiarly the pro-
> posal of the United States. Action of any international group of
> nations, including many small nations who have not demonstrated
> their potential power or responsibility in this war would not, in
> my opinion, be taken seriously by the Soviets.[24]

Stimson repeated these sentiments to the President and the
cabinet on the day of his retirement, September 24, 1945. The
cabinet discussion that followed, according to Dean Acheson,
who attended as Acting Secretary of State, was "unworthy of the
subject." Acheson further notes: "The discussion got nowhere,
but distorted accounts of it to the effect that the President was
contemplating sharing the bomb were leaked to the press, putting Congress into an uproar." [25]

Acheson's attitude at the time is reflected in a letter he wrote
to his daughter, with whom he apparently shared cabinet discussions. Others, he reported, had "expressed more or less agreement
with Colonel Stimson. Henry Wallace soared into abstractions,
trailing clouds of aphorisms as he went." [26]

Stimson later came to regard the views stated in this memo as
having been "seriously incomplete." The behavior of the Soviet
leadership between 1945 and 1947 filled Stimson with "astonish-
ment and regret." Stimson was convinced that it was the Soviet
leaders who had ended the wartime relationship.

Stimson was not involved in the decision to end Lend-Lease,
an action announced by President Truman on August 21. In making the decision, Truman announced to the press: "The reason
is that the bill passed by Congress defined Lend-Lease as a
weapon of war, and after we ceased to be at war, it is no longer
necessary." [27]

Acheson, possibly Truman's most gallant defender across the
years, later found the statement to be untrue and the decision
disastrous. Truman told Acheson he himself had come to regard
the abrupt ending of Lend-Lease as "a grave mistake." Given the
context of events in July and August 1945, one can imagine
the kind of reading the President's announcement received in

the Kremlin. (It may be safely assumed that it was not the effect on the Russians that caused Truman and Acheson to regard the decision as a grave mistake.)

This "test boring" has probed beneath the surface far enough to reveal certain aspects of national security decision-making that may also be present in subsequent decisions.

THE CIVILIAN POLICY-MAKERS

One especially notes the large and significant part that civilian leaders and their key subordinates played in the development of atomic weapons and in making the decision to use these instruments of mass destruction against inhabited cities. The decision was influentially shaped by eminent civilians, including leading members of the educational-scientific establishment. For obvious reasons the decision to use the bombs against Japanese cities was not a matter of public discussion; indeed, only a select few among Congressional leaders were privy to the fact that a bomb was being built. For less obvious reasons, there is reason to believe that no serious consideration was given by the Secretary of War or his civilian advisers to the possibility of not using the bomb.

The advisory committee, which included the presidents of Harvard, the Massachusetts Institute of Technology, and the Carnegie Institution of Washington, evidently did not discuss the moral issue involved in the use of atomic weapons. Indeed, as Alperovitz has shown, it was James B. Conant who suggested, and Stimson agreed, that "the target would be a war plant employing a large number of workers closely surrounded by workers' houses." At the meeting of the Interim committee one day later, Secretary of State James Byrnes formally proposed that the committee recommend that the bomb be used as soon as possible and without warning against a Japanese war plant surrounded by workers' houses.[28] The bomb was viewed, officially and surgically, as a unique instrument that would lead to prompt surrender on the part of the Japanese war machine. The clear impression given in Stimson's semiofficial biography is that the bomb was received in his office with a sense of pride and confidence, not in any mood of moral anguish.

Who were the civilian policy-makers who helped shape the decision in the higher levels of the War Department? The backgrounds of Colonel Henry L. Stimson and his Special Assistant Harvey Bundy have already been indicated. Stimson retired in September 1945; he was then seventy-eight years of age. Bundy has not been active in national security matters since World War II, although his sons, McGeorge and William, came to play prominent roles in the 1960s. John J. McCloy and Robert A. Lovett were two of Colonel Stimson's protégés who served as influential Cold War policy-makers over a long period of time. A brief sketch of each of their careers follows:

John J. McCloy

John J. McCloy was born in Philadelphia in 1895. He prepared for college at the Peddie School, was graduated from Amherst College in 1916, and then studied law at Harvard. McCloy was admitted to the bar of New York in 1921 and for the next two decades practiced law in large New York firms, principally Cravath, Swaine and Moore, of which he was a member from 1929 until 1940. (Roswell Gilpatric, Robert McNamara's deputy at the time of the TFX contract award, was a member of the same law firm, and, indeed, had previously represented General Dynamics, recipient of the controversial contract to build the TFX.)

McCloy served as Assistant Secretary of War under Colonel Stimson from April 1941 until November 1945 and was especially active in plans for the postwar development of both Germany and Japan. He was a member of the law firm of Milbank, Tweed, Hope, Hadley and McCloy in 1946 and 1947 until he assumed the presidency of the World Bank, a position he held between 1947 and 1949. McCloy next served as the United States Military Governor and High Commissioner for Germany in the years 1949 to 1952. In 1953 McCloy became chairman of the board of Chase National Bank in New York City. Two years later he was chairman of the board of Chase-Manhattan Bank, following the merger of Chase with the Bank of Manhattan. He served in this capacity until 1961.

Between 1961 and 1963, McCloy served at President Kennedy's request as Coordinator of United States Disarmament Activities. McCloy had previously established a reputation in this field, having served as unofficial, unpaid adviser on disarmament matters to John Foster Dulles, who was not generally considered a passionate disarmer.

McCloy has been a member of the Milbank, Tweed, Hadley and McCloy firm since 1963. He served as chairman of the Ford Foundation from 1953 until 1965. He has also been active in the Council on Foreign Relations, and served as chairman at one time.

Dean Acheson offered the following description of McCloy's qualities:

> McCloy belongs in the first rank of men with whom I have worked. He came to the War Department at Secretary Henry L. Stimson's call, from a successful New York legal practice to serve as Assistant Secretary during the Second World War, having been an infantryman in the First. In 1947, President Truman put him forward to be President of the International Bank for Reconstruction and Development, and as soon as civilian high commissioners replaced military governors in Western Germany, the President sent him there. The fundamental quality in McCloy's nature is vitality, a rare and priceless gift. He never tires, never flags. His mind stays fresh, imaginative and vigorous throughout a whole night of complex negotiations. Physically he bounces. Jack McCloy has been known to wear to tatters two pairs of socks during a tennis match, a game at which he excels. A man of his temperament is forthright. Where security is necessary, he can keep quiet; but if an argument is going on, his views are pretty likely to pop out.[29]

Robert A. Lovett

Robert A. Lovett was born in Huntsville, Texas, in 1895. He was graduated from Yale in 1918. He was a highly decorated pilot in the First World War. After the war Lovett studied law and business administration at Harvard. His business career, beginning in the 1920s, has been with Brown Brothers, Harriman, the international investment banking firm. Lovett resigned from the firm in 1940 when he went to Washington to serve as a special assistant to Secretary of War Stimson. In April 1941 he was appointed Assistant Secretary of War for Air, a post he held until December 1945. Thus Lovett was the civilian official most directly responsible for the growth of American military air power during World War II. It was during this period that Lovett came to be closely associated with General George C. Marshall. In July 1947 Marshall asked Lovett to serve as his Undersecretary of State, succeeding Dean Acheson.

Acheson offered this commentary:

> General Marshall went about choosing my successor as he did other decisions—no meetings, no lists of names, no papers on desired qualifications. He thought about the question and came to a conclusion. What would I think, he asked me, of Robert A. Lovett? He had been an Assistant Secretary of War for Air during the war and had gone back to his banking business in New York. We had known each other since Yale days. He had all the necessary requirements of mind, character, and Washington experience. Most importantly, that experience included years of working with General Marshall under the severe pressures of wartime. He knows Europe well. I thought it an excellent idea.[30]

Lovett served as Undersecretary until January 1949.

In 1950 Lovett was appointed Deputy Secretary of Defense, and in 1951 he was appointed Secretary, a position he held until 1953. Thus, Lovett served at the highest levels of defense decision-making during the Korean war as he had during World War II.

Since 1953 Lovett has been a general partner in Brown Brothers, Harriman and Company, returning only briefly to Washington from time to time when his advice is solicited in moments of crisis as, for example, the Cuban missile crisis, October 1962.[31]

John McCloy, Robert Lovett, and Harvey Bundy were all successful attorneys experienced in the world of high finance. One would expect that Colonel Stimson, a successful lawyer in New York City, who took the time during the 1920s to make himself rich, would attract bright and energetic younger men with similar interests and background, as his protégés. The esteem that Stimson felt for his younger civilian assistants was indicated when he personally wrote the citations for awards of the Distinguished Service Medal that each received for services to the

Army and the nation. There is also evidence that Stimson's public career served as a model for other men of similar background who were to play prominent roles in Cold War national-security policy-making. McGeorge Bundy and Dean Acheson are notable examples, and so, one assumes, is William Bundy.

TIES AMONG THE ELITES

If we see here preliminary data that might be consistent with a Cold War policy elite, it is well to realize that the unity may be that of men who enjoy close personal and social ties, plus perhaps the additional effect of the old school tie. Some of these social and political relationships are quite well known. Harvey Bundy served as a principal aide to Colonal Stimson in two cabinet positions. McGeorge Bundy served as Stimson's official biographer and was later to perform a somewhat similar function for Dean Acheson, although Bundy was then a Republican foreign policy adviser. William Bundy is married to Dean Acheson's daughter.

Each of the men mentioned in the previous two paragraphs was graduated from Ivy League institutions (with Yale predominating) except for McCloy, who chose Amherst among the little ivies. All are graduates of Harvard Law School except McGeorge Bundy, who did not study law. The careers of all of these men mesh nicely with Mills's notion of "the interchangeability of positions" open to members of the elite in a society where economic, political, and military bureaucratic structures are closely linked.

How closely are leading members of this elite linked with an American establishment? Professor Galbraith offers the following view:

> The Roosevelt administration had been in the closest wartime association with the Soviets under Stalin; most of its members had taken the association very seriously. Some had been romantic. Now with Stalin the archenemy and the Soviet Union the international villain, those who had been involved were not the sort of men to be entrusted with the new policy. It had better be someone whose intelligence was considerable, whose respectability was impeccable and whose anti-Communist sympathies were beyond doubt.[32]

So the business community and the bar, and especially "the New York legal establishment," recruited, Galbraith tells us, Robert Lovett, Paul Hoffman, John J. McCloy, the Dulles brothers, William Foster, Paul Nitze, and many others. David Halberstam portrays McGeorge Bundy in Washington during the early 1960s as "one of the Establishment's key men," a man who seemed to be another John J. McCloy. Halberstam continues, "In succeeding to the Ford Foundation, indeed, there was a feeling that he had succeeded McCloy ... as head of the Establishment for a generation." [33]

Graham Allison places Acheson, McCloy, and Lovett, who were private citizens at the time, within the inner circle of closed Presidential decision-making during the Cuban missile crisis in October 1962. In doing so, he identified these three men as "representatives of the bipartisan foreign policy establishment" who joined JFK's ExCOM (Executive Committee of the National Security Council) group as "Presidentially selected surrogates for major segments of the public." Allison makes nothing of the fact that no member of the Congress participated in the ExCOM meetings, nor does he explain which major segments of the public Acheson, McCloy, and Lovett represented at the brink of nuclear Armageddon.[34]

The preliminary analysis in this chapter suggests McCloy, Lovett, Acheson, Stimson, and the Bundys as prime candidates for membership in a national security policy elite, an elite with a *potential* for exercising an enormous influence on policy. We have discovered that a small group of civilian officials in Secretary Stimson's office was extremely influential in linking the development of atomic weapons with a policy of firm resistance to Soviet objectives in Europe. The A-bombs were dropped on Japanese cities to "impress" Soviet leaders as well as the Japanese. Within the inner circle of closed politics a secret decision was made that simply ignored the possibility of *not* using the bombs. This poses a fundamental, and, as Alperovitz has noted, an extremely subtle, question:

> Why did men whose ultimate motives are not in doubt, come to ignore information? Why did they blot out other possibilities? And why did they consciously or unconsciously refuse to con-

sider different approaches? It is not why they cruelly "decided" to destroy large numbers of Japanese civilians, but why they never even thought this was an issue.[35]

BUREAUCRACY AND THE MORAL FACTOR

The failure of intelligent and honorable men to see the issue is an aspect of elite behavior calling for deeper study. Other observers have noted similar behavior patterns in later decisions. James Thomson, Jr., has written about the factor of "bureaucratic detachment" in relation to Vietnam decision-making.[36] Richard J. Barnet, reflecting on the Cold War as a whole, is closer to the finding in this chapter. Barnet refers to men committing "bureaucratic homicide" in situations where "their official roles insulate them from personal responsibility for their actions." [37] Robert Jervis's pioneering study of the manner in which the political-bureaucratic actor misperceives the actions and intentions of other actors may have a bearing on this problem. Jervis hypothesizes that decision-makers tend to fit incoming information into their existing theories and images. He further assumes that men's theories and images play a large part in determining *what they notice*.[38] Bureaucratic detachment, bureaucratic arrogance, bureaucratic homicide may be related to a basic misperception of external reality; indeed, such bureaucratic behavior may be *eased* by misperceptions based upon image, myth, and theory. In any event, in this instance we have glimpsed an elite group, centering in the office of the Secretary of War, deciding (or assuming) in secret to use atomic weapons against cities crowded with hundreds of thousands of civilians; the bombs were used in this fashion partly as an instrument of diplomacy in a political struggle with the Soviet Union over patterns of control in postwar Europe. The decision was heavily influenced by elite-held theories and images of Soviet *intentions*.

A small group of key civilian officials having strong personal and social ties with centers of economic and political orthodoxy heavily influenced the decision to drop atomic bombs on two Japanese cities. Ostensibly this was done as a means of effecting a surrender. Actually the bombs were used because a policy-making elite held profound apprehensions about the role the Soviet Union might be expected to play in world affairs after the Japanese surrender. Leading members of the same policy elite rapidly developed views about ways in which Germany and Japan might be revived partially to counterbalance Soviet power and ambitions.

This preliminary analysis has brought forth little which would suggest that the first generation of Cold War civilian militants felt any urgent need to have their policy biases exposed to public debate or to critical analysis. To the contrary, these were men whose careers essentially lay outside the thrust and clash of democratic political action. The general operating assumption of the Stimson-Bundy-McCloy-Lovett group seemed to be that their policy views coincided with the public interest. Certainly the Congressional checks and balances had no functional relevance in this situation. The attentive public could have had no awareness of the decision or of the factors that entered into it. There is abundant evidence showing that Stimson's men were active in promoting their views within the higher levels of the executive establishment. These men had a special "view of the world" and of the role American technocratic power, armed with nuclear weapons, ought to play in the postwar era. This is not to suggest that there were not other men, influentially located, with different views. A number of leading military men are known to have believed that the use of the A-bomb was *not* a military necessity. Whose views prevailed? The question that must be examined further is whether the Cold War ideology adumbrated in the thinking of Secretary Stimson and his key men in 1945 bears a strong resemblance to views subsequently held by a similar national security policy elite whose views also tended to prevail over a long period of time. We shall also be curious to see how influential Stimson's men may have been in later years.

CONCLUSION

Before moving on to an analysis of subsequent Cold War decisions, it seems appropriate to review what Henry L. Stimson had to say about the American world mission on the occasion of his eightieth birthday:

> Americans must now understand that the United States has become, for better or worse, a wholly committed member of the world community. . . . It is the first condition of effective foreign policy that this nation put away forever any thought that America can again be an island to herself. . . . Atomic energy and Soviet Russia are merely the two most conspicuous present demonstrations of what we have at stake in world affairs. . . . As a corollary to this first great principle, it follows that we shall be wholly wrong if we attempt to set a maximum or margin to our activity as members of the world. The only question we can safely ask today is whether in any of our actions on the world stage we are doing enough. . . . How soon this nation will fully understand the size and nature of its present mission, I do not dare to say. But I venture to assert that in very large degree the future of mankind depends on the answer to this question.[39]

These were Henry L. Stimson's views in 1947.

Two decades later James C. Thomson, Jr., who served as a Cold War technician in Washington from 1961 through 1966, reflecting on escalation in Vietnam—and asking, "how could it happen?"—pointed to "a new breed of American ideologue":

> I have in mind those men in Washington who have given a new life to the missionary impulse in American foreign relations: who believe that this nation, in this era, has received a three-fold endowment that can transform the world. As they see it, that endowment is composed of first, our unsurpassed military might; second, our clear technological supremacy; and, third, our allegedly invincible benevolence, our "altruism," our affluence, our lack of territorial aspirations. Together, it is argued, this three-fold endowment provides us with the opportunity and the obligation to ease the nations of the earth toward modernization and stability: toward a full fledged PAX AMERICANA TECHNOCRATICA.[40]

Perhaps the question is: How new was the "new breed" American ideologue of the 1960s; was his ideology common among members of a national-security policy elite? Are the Cold War ideologues of the 1960s, as portrayed by Thomson, Barnet, and others, directly related to their counterparts in the 1940s and 1950s? Are they often the same people? Do certain individuals appear and reappear in key positions within the inner circle of closed politics during a number of vital periods throughout the Cold War? Have we focused on members of a distinct, well-defined elite group? Does this particular group's potential for "control" of national security policy appear to be something more than "potential"? Do the policy preferences of this elite group tend to prevail, in a presumably pluralistic system, over long periods of time? Who poses the alternative policies? Who checks the Cold War civilian militants?

Chapter Two Notes

1. Gar Alperovitz has shown in *Atomic Diplomacy: Hiroshima and Potsdam* (1965) how possession of nuclear weapons gave American policy-makers an exaggerated sense of confidence, what Sir Denis Brogan called the American "sense of omnipotence," in their dealings with the Soviet Union. See also William Appleman Williams's *The Tragedy of American Diplomacy* (1959), which portrays United States policy in the early years of the Cold War as part of a larger pattern of globalism reaching back to 1898. According to this interpretation, our diplomacy has followed the "open door" policy, a policy of expansionism that seeks to extend United States influence across the globe. Hence, Williams argues that most American leaders were operating on assumptions that defined the world in terms of a cold war long before anyone knew the bomb would work. D. F. Fleming's two-volume study, *The Cold War and Its Origins* (1961), argues that Russia's military weakness following the war dictated a policy of postwar cooperation, but Western leaders' hostility to Communism prevented them from seeing this. Fleming writes at one point: "The Cold War as proclaimed by Churchill and Truman would have been impractical from the start had it not been for the American A-bomb monopoly, in which both leaders took the deepest satisfaction."

2. Henry L. Stimson and McGeorge Bundy, *On Active Service in Peace and War* (New York: Harper, 1947).

3. See David Halberstam, "The Very Expensive Education of McGeorge Bundy," *Harper's Magazine,* July 1969, for more detail concerning the Bundy-Stimson relationship. Halberstam sees McGeorge Bundy as a key establishment representative in Washington in the 1960s.

4. Stimson and Bundy, *On Active Service,* p. 617. Much of the material in this chapter concerning Stimson's role in the decision is drawn from his authorized biography.

5. Ibid., p. 631.

6. See Gar Alperovitz, *Cold War Essays,* introduction by Christopher Lasch (New York: Doubleday-Anchor, 1970), pp. 62–63. Feis was appointed economic adviser to Secretary of State Henry

L. Stimson in 1931. He remained in the State Department until 1943, when he moved to the War Department, where Stimson had become the Secretary of War. In 1947 Feis left the War Department and began writing history, including a five-volume diplomatic history of World War II.

7. Stimson and Bundy, *On Active Service,* p. 633.

8. Ibid.

9. Ibid.

10. Ibid., pp. 628–29.

11. Ibid., p. 629.

12. Alperovitz, *Cold War Essays,* pp. 53–54.

13. Stimson and Bundy, *On Active Service,* pp. 629–30.

14. Walter S. Schoenberger, *Decision of Destiny* (Columbus, Ohio: Ohio University Press, 1969), p. 127.

15. Ibid., p. 138.

16. Elting E. Morrison, *Turmoil and Tradition: A Study of the Life and Times of Henry L. Stimson* (Boston: Houghton Mifflin, 1960), p. 630.

17. *The Forrestal Diaries,* ed. Walter Millis (New York: Viking, 1951), is the best source of his views. Alperovitz finds that James Byrnes, not Stimson, was President Truman's "closest confidant on the role of the new weapon" (Alperovitz, *Cold War Essays,* p. 65). This is Alperovitz's summary view of Byrnes as "cold warrior" (p. 73):

> Truman's personal representative for atomic matters and his Secretary of State—the forgotten man of Cold War history—almost always urged the hard line: in April 1945, his recommendation that the bomb would permit America "to dictate our own terms"; in May 1945, his view that the bomb would make Russia more "manageable"; in July–August 1945, his hope that it would keep Russia out of Manchuria; his need, in September 1945, to have the weapon "in his pocket" to impress Molotov; his complaint to Forrestal, early in 1947, that the Russians "don't scare"; and finally, his demand, in mid-1947 for "measures of the last resort" to force Russia to yield in European negotiations.

See also James Byrnes, *Speaking Frankly* (New York: Harper, 1947).

18. Stimson and Bundy, *On Active Service,* p. 637.

19. Quoted by Alperovitz, *Cold War Essays,* p. 69.

20. Ibid., p. 68.

21. Stimson and Bundy, *On Active Service*, pp. 639–40.

22. Ibid., pp. 640–41.

23. Ibid., p. 641.

24. Ibid., pp. 644–45.

25. Dean Acheson, *Present at the Creation* (New York: W. W. Norton, 1969), p. 124.

26. Ibid.

27. *New York Times*, August 22, 1945.

28. Alperovitz, *Atomic Diplomacy*, p. 115.

29. Dean Acheson, *Sketches from Life* (New York: Harper, 1960).

30. Ibid., p. 236.

31. See Graham T. Allison, *Essence of Decision* (Boston: Little, Brown, 1971), p. 215.

32. John Kenneth Galbraith, *Who Needs the Democrats and What It Takes to Be Needed* (New York: Signet Broadside, 1970), p. 36.

33. Halberstam, "The Very Expensive Education," p. 37.

34. Allison, *Essence of Decision*, p. 215.

35. Alperovitz, *Cold War Essays*, p. 72.

36. James C. Thomson, Jr., "How Could Vietnam Happen? An Autopsy," *The Atlantic Monthly*, April 1968, pp. 49–53.

37. Richard J. Barnet, *Roots of War* (New York: Atheneum, 1972), pp. 13–16.

38. Robert Jervis, "Hypotheses on Misperception," *World Politics*, Vol. 20, No. 3 (April 1968), 454–79.

39. Stimson and Bundy, *On Active Service*, pp. 652–55.

40. Thomson, "How Could Vietnam Happen?", p. 53.

3 CONTAINMENT: THE NEW AMERICAN STRATEGIC-POLITICAL DOCTRINE, 1947

. . . it is clear that the main element of any United States policy toward the Soviet Union must be that of a long-term, patient but firm and vigilant containment of Russian expansive tendencies.

Mr. X article (July 1947)

This chapter examines the origins of containment in the Truman Doctrine and in the Mr. X article, although the preliminary analysis undertaken in chapter 2 indicates that the assumptions on which containment was based were taking shape in official thinking as early as the summer and autumn of 1945, before the Japanese surrender. The Cold War started in men's minds before the hot war had ended. Fortunately for this analysis of Cold War national security decision-making, there is a rather full record concerning the containment concept, especially as it figured in the making of United States policy in 1947. The principal author of the containment concept, so far as the attentive public was concerned, was George Kennan, a career Foreign Service officer chosen to head the State Department's new Policy Planning Staff, a creation of General Marshall's, just as United States relations with Russia in Europe reached a point of severe crisis during the harsh winter of 1947.

Kennan formally assumed the chairmanship of the Policy Planning Staff on May 5, 1947, after having been advised some months earlier by Undersecretary Dean Acheson that such a planning staff was soon to be created with Kennan to head it. The establishment of the Policy Planning Staff was accelerated by the crisis in Europe that led to the Truman Doctrine and the Marshall Plan.

Kennan seemed admirably suited by training and background for the new post. A career Foreign Service officer, well seasoned in a number of important positions in our European embassies during the 1930s, he had spent the latter war years in Moscow. Kennan knew the Russian language and culture; his interpretations of Russian society were based on years of study and reflection. By 1946 Kennan, filled with foreboding about future relations between the United States and the USSR and troubled by what he regarded as falsely optimistic American expectations about Soviet behavior, had decided to let his superiors in Washington "have it." On February 22, 1946, in response to an official inquiry, Kennan, who was acting head of our Moscow embassy, fired off an eight-thousand-word telegram to the State Department.[1]

THE KENNAN TELEGRAM

The telegram offered a five-part (all neatly divided, like an eighteenth-century Protestant sermon, Kennan later mused) analysis presenting:

a) the basic features of the Soviet postwar outlook;
b) the background of that outlook; ·
c) its projection on the level of official policy;
d) its projection on the level of unofficial policy, that is, policy implemented through front organizations, etc., and
e) the implications of all this for American policy.

Kennan justified the length of his telegraphic response by noting that the department's query had involved "questions so intricate, so delicate, so strange to our form of thought, and so important to the analysis of our international environment that I cannot compress the answers into a single brief message without yielding to ... a dangerous degree of oversimplification." The effect produced in Washington by Kennan's long telegram was, in his words, "nothing less than sensational." Dean Acheson, who was later to disagree with Kennan fundamentally on issues relating directly to the nature of the Soviet threat, termed it a "truly remarkable" dispatch, which had "a deep effect on thinking within the Government." [2]

More specifically, Kennan's dispatch had a deep effect on the thinking of certain key members of the policy elite within the national security bureaucracy.

Acheson summarized Kennan's thesis:

> He found "at the bottom of the Kremlin's neurotic view of world affairs" centuries of a Russian fear of physical, and a tyranny's fear of political, insecurity. To the Government, whether czarist or bolshevik, penetration by the Western world was its greatest danger. Marxism, "with its basic altruism of purpose" furnished them with justification for their "fear of [the] outside world. . . . In the name of Marxism they sacrificed every single ethical value in their methods and tactics. Today they cannot dispense with it. It is [the] fig leaf of their moral and intellectual respectability." [3]

Acheson continued:

> Kennan predicted that Soviet policy would be to use every means to infiltrate, divide, and weaken the West. Means would include the foreign communist parties, diplomacy, international organizations—blocking what they did not like, starting false trails to divert—probing weak spots by every means. To seek a *modus vivendi* with Moscow would prove chimerical, a process leading not to an end but only to political warfare. [4]

While Undersecretary Acheson felt that Kennan's historical analysis "might or might not have been sound," he was certain that "his predictions and warnings could not have been better." [5] Acheson was not alone in his reaction to Kennan's message. James Forrestal, energetic Secretary of the Navy, the former president of Dillon, Read Company, became an enthusiastic Kennan booster. Forrestal not only circulated Kennan's views throughout the higher echelons of the national security bureaucracy, he also sponsored Kennan as the only civilian leader in a quadrumvirate chosen to head the newly established National War College. The War College was intended as the senior establishment for in-service training in the problems of national policy, military and political; the institution owed its existence principally to Forrestal, who early saw the need for special training in strategic-political doctrine on the part of Cold War technocrats.

Kennan, whose career was transformed overnight by the "success" of his long telegram, entered into the War College directorship with enthusiasm. It is best to let Kennan describe the purpose of the War College as he viewed it in 1946:

Not only were we all new to this subject [strategic-political doctrine], personally and institutionally, but we had, as we turned to it, virtually nothing in the way of an established or traditional American doctrine which we could take as a point of departure for our thinking and teaching. It was a mark of the weakness of all previous American thinking about international affairs that there was almost nothing in American political literature of the past one hundred years on the subject of the relationship of war to politics. American thinking about foreign policy had been primarily addressed to the problems of peace, and had taken place largely within the frameworks of international law and international economics.[6]

Kennan saw the need for a fundamental rethinking of the use of American power in the atomic age:

A strategic-political doctrine would have to be devised for this country which gave promise not simply of expanding the material and military power of a single nation but of making the strength of that nation a force for peace and stability in international affairs and helping, in particular, to avoid the catastrophe of atomic war.[7]

As Kennan and his military colleagues, Admiral Harry W. Hill and Generals Alfred M. Gruenther and Truman H. Landon, proceeded "so buoyantly" to the inauguration of this new institution, a Cold War academy, he hoped that it would come to serve "as a home for the development of such a doctrine."

The doctrine, as it turned out, was the doctrine of containment, and one of its principal authors was George F. Kennan, a role he later found uncongenial. Kennan was soon called away from the War College, where, "all in all" he had never known "a more enjoyable professional experience."

Kennan was summoned to the office of the Secretary of State, General George C. Marshall, on April 29, 1947, one day after the general's return from the Moscow conference. Kennan was told to leave the War College immediately and to come to the State Department in order to set up the Policy Planning Staff without delay. The Staff was formally established on May 5, 1947. Its first assignment was the problem of European economic recovery, its first policy "input" the series of decisions that led to the Marshall Plan.

AID TO GREECE AND TURKEY

Actually, Kennan had been drawn into State Department activity in connection with the crisis in Greece and Turkey in response to a summons from Undersecretary Acheson on February 24. He served briefly as a member of a special committee that Acheson set up to study the whole problem of assistance to Greece and Turkey under the chairmanship of Loy Henderson.

Kennan later recalled that "we had before us ... the task of recommending whether to respond affirmatively at all to the problem posed for us by the British withdrawal, or whether to leave the Greeks and Turks to their own devices." [8]

Henderson's recollection was that this question, so far as the State Department was concerned, had already been decided in principle by Acheson and himself over the preceding weekend; hence, the committee's task was simply to recommend in more detail the course of action to be taken by the President.

Henderson's view has been confirmed by Acheson, who had been instructed by General Marshall on Friday, February 21, to prepare the necessary steps for sending economic and military aid. Henderson's staff worked all weekend preparing the preliminary papers. On Sunday, February 23, the results of this hasty effort were brought to Acheson's home in Georgetown for final review. The Undersecretary found them to be in good shape. When Henderson asked whether they were still working on papers bearing on the making of a decision or the execution of one, Acheson recalls: "I said the latter; *under the circumstances there could be only one decision.* At that we drank a martini or two toward the confusion of our enemies." [Italics mine.] [9]

It would appear, therefore, that the decision to send American military aid to Greece and Turkey, following the sudden British announcement of the termination of their aid, was taken as early as February 21 in the case of General Marshall, the Secretary of State, and no later than February 23 in the case of Undersecretary Acheson.

On Monday, February 24, the day Kennan was first summoned to participation by Acheson, General Marshall was already discussing his recommendation with the President and with the Secretaries of War and Navy. The next day the President approved for action the paper that had been prepared under Acheson's direction the previous weekend. The committee that Kennan had joined prepared the papers which led to the Presidential decision, but the decision to extend American aid to Greece and Turkey was well advanced before the summoning of Kennan to participate in the staff work leading to the ultimate formal decision.

THE TRUMAN DOCTRINE

It seems more than a little ironic that Kennan later came to be viewed by many in the attentive public as a principal architect of the Truman Doctrine, when, in fact, his own direct impact on the literary effort preceding the President's message of March 22, 1947, was slight, if indeed it was not nonexistent.[10] When Kennan, on or about March 6, first saw the State Department's draft of the Presidential message to Congress, he was "extremely unhappy." The rationale for the President's decision had been framed in language "more grandiose and more sweeping" than anything the author of the long telegram had ever envisaged. When Kennan remonstrated to Acheson and suggested alternative language, his effort proved abortive. Kennan himself was later unable to remember whether his remonstrations were met with much understanding inasmuch as the die had been cast. "No one wanted to repeat the agony of collective drafting that had been invested over the preceding days in the production of this historic piece of paper," Kennan drearily recorded in his memoirs.[11]

What the historic piece of paper said, of course, was:

We shall not meet our objectives ... unless we are willing to help free people to maintain their free institutions and their national integrity against aggressive movements that seek to impose upon them totalitarian regimes. This is no more than a frank recognition that totalitarian regimes imposed upon free peoples, by direct or indirect aggression, undermine the foundations of internal peace and hence the security of the United States. ...
At the present moment in world history nearly every nation must choose alternative ways of life. The choice is too often not a free

one. . . . I believe that it must be the policy of the United States to support free peoples who are resisting attempted subjugation by armed minorities or by outside pressure.[12]

The Truman Doctrine, aimed at a particular situation in Greece and Turkey in the winter and spring of 1947, was phrased in universal language. Its simplistic Cold War language was the work of Joseph Jones and his fellow draftsmen in the foreign policy bureaucracy. Kennan thought the use of such sweeping language a mistake and he said so—but to no avail.

Two decades later Kennan had an opportunity to reflect on "this persistent American urge to the universalization or generalization of decision."

"We obviously dislike to discriminate," he observed.

We like to find some general governing norm to which in each instance, appeal can be taken, so that individual decisions may be made not on their particular merits but automatically, depending on whether the circumstances do or do not seem to fit the norm. We like, by the same token, to attribute a universal significance to decisions we have already found it necessary, for limited or parochial reasons, to take.[13]

The record seems fairly clear that weeks before he formally assumed the chairmanship of the State Department's new Policy Planning Staff, George Kennan entertained real, if initial, doubts about the manner in which the thoughts he poured forth in the long telegram, a year earlier, had been translated into public language and Presidential message. Kennan's role as articulator of Cold War doctrine for the attentive public had not yet begun.

It would be a mistake, of course, to assume that Kennan's long telegram was the only substantial document circulating within the inner circle that was to have an impact in crystallizing a hard American position vis-à-vis the Soviet Union. Arthur Krock's *Memoirs,* published in 1968, carried as an Appendix a top secret document prepared in the office of Clark Clifford, Special Counsel to President Truman, in September 1946, advocating a global policy of military strength based upon atomic weapons, "to restrain the Soviet Union and to confine Soviet influence to its present area." [14]

Until the summer of 1947, Kennan's views were known only

to other key participants within the national security decision-making elite. Any misinterpretations, up to that point, had occurred within the inner circle of closed politics.

THE MR. X ARTICLE

In July 1947, *Foreign Affairs* published the since-famous Mr. X article, "The Sources of Soviet Conduct." The author was George Kennan, a fact soon to become public knowledge. Once again, as in the case of the long telegram, a statement analyzing Soviet behavior and suggesting an appropriate American reaction quickly established Kennan as a principal shaper of Cold War policy. This was a role Kennen later found to be as uncomfortable as it was misleading. The Mr. X article also resembles the long telegram in the thesis it presents: Soviet power is viewed as being the product of ideology and circumstances:

> Now the outstanding circumstance concerning the Soviet regime is that down to the present day this process of political consolidation has never been completed and the men in the Kremlin have continued to be predominantly absorbed with the struggle to secure and make absolute the power which they seized in November 1917. They have endeavored to secure it primarily against forces at home, within Soviet society. But they have also endeavored to secure it against the outside world. . . .
>
> . . . it will be clearly seen that the Soviet pressure against the free institutions of the Western world is something that can be contained by the adroit and vigilant application of counter-force at a series of constantly shifting geographical and political points, corresponding to the shifts and maneuvers of Soviet policy, but which cannot be charmed or talked out of existence. . . .[15]

These brief excerpts from Kennan's paper hardly do justice to his thesis, but they do present two basic points that were to prove extremely troublesome: the nature of the internal Soviet regime as related to its external drives and the necessity of meeting Soviet external moves by the application of counterforce.

On the first point, Kennan was shortly to be overruled by his superiors within the policy-making elite. This aspect will be examined in some detail when Dean Acheson's contributions to

Cold War policy are reviewed in the next chapter. Briefly, Kennan's views on the relative weight to be assigned to the various factors pushing Soviet expansion came to be regarded within the inner circle as being merely technical and hence irrelevant to the objective of containing Soviet power.

Kennan himself realized, albeit belatedly, that his language concerning the application of counter-force was ambiguous. Perhaps the most serious defect of the X article, in Kennan's retrospective judgment

> was the failure to make clear that what I was talking about when I mentioned the containment of Soviet power *was not the containment by military means of a military threat, but the political containment of a political threat.* [Italics mine.] [16]

The publication of the X article led to a lengthy and biting attack by Walter Lippmann, an attack steeped in irony inasmuch as Kennan was soon to fall from grace within Acheson's policy-making elite for expressing views within the inner circle remarkably similar at certain points to those publicly advanced by Lippmann in his critique.[17] Lippmann deemed it a fundamental error in statecraft to base United States policy on the dubious assumption that Soviet power bore "within itself the seeds of its own destruction" and that "the sprouting of the seeds was well advanced." The notion that United States policy should seek to "contain" the Soviet Union by attempting to make "unassailable barriers" out of surrounding border states also seemed unrealistic to Lippmann. Such states, he warned, are likely to be *weak* states:

> Now a weak ally is not an asset. It is a liability. It requires the diversion of power, money, and prestige to support it and to maintain it. These weak states are vulnerable. Yet the effort to defend them brings us no nearer to a decision or to a settlement of the main conflict.[18]

The key factor was not Marxist ideology, as Mr. X seemed to imply, but the presence and the power of the Red Army. Hence, Lippmann urged a major American diplomatic effort aimed at getting the Red Army back to Soviet territory. The central issue was to "negotiate, sign and ratify a treaty of peace for Germany and Austria to which the Soviet government is a party." There was a fundamental difference, he thought, between the approach found in the Marshall Plan, which viewed European governments as independent powers, and the Truman Doctrine, which treated those it was supposed to benefit as "dependencies of the United States, as instruments of the American policy for 'containing' Russia." Finally, Lippmann noted the crucial flaw:

> The policy of containment, as Mr. X has exposed it to the world, does not have as its objective a settlement of the conflict with Russia. . . . At the root of Mr. X's philosophy about Russian-American relations and underlying all the ideas of the Truman Doctrine there is a disbelief in the possibility of a settlement of the issues raised by this war.[19]

One of the difficulties to be faced in making an assessment of the X article is that it did not always state clearly the views of the man who wrote it. This may be explained, at least in part, by the fact that the essay was not written for publication but was simply a paper prepared by Kennan for the "private edification," as he so felicitously put it, of Secretary of the Navy James Forrestal. Why Kennan ever assumed that anything as momentous as Soviet behavior in the Cold War could be discussed with Forrestal on a simple basis of his "private edification" must remain an unresolved mystery, at least so far as this analysis goes.

Why then was the X article published in *Foreign Affairs,* the journal of the Council on Foreign Relations, unofficial voice of the foreign policy establishment? The trail of the X article is worth tracing since it sheds light on elite behavior in relation to the attentive public. In December 1946 Forrestal sent Kennan a paper on Marxism and Soviet power (a subject soon to preoccupy the Secretary of the Navy), soliciting Kennan's comments. After reading the paper, which had been prepared by a member of Forrestal's entourage, Kennan replied by saying that he would prefer addressing himself to the same subject in his own words. On January 31, 1947, Kennan sent Forrestal "for his private and personal edification" a paper later known as the X paper. Forrestal read Kennan's paper and acknowledged it, saying that he found it "extremely well done." He added that he was going to suggest "the Secretary" read it. Kennan assumed he meant the Secretary of State. Whether General Marshall read the paper or not is unclear, but Forrestal did share the paper with Arthur Krock of the *New York Times,* who later had no trouble in identifying the author when the article appeared in *Foreign Affairs.*

In the meantime, Kennan was busy speaking on the same subject, notoriously a far more ambiguous way of communicating a complicated subject than by way of the written word. Early in January Kennan spoke on the same subject informally at the Council on Foreign Relations in New York. Hamilton Fish Armstrong, editor of *Foreign Affairs,* recognized this as a piece for his journal. Since Kennan had no text for his council talk, he thought immediately of the paper he had previously prepared for Forrestal.

It is well to let Kennan describe the rest of the route to publication:

> In early March . . . I sought and obtained Mr. Forrestal's assurance that he had no objection to its publication. I then submitted it (March 13) [the day after the President's message to Congress enunciating the Truman Doctrine] to the Committee on Unofficial Publication, of the Department of State, for the usual official clearance. In doing so, I explained that it was the intention that it should be published anonymously. The committee pondered it at leisure, found in it nothing particularly remarkable or dangerous from the government's standpoint, and issued, on April 8, permission for its publication in the manner indicated.[20]

All that remained was for Kennan to cross out his own name, replacing it with an X to assure anonymity, and to send the paper on to Armstrong, with whom this association was to initiate a long and close friendship.

Kennan appears mystified by the manner in which his X article launched the containment dogma. This is a matter we return to shortly. But why was Kennan, a sophisticated and intelligent man, so careless about an essay on a matter of such obvious importance, at a moment so close to an hour of great—even ominous —national decision? Kennan had just come from a losing battle in an internal struggle within the policy elite concerning the language that was used in the Presidential message when he submitted his X paper to the State Department committee for clearance, and yet his article is subject to the same flaw; that is, it seems to be enunciating a doctrine of universal scope. Why was the author less sensitive to his own language in an essay he had recently written on a subject about which he obviously felt strongly?

Kennan did have a choice in the matter after all. He might have declined to have his views published in *Foreign Affairs,* or he might have taken pains to rewrite a paper that he admits was prepared with no thought of publication in a journal widely read by people seriously interested in American foreign policy. Kennan is a serious and committed man. Armstrong was a serious and committed editor. Is it not reasonable to assume that the X article was published in order to broaden understanding among the attentive public of American foreign policy as it was being formulated in the early months of 1947? Whether Kennan fully realized it or not, what alternative was there but to regard the publication of the X article as a semiofficial effort to popularize the new Cold War rationale? Kennan, who had been outside the United States most of the time between the early 1930s and 1946, may have held a naïve view of the nexus of relationships among foreign policy elite, the mass media, and the attentive public in the shaping of public attitudes on foreign policy issues. In any event, Kennan appears to have been unprepared for the sequence of events that followed publication of his anonymous article.

On July 8 Arthur Krock hinted at the official origin of the X article in his *Times* column; shortly thereafter, the authorship of the article became common knowledge. *Life* and *Reader's Digest* reprinted long excerpts. In all of this Kennan remained "innocent and unsuspecting." As he later reflected in his *Memoirs:*

> What I said in the X article was not intended as a doctrine. I am afraid that when I think about foreign policy, I do not think in terms of doctrines, I think in terms of principles.[21]

Kennan has his own view of how these things happen:

> The term "containment" was picked up and elevated, by common agreement of the press, to the status of a "doctrine," which was then identified with the foreign policy of the administration. In this way there was established—before our eyes so to speak—one of those indestructible myths that are the bane of the historian.[22]

In this way, everyone involved in creating the containment doctrine, except the press, gets off the hook.

Obviously, the article was published to serve a purpose. Once the identity of Mr. X had been established, the Mr. X article was "no longer just one more report on the Soviet regime and what to do about it. It was an event, announcing that the Department of State had made up its mind, and was prepared to disclose to the American people, to the world at large, and of course to the Kremlin the estimates, the calculations, and the conclusions on which the Department was basing its plans," Walter Lippmann observed.[23]

Why is it difficult for Kennan to understand what transpired at this stage in the process, when he readily appreciated what was happening as his long telegram bounced around the corridors of power?

This is his insightful view of the official reaction to the long telegram:

> Six months earlier this message would probably have been received in the Department of State with raised eyebrows and lips pursed in disapproval. Six months later, it would probably have sounded redundant, a sort of preaching to the convinced. . . . All this only goes to show that more important than the observable nature of external reality, when it comes to the determination of Washington's view of the world, is the subjective state of readiness on the part of Washington officialdom to recognize this or that feature of it.[24]

About a year and a half before the appearance of the X article, Kennan set out to influence Washington's view of the world on a matter of the greatest importance, our relations with the Soviet Union. His long telegram sent in February 1946 had a more pronounced effect in crystallizing the Cold War policy views of the national security elite than he could have possibly imagined. His own professional career prospered as a result. He became a leading architect of official Cold War thinking. His own view of his purpose at the War College was to create a new strategic-political doctrine. The paper he prepared for James Forrestal appears to have been a reasonably accurate reflection of the doctrine he was helping to create. Kennan experienced no difficulty in talking about the doctrine with select audiences at the War College, at the Council on Foreign Relations, and elsewhere. He was perfectly willing to have his views, as expressed in the X article, appear in *Foreign Affairs*. He must have known that people outside the inner circle of closed politics read *Foreign Affairs*.

Kennan's explanation contains an unstated (was it also unconscious?) assumption: that it is appropriate and fitting for the strategic-political doctrine to be discussed in elite circles where these matters, in all their complexity and subtlety, are understood; but it is a mistake and a perversion of the "process" for these esoteric views to appear in the mass media where they will inevitably find simplistic and crude expression—and where they are certain to be misunderstood! In putting the matter so bluntly, because it seems important to an understanding of elite mentality, there is no suggestion that Kennan was being disingenuous. He *was* in danger of being misunderstood, and not necessarily only by the readers of *Life* and *Reader's Digest*. (I recall having read the X article as a young political scientist, and I certainly did not read it as Kennan presumably hoped a student of public policy would read it: that is, it seemed to be urging political *and military* containment on a universal scale.) Kennan's concern, we learn in reading his *Memoirs* two decades after the X article first appeared, was that many people were "falling into despair" about our relations with the USSR and some were jumping to the panicky conclusion that an eventual war between the two super-powers was inevitable. It was this conclusion Kennan sought to dispute. "I saw no necessity of a Soviet-American war, nor anything to be gained by one, then or at any time," Kennan now advises us.

> There was, I thought, another way of handling this problem—a way that offered reasonable prospects of success, at least in the sense of avoiding a new world disaster and leaving the Western community of nations no worse off than it was. This was simply to cease at that point making fatuous unilateral concessions to the Kremlin, to do what we could to inspire and support resistance elsewhere to its efforts to expand the area of its dominant political influence, and to wait for the internal weaknesses of Soviet power, combined with frustration in the external field, to

moderate Soviet ambitions and behavior. The Soviet leaders, formidable as they were, were not supermen. Like all rulers of great countries, they had their internal contradictions and dilemmas to deal with. Stand up to them, I urged, manfully but not aggressively, and give the hand of time a chance to work.[25]

This is all that the X article was meant to convey.

Kennan was happier as Chairman of the Policy Planning Staff preparing the way for the Marshall Plan; this was the first assignment he received from General Marshall, the Secretary of State. Kennan felt then and later that the new staff made a notable contribution to the concepts on which the Marshall Plan was built. On the other hand, Dean Acheson, who served as Undersecretary under Marshall, assigns a modest role to the Policy Planning Staff during its early months. In Acheson's words:

> He [Marshall, following his return from Moscow on April 28, 1947] immediately put the Policy Planning Staff to work on suggestions for a plan of action to deal with facts already known. It accomplished little more than reiteration that the crisis was immediate and desperate and called urgently for action. Not until a month later, when Clayton returned from Europe with a memorandum written on the plane, did a concrete outline for the Marshall Plan emerge.[26]

One would have to read Acheson's memoirs in full to appreciate how large a responsibility he ascribes to Will Clayton, the Assistant Secretary for Economic Affairs, in preparing other leading members of the State Department policy-making team for the necessity of an American program to undergird European economic recovery. Clayton, who had come to the State Department after heading the Anderson, Clayton Company of Houston, largest cotton exporting company in the world, is portrayed as the leading advocate of massive United States economic assistance to Western Europe in Acheson's account of these events.

KENNAN AND ACHESON: PARTING WAYS

Although it is not possible, reading the Kennan and Acheson memoirs, to pinpoint the time or the occasion of their first major policy disagreement, it is apparent that Acheson relied less and less on Kennan's judgment as time went on. They differed significantly on the crucial issue of Soviet behavior in international politics. This much is clear. Dean Acheson took the oath of office as Secretary of State on January 21, 1949. By September of the same year, Kennan asked to be relieved of his duties as Chairman of the Policy Planning Staff. He had developed substantial doubts about the usefulness of such a body in the State Department, especially under the new Acheson ground rules (put into effect by Undersecretary James Webb) whereby the Assistant Secretaries were free to rewrite Policy Planning documents which no longer went directly to the Secretary. What is more to the point in terms of this study, Acheson had found a man who agreed with his policy premises to head the Policy Planning Staff. Paul Nitze took over the position on January 1, 1950. Within a matter of weeks, Nitze, with Acheson's enthusiastic backing, had guided the development of a national security document of singular importance. NSC–68 called for a major American rearmament, an increase in defense expenditures on an annual basis from less than $14 billion to as much as $50 billion. The principal architects of NSC–68 were Dean Acheson and Paul Nitze, who prevailed against the active opposition of Louis Johnson, the Secretary of Defense, a man politically committed to a $14 billion ceiling. A few months later George Kennan left the department on an extended leave of absence from the Foreign Service in order to assume a more scholarly and reflective position as a member of the Institute for Advanced Study, Princeton.

Neither Kennan nor Acheson appears to have been completely candid in explaining their policy differences, although both men have assumed that their public careers were worthy of being memorialized, as they undoubtedly were. What it comes down to, in essence, is a crucial disagreement in assessing Soviet expansionist tendencies and the appropriate American response. Kennan's view has already been explained. He did not place a high value on the possibility that the Soviets might use overt military force to expand the Russian empire into Western Europe. He was convinced that the Soviet leaders were primarily concerned with protecting the regime from external encroachment.

Acheson, after listening to Kennan and other Soviet experts in the State Department, regarded the argument as stultifying, sterile, and semantic. As he explained it:

> we ran into a stultifying and so I thought, sterile argument between the Planning Staff and the Soviet experts. The latter challenged the belief which I shared with the planners that the Kremlin gave top priority to world domination in their scheme of things. They contended that we attributed more of a Trotskyite than Leninist view to Stalin and that he placed survival of the regime and "communism in one country" far ahead of world revolution. We did not dissent from this, but pointed out that, assuming the proper semantic adjustment, the effect of their point bore on the degree of risk of all-out war which the Soviet government would run in probing a weak spot for concessions.[27]

Since the judgment had to do with the probability of Soviet military aggression into the industrial heart of Western Europe, it seems odd that it was regarded as a matter of mere semantic adjustment. *In any event, George Kennan was gradually excluded from the policy elite in the State Department because his views of these matters differed significantly from those held by Dean Acheson, the leading civilian militant in the national security policy elite.*

Kennan has described these differences as they appeared in September 1949. There were, he felt, two divergences of basic outlook:

> I was trying, as I think befitted one who directed a governmental unit concerned with "planning," to look ten to twenty years into the future. My friends in Washington, London, Paris, and The Hague were thinking of the problems we had immediately before us. But secondly, and even more important, *I did not believe in the reality of a Soviet military threat to Western Europe.* Not believing it, I was concerned not so much to provide protection against the possibility of such an attack (although I recognized the need for some sort of military facade to quiet the anxieties of the jittery Western Europeans) as to facilitate the retirement of Soviet forces, and with them dominant Soviet political influence, to limits closer to the traditional boundaries of the Russian state. [Italics mine.] [28]

On the other side, as Kennan makes clear, the assumption was that American policy should be less concerned about the division of Europe (and perhaps even be content with it) and should concentrate on finding means of deterring a Soviet attack envisaged as likely to take place in the early 1950s.

The intensity of the feelings aroused is suggested in an exchange that occurred in 1957, long after Kennan and Acheson had retired from active policy-making roles. Kennan delivered the BBC Reith lectures in London in December 1957, advocating the withdrawal of American, British, and Russian military forces from the center of Europe and also inveighing against basing the defenses of the continental NATO members on nuclear missiles. Acheson was furious that Kennan had chosen to discuss these basic issues in public (albeit on the other side of the Atlantic). On the ludicrous pretext that the impression existed in Europe that Kennan's Reith lectures somehow represented the views of the Democratic party, Acheson, presuming to speak for the Democratic party, issued a public statement to set the record straight. "Mr. Kennan has never, in my judgment, grasped the realities of power relationships, but takes a rather mystical attitude toward them. To Mr. Kennan there is no Soviet military threat in Europe," Acheson complained.[29]

No one in his right mind ever accused Acheson of holding mystical views of power relationships. Nor apparently was there the slightest element of doubt in Acheson's mind that the use of American power during the Cold War has been both benign and effective.

> In the present state of the distribution of power in this world, and in the light of the use made by the Russian Communist regime of its power to extend its authority, can one doubt that, were it not for the American connection, there would be no more independent national life in Western Europe than there is in Eastern Europe? [29]

There are informed critics who profoundly disagree with Acheson's view of the Cold War. He in turn was far too intelligent not to know that the criticism existed and had to be dealt with. And he did so in a footnote:

A decade and a half later a school of academic criticism has concluded that we overreacted to Stalin, which in turn caused him to overreact to policies of the United States. This may be true. Fortunately, perhaps, these authors were not called upon to analyze a situation in which the United States had not taken the action which it did take.[30]

Dean Acheson has emerged as a Cold War policy-maker of formidable proportions. The next chapter is devoted to a review of his stewardship as Secretary of State during a period of intense Cold War struggle, a struggle which turned "hot" in Korea.

CONCLUSION

Containment, the new American strategic-political doctrine based on the reality of American atomic power, received its most significant popular expression with the publication of the X article in *Foreign Affairs* magazine, July 1947. The article followed the enunciation of President Truman's doctrine of economic and military assistance to peoples struggling against Soviet pressure and of General Marshall's Harvard address calling upon Europe to organize in order to receive large-scale American assistance. The X article, authored by George Kennan, who served as the first chairman of the State Department Policy Planning Staff, presented a view of Soviet society and motivation similar to that which appeared in Kennan's "long telegram" sent from Moscow, February 22, 1946. The telegram fed into the mounting Cold War atmosphere in Washington and led to Kennan's promotion to an active directorship of the new National War College.

The War College, a unique instrument of the Cold War sponsored by James Forrestal, was created for the better training of military and foreign service officers in strategic-political thinking in the nuclear age. Kennan deeply enjoyed his role in establishing the War College and in developing its course devoted, as he saw it, to the articulation of a new strategic doctrine unlike anything in previous American experience. Kennan later wished to reinterpret his own role as an early Cold Warrior, and, indeed, he left Washington in 1950 for more scholarly pursuits.

Nevertheless, his own *Memoirs* amply support the conclusion that George Kennan was, more than any other single individual, the original popularizer of the containment doctrine, a doctrine that he himself soon came to wish had not been so easily reduced to dogma and cliché.

Kennan's public career is full of irony. A highly trained Soviet expert, Kennan seemed ideally equipped to play a major role within the policy elite shaping postwar United States policy vis-à-vis the Soviet Union. His appointment to the War College Staff and his selection as first chairman of the State Department's Policy Planning Staff provided unusual opportunities to promote his views on these vital matters within elite circles. But Kennan's views shortly proved unacceptable in elite circles as the Cold War intensified. He did not agree with the dominant view in the national security hierarchy concerning Soviet military intentions. He was gradually and subtly moved to the periphery of national security elite decision-making. Realizing that his views were not acceptable to the men who were making national security policy, Kennan decided in 1950 to take a leave of absence. When he left the department, it was his own estimate that probably no other senior officer in the State Department agreed with his views. Yet years after these events Kennan was chiefly known as the author of the containment doctrine largely because his X article served as a popular device for spreading Cold War doctrine in non-elite circles. Kennan, who has said that he preferred dealing in principles rather than doctrines, finally disavowed the containment doctrine in its later distorted versions.

Writing in 1967 during the period of escalation in Vietnam and mounting dissension at home, Kennan said:

> If . . . I was the author in 1947 of a "doctrine" of containment, it was a doctrine that lost much of its rationale with the death of Stalin and with the development of the Soviet-Chinese conflict. I emphatically deny the paternity of any efforts to invoke that doctrine today in situations to which it has, and can have, no proper relevance.[31]

Kennan had an important part in constructing the political-strategic doctrine that has undergirded United States Cold War policy. The containment doctrine was the creation of a small, civilian-led elite within the inner circle of closed politics. The doctrine prevailed although policy alternatives were available, as the publication of Lippmann's critique in 1947 indicates. When Kennan turned critic of the doctrine—thus moving closer to the position stated by Lippmann—his influence within the policy elite declined rapidly. It is clear that Secretary Acheson did not actively seek an alternative to a policy that he knew best fitted his own perception of Soviet intentions and actions. Kennan's experience in 1946–47 is suggestive in terms of the relationship between policy elite and attentive public. As a case study it also tells something about the manner in which a dominant elite disciplines dissident views within its own ranks.

The Kennan experience with the containment doctrine calls to our attention the special nature of the policy elite's mind-set. The next chapter shows the elite shaping national security policy in keeping with a view of the world that was based upon lessons derived from experiences with Hitler.

Chapter Three Notes

1. See George F. Kennan, *Memoirs, 1925–1950* (Boston: Little, Brown, 1967). Excerpts from the long telegram appear as Appendix C in the *Memoirs*.

2. Dean Acheson, *Present at the Creation* (New York: W. W. Norton, 1969), p. 151.

3. Ibid.

4. Ibid.

5. Ibid.

6. Kennan, *Memoirs*, p. 308.

7. Ibid., pp. 308–9.

8. Ibid., p. 314.

9. Acheson, *Present at the Creation*, p. 218.

10. For more detail on the literary effort that preceded the President's announcement of the Truman Doctrine, see Joseph Jones, *The Fifteen Weeks* (New York: Harcourt, Brace and Co., 1955). Jones presents a lyrical account of the detailed discussions that went into the formulation of the Truman Doctrine and the decision to launch the Marshall Plan. Since Jones was a Public Affairs officer in the State Department at the time, with responsibility for drafting a number of documents, including President Truman's message of May 12, 1947, and General Marshall's famous Harvard commencement address, he proves to be both a knowledgeable and also an extraordinarily subjective observer of these events.

11. Kennan, *Memoirs*, p. 315.

12. Ibid., p. 320.

13. Ibid., p. 322.

14. Arthur Krock, *Memoirs—Sixty Years on the Firing Line* (New York: Funk and Wagnalls, 1968). It is not clear how Krock gained access to this document, which appears as Appendix A. James Forrestal was a close friend who revealed to Krock the authorship of the X article. See also Richard J. Powers, "Clark Clifford, The Wisdom of Hindsight," *The New Republic*, Vol. 166, No. 14 (April 1, 1972).

15. "The Sources of Soviet Conduct" by X has been reprinted in Walter Lippmann, *The Cold War, A Study in U.S. Foreign Policy* (New York: Harper & Row, 1972). The quotations appear on pages 59 and 68.

16. Kennan, *Memoirs,* p. 358.

17. Lippmann, *The Cold War.* All quotations from Lippmann in this paragraph are taken from this book.

18. Ibid., p. 17.

19. Ibid., pp. 49–50.

20. Kennan, *Memoirs,* p. 355.

21. Ibid., pp. 363–64.

22. Ibid., p. 356.

23. Lippmann, *The Cold War,* pp. 3–4.

24. Kennan, *Memoirs,* p. 295.

25. Kennan, *Memoirs,* p. 364.

26. Acheson, *Present at the Creation,* p. 228.

27. Ibid., pp. 752–53.

28. Kennan, *Memoirs,* p. 464.

29. *New York Times,* Jan. 12, 1958.

30. Acheson, *Present at the Creation,* p. 753.

31. Kennan, *Memoirs,* p. 367.

4 NSC–68: THE ACHESON-NITZE HARD LINE, 1950

The task of a public officer seeking to explain and gain support for a major policy is not that of the writer of a doctoral thesis. Qualification must give way to simplicity of statement, nicety and nuance to bluntness, almost brutality, in carrying home a point. It is better to carry the hearer or reader into the quadrant of one's thought than merely to make a noise or to mislead him utterly.

Dean Acheson

Present at the Creation (1969)

Soviet menace always made it easier for Acheson to persuade Congress and people to do the things he deemed necessary for security.

Gaddis Smith

Dean Acheson (1972)

This chapter examines the role played by two leading civilian militants in preparing National Security Council Document Sixty-eight (referred to henceforth as NSC–68), an influential Cold War policy paper.[1] NSC–68 was the special project of Dean Acheson, the new Secretary of State, and Paul Nitze, his hand-picked Chairman of the State Department's Policy Planning Staff. NSC–68 was the product of a major review of the United States' position in relation to the Soviet Union following the Soviets' explosion of an atomic bomb. The review was undertaken by a small State Department–Defense Department study group under the chairmanship of Nitze early in 1950, shortly after Acheson succeeded General Marshall as Secretary, and immediately after Nitze had replaced George Kennan. NSC–68 was put together after several weeks of intensive discussion by a small group of technicians from State, Defense, and the Joint Chiefs of Staff, in which the State Department representatives provided the main policy leadership. Although NSC–68 promulgated a theory of Soviet military expansion that was at odds with the views of the State Department's leading Soviet experts (especially George Kennan and Charles Bohlen), Acheson and Nitze supported NSC–68 for its "rhetorical" and "polemical" advantages in moving national policy in the direction they thought it ought to move. This review of the American position was undertaken following a Presidential directive calling for the new assessment in the light of Soviet atomic capability (the USSR had tested an A-bomb in August 1949), the triumph of Mao Tse-tung's forces in China (also substantially accomplished by August 1949), and the necessity of an expanded program of American military assistance to NATO countries.

NSC–68 was promulgated without having had the usual "clearance" by interested agencies. Since it contemplated an increased level of defense spending totally at odds with existing administration policy, NSC–68 was opposed initially by the Secretary of Defense, who regarded the Nitze group's policy recommendations as unwarranted intrusions in his area of responsibility.[2]

Acheson and Nitze, the two principal protagonists of NSC–68, appear to be leading candidates for membership in a national security policy elite. Indeed, it would be hard to imagine two men better qualified by way of background and training to fit Domhoff's thesis that the policy elite is also an upper-class institution.

DEAN ACHESON AS ELITE LEADER

Dean Acheson was born in Middletown, Connecticut, in 1893. His father, Edward Campion Acheson, was the Episcopal Bishop of Connecticut. Acheson studied at Groton, Yale, and Harvard Law School, the appropriate educational experience for a member of an upper-class elite. He served as private secretary to Justice Brandeis, 1919–21. He was later to become a warm personal friend of Brandeis's colleague, Justice Felix Frankfurter. In 1921 Acheson joined the Washington law firm, Covington and

Burling. He remained a member of the firm through his adult life except during periods of active public service. Acheson served briefly in FDR's first subcabinet. He was Undersecretary of the Treasury May 19, 1933, to November 15, 1933, resigning from this position in a policy disagreement. Apparently Acheson's feelings toward Roosevelt were not warm. Acheson felt that FDR "condescended." He comments: "Many reveled in apparent admission to an inner circle. I did not . . . ."

Instead Acheson found the atmosphere of FDR's inner circle "patronizing and humiliating." He continues:

> This, of course, was a small part of the man and the impression he made. The essence of that was force. He exuded a relish of power and command. His responses seemed too quick; his reasons too facile for considered judgment; one could not tell what lay beneath them. He remained a formidable man, a leader who won admiration and respect. In others he inspired far more, affection and devotion. For me, that was reserved for a man of whom at that time I had never heard, his successor.[3]

It was Harry Truman, of course, who appointed Acheson Secretary of State in January 1949, a position he held until the 1952 election placed a Republican President in the White House. Acheson brought a solid background of previous high-level experience in the State Department to the cabinet post. He had served as an Assistant Secretary between 1941 and 1945, first in the field of economic affairs and later in the area of Congressional relations. Acheson served as Undersecretary of State between 1945 and 1947.

Acheson's role as Undersecretary under General Marshall has been described by Joseph Jones, who served as a State Department public affairs officer during the same period:

> When he [Marshall] gave Dean Acheson, under his command, full authority over policy, administration, and operations, the Department of State for the first time in years became an integrated institution subject to the authority of the President, capable of conducting foreign relations in an orderly manner. Acheson, rather than competing with members of his staff, knew how to draw from them wise counsel, harmony, and constructive effort.[4]

Gaddis Smith, Acheson's biographer, goes beyond the admiring Jones in his assessment of the role Acheson played as Undersecretary:

> Never in American history has the second-ranking officer of the Department of State exerted as much influence on foreign policy as did Under Secretary of State Acheson from August 1945 through June 1947. He was the balance wheel, the coordinator, the provider of continuity and sense of direction during an extraordinarily baffling time. His ideas and direction contributed substantially and continuously to the sharpening and hardening of American policy toward the Soviet Union in an era now recognized as the unequivocal outbreak of the Cold War.[5]

Shortly after he became Secretary, Acheson added Paul Nitze to the Policy Planning Staff. Kennan remained chairman for several months thereafter, while Nitze on special assignment was charged with establishing better liaison with the strategic planners in the Defense Department. Kennan was personally in favor of the $13.5 billion limitation on annual defense expenditures, a limit imposed by the White House with the active support of the Bureau of the Budget and of Louis Johnson, the Secretary of Defense. As noted in the previous chapter, Kennan was opposed to an increasing tendency of imposing a military interpretation on the containment doctrine. Kennan also favored the development of small unified military task forces, highly qualified, mobile, and mechanized to fight limited wars as an alternative to the overwhelming emphasis on atomic air power. Paul Hammond, the leading authority on NSC–68, reports: "Nitze was more concerned about the overall threat of Soviet arms, necessitating the achievement of superiority over them in an all-out war."[6] Hammond also speculates that Nitze was influenced by his earlier participation as a member of the Joint Strategic Bombing survey.

Paul Nitze, born in Amherst, Massachusetts, in 1907, was graduated from Harvard in 1928 and the following year joined Dillon, Read, investment bankers, a firm he stayed with until 1941 with the exception of a brief period as president of P. H. Nitze and Company, 1938–39. Nitze first entered government service in World War II, serving at one time or another as financial director for the Coordinator of Inter-American Affairs, as chief of the metals and materials branch of the Board of Economic Warfare, as Director of Foreign Procurement and Development branch of the Foreign Economic Administration, as a special consultant to the War Department, and as Vice Chairman of the U.S. Strategic Bombing Survey, 1944–46.

Nitze then moved to the State Department, serving as Deputy Director, Office of International Trade Policy, 1946; as Deputy to the Assistant Secretary for Economic Affairs, 1948–49; and as Acheson's Director of the State Department Planning Staff, 1950–53. During the Eisenhower years, Nitze served as president of the Foreign Service Educational Foundation in Washington. During this period he also played an active role in the preparation of the Gaither report and the Rockefeller Brothers study, both of which recommended major rearmament programs. The Kennedy administration brought Nitze back to active participation at the highest levels of national security decision-making. From 1961 to 1963 Nitze served as Assistant Secretary of Defense for International Security Affairs; from 1963 to 1967 he was Secretary of the Navy; and he served as Deputy Secretary of Defense between 1967 and 1969.

As this brief résumé shows, Paul Nitze has been since early World War II days a Cold War professional functioning originally in high-level technical positions within the bureaucracy and then during the 1960s at the highest level of executive decision-making. His departure from the world of investment banking in 1941 apparently was a permanent one. Acheson found Nitze "a joy to work with because of his clear, incisive mind." More importantly, Nitze shared Acheson's view of Soviet military intentions and of the need for a major American rearmament effort in 1950.

Policy differences between Acheson and Kennan help explain the real significance of NSC–68; equally important to this analysis, the Acheson-Kennan disagreement also affords some insight into the way in which Acheson's policy elite "handled" opposing views within the elite. Gaddis Smith reports that as early as May 1949 Kennan had come to believe that agreement with Russia over a neutral, demilitarized Germany was possible. Acheson thought otherwise. As Kennan viewed it, Acheson offered the

Soviet Union nothing less than "unconditional capitulation of their position in Germany." And Germany was the key. Here again Smith is helpful: "Stated baldly, the policy of the United States under Acheson's direction, was to press for the maximum development of German power as a counterpoise to the Soviet Union and as an essential foundation for European recovery." [7] It was a policy that John J. McCloy and Robert Lovett could support with genuine enthusiasm. The fundamental difference between Acheson and Kennan, of course, had to do with the nature of the Soviet regime.

> Kennan believed that military strength in the West had to be tempered with a readiness to understand Moscow's concern for Russian security and a willingness to seek and accept compromises which met both the interests of the Soviet Union and the West. Acheson denied that such negotiated, mutually acceptable compromises were possible. [8]

And so it was agreed that Kennan would leave the staff, accept the position of counselor on a temporary basis, and sometime in 1950 take a leave of absence from the department.

BACKGROUND TO NSC–68

NSC–68 is a curious product because of the circumstances that gave rise to its birth. The Secretary of Defense was committed to an annual figure of $13.5 billion for national defense. The White House presumably was committed to the same figure. The prevailing assumption held that there were fiscal grounds for establishing a rigid budget ceiling on expenditures; military expenditures had to fit beneath this arbitrary ceiling. But Dean Acheson came to the State Department cabinet post in January 1950 holding a sharply different view.

Smith reports that Acheson considered the $13.5 billion figure "pitifully inadequate... a mere fraction of what the United States could afford."

> Indeed the word "afford" struck him as silly. The one thing no nation could afford was insufficient defense; therefore it bordered on insanity for a government to adjust military requirements to the budget rather than the other way around. [9]

There had been two huge shocks in August 1949: the Soviet A-bomb success and the collapse of Chiang Kai-shek's regime on mainland China. These events in themselves would probably have moved Acheson away from his predecessor's preference for a relatively modest defense budget. In addition, Acheson was ready for a program in which increased American military strength would provide the center for a system of Western military defense based in NATO. Acheson's views in 1950 reflected his earlier personal involvement as one of the principal architects of the Truman Doctrine and the Marshall Plan. For example, when the time came in March 1947 to unveil the proposed Truman Doctrine at the first meeting with selected Congressional leaders, headed by Senator Vandenberg, the White House briefing was led off by Secretary Marshall who did not impress with his presentation.

Acheson recalls:

> My distinguished chief, most unusually and unhappily, flubbed his opening statement. In desperation I whispered to him a request to speak. *This was my crisis. For a week I had nurtured it. These congressmen had no conception of what challenged them; it was my task to bring it home.* Both my superiors, equally perturbed, gave me the floor. Never have I spoken *under such a pressing sense that the issue was up to me alone.* [Italics mine.][10]

The Undersecretary spoke with passion. After describing the perilous situations in Greece and Turkey, Acheson addressed himself to the Russian menace. "The Russians had any number of bets."

Acheson continued:

> If they won any one of them, they won all. If they could seize control of Turkey, they would almost inevitably extend their control over Greece and Iran. If they controlled Greece, Turkey would sooner or later succumb, with or without a war, and then Iran. If they dominated Italy, where Communist pressures were increasing, they could probably take Greece, Turkey, and the Middle East. Their aim,

Acheson emphasized,

was control of the eastern Mediterranean and the Middle East. From there the possibilities for penetration of South Asia and Africa were limitless.[11]

There is no public record that Acheson thought of calling this the domino theory.

Acheson continued:

> As for Europe, it was clear that the Soviet Union, employing the instruments of Communist infiltration and subversion, was trying to complete the encirclement of Germany.... Only two great powers remained in the world ... the United States and the Soviet Union. We had arrived at a situation unparalleled since ancient times. Not since Rome and Carthage had there been such a polarization of power on this earth. Moreover, the two powers were divided by an unbridgeable ideological chasm.[12]

There was a long silence after Acheson finished speaking.

> Then Arthur Vandenberg said solemnly, "Mr. President, if you will say that to the Congress and the country, I will support you and I believe that most of its members will do the same." [13]

Acheson believed the danger of Russian expansion was great; he also knew that this kind of language would get through to the Congressional leaders.

When Marshall, in delivering his famous commencement address at Harvard, spoke of a policy "directed not against any country or doctrine, but against hunger, poverty, desperation and chaos" (phrases attributed to Charles Bohlen), Acheson held a less lofty view.

Acheson later mused:

> If General Marshall believed, which I am sure he did not, that the American people would be moved to so great an effort as he contemplated by as Platonic a purpose as combatting "hunger, poverty, desperation, and chaos," he was mistaken. But he was wholly right in stating this as the governmental purpose.[14]

"CLEARER-THAN-TRUTH" SYNDROME

Acheson offered no explanation in his memoirs as to how he gained his understanding of those purposes which would or would not move the American people in this historic national effort. But he did reflect on the importance of oversimplifying the reality of the Soviet threat:

> In the State Department we used to discuss how much time that mythical "average American citizen" put in each day listening, reading, and arguing about the world outside his own country. Assuming a man or woman with a fair education, a family, and a job in or out of the house, it seemed to us that ten minutes a day would be a high average. If this were anywhere near right, points to be understandable had to be clear. If we made our points clearer than truth, we did not differ from most other [sic] educators and could hardly do otherwise.[15]

This we may tentatively label, "the clearer-than-truth" syndrome, a disease of the intellect that started with the Grand Inquisitor.

The effect that the "loss" of China may have had on men such as Acheson and Nitze in hardening their attitudes toward Communist expansion must remain speculative. It may well be that the spirit of civilian militancy in the State Department was intensified by an unconscious urge to show that the foreign policy elitists were "true" Americans after all; but, if Acheson's presentation to Congressional leaders at the time of the Truman Doctrine is any indication, the official attitude was hard-nosed before Chiang Kai-shek was driven from the mainland. What does seem strange is that Acheson, who was prepared to say that we never "had" China to lose, did not make a similar assessment of Indochina.

Still smarting from his experience with the X article, Kennan not only disagreed with the assumptions on which the analysis in NSC–68 was based, he also objected to the art form. He had come at last to the painful conclusion that national policy on a matter of such grave importance could not usefully be written in the simplistic clichés of Cold War bureaucratese—not if it were to be used as a guide to policy-making. In any event, NSC–68 managed to combine the ideology of Communist doctrine with the power of the Russian state into one simple expansionist drive. Kennan and Bohlen had difficulty with this line of analysis. Trained Soviet experts and experienced Foreign Service officers,

Kennan and Bohlen thought it made a difference whether the USSR was or was not likely to engage in military expansion; they deemed it important to distinguish between those forces that motivated Soviet expansionist tendencies and those factors that militated against expansion. Nitze, on the other hand, felt that Kennan's view in particular failed to give proper weight to the contingency of a major aggressive move by the Russians.

Paul Hammond explains Nitze's reaction when he learned that military planning in the Defense Department was concentrating on strategic air retaliatory capacity.

> Nitze took back to his work in the Policy Planning Staff of the State Department a deep concern over the budgetary limits imposed upon American defense policy, and over the relative importance of military and non-military factors in foreign policy. During the latter part of the summer of 1949, the Policy Planning Staff interested itself in a comparative analysis of military costs between the Soviet Union and the United States, and the capability of the Soviet economy to depress consumption and carry a high rate of capital investment simultaneously with a high rate of military expenditure.[16]

Acheson and Nitze, deeply involved in developing a program of mutual defense assistance for Europe, were distressed to find that the Defense Department strategic thinking was limited by the rigid budget ceiling. The new civilian militancy, as it took form in the State Department in 1949–50, looked to both a big war and a limited war capability requiring an enormous increase in defense spending. This is a major policy strand that feeds directly into NSC–68.

NSC–68 AND THE H-BOMB

NSC–68 was also related directly to the decision taken by President Truman to build the hydrogen bomb. David Lilienthal, Chairman of the Atomic Energy Commission, advised Secretary Acheson that he was opposed to the H-bomb development because State and Defense had not thought through the strategic implications of nuclear weapons. Lilienthal's criticism proved timely for Acheson and Nitze. The State Department leadership, according to Hammond, was "delighted at the opportunity which might now be afforded them to follow through with the Defense Department to a greater integration between strategic and foreign policy planning." [17]

Acheson finally had the decisive hand in making the recommendations that led to the building of the H-bomb. Schilling reports that it was

> the Secretary of State who spoke with authority, so far as the President was concerned, with regard to the various foreign policy hopes and fears that had conditioned the views of many of the other participants. It was also the Secretary of State who held the balance of persuasion, so far as the President was concerned, on those issues on which the representatives of the Department of Defense and the Atomic Energy Commission were divided. [18]

President Truman signed the directive initiating the H-bomb program on January 30, 1950. At the same time, he also signed a letter that had been drafted in the State Department directing the Secretaries of State and Defense to undertake an overall review and reassessment of American foreign and defense policy in the light of (a) the loss of China; (b) Soviet mastery of atomic energy; and (c) the prospect of the fusion bomb. The Presidential letter gave Secretary Acheson the leverage he needed to provide policy leadership in this fundamental reassessment of national security policy. Actually, both the National Security Council staff and State Department planners were already at work on just such a reappraisal *before* the President signed the letter. The operational effect of the Presidential letter (carefully drafted in State) was to take the review out of regular NSC channels and place the leadership squarely in the hands of Acheson. When the review was completed, the results and recommendations would go directly to the President "rather than through NSC, where it might have been delayed or picked to pieces," Hammond notes.

Acheson looked to Nitze, his new Policy Planning chief, to lead the review. NSC–68 was drafted in six weeks by a study group chaired by Nitze. The members of the group included representatives of both State and Defense including General Truman

H. Landon, an Air Force general assigned to the Joint Strategic
Survey Committee, a unit within the JCS staff structure concerned with advising the Joint Chiefs on the overall national
security implications of their strategic plans. Nitze brought to
the group Acheson's belief, which he fully shared, that the American response to the Soviet challenge was inadequate. According
to Hammond the members of the study group were able to
anticipate from the beginning the direction in which the study
ultimately would move.

In fact, General Landon originally came to the study group
committed to existing budget programs and plans. The first draft
paper that General Landon presented was optimistic with respect to the relative military capabilities of the United States
and the USSR. Then Nitze's Policy Planning staff presented its
draft, which, compared with Landon's paper, appeared "pessimistic" about relative military capabilities. When PPS representatives attacked Landon's thesis, they found, presumably not to
anyone's great surprise, that the general was not really convinced
by his own document. Hammond explains the situation then
facing the study group:

> It was . . . an invitation to break out of the strait jacket of De-
> fense Department strategic thinking and to explore, unencum-
> bered by the severe budgetary pressure of the Truman-Johnson
> administration, the strategic requirements of national security.[19]

The invitation, so cordially rendered, was accepted.

Nitze held the chair. More important, he was fully in Acheson's confidence. Thus, he was able to move throughout this
period knowing that he had the support of the Secretary. The
Defense Department representatives, by way of contrast, found
that they were "walking on eggs" during their participation in
the study group. Landon did not directly represent the JCS while
General James H. Burns (ret.) was a member of the study group
for procedural and protocol reasons (he was personal aide to
Secretary of Defense Louis Johnson). Burns tended to keep out
of the detailed considerations that came before the study group
presumably so the review would not be limited by Johnson's
strong commitment to the existing budgetary ceiling.

NSC–68 VIEW OF SOVIET GOALS

With Nitze and Acheson in command, the study group prepared the document which later became NSC–68 and which, despite its top secret rating, was paraphrased by Cabell Phillips in his book on the Truman Presidency:

Events since the end of World War II have created a new power relationship in the world which must be viewed not as a temporary distortion but as a long-range and fundamental realignment among nations. This has arisen out of two historical events: the Russian revolution and the growth of the Communist movement throughout the world; and the development of nuclear weapons with their capacity for unlimited destruction. The U.S. and the U.S.S.R. are the terminal poles of this new international axis.

Kremlin policy has three main objectives: (1) to preserve and to strengthen its position as the ideological and power center of the Communist world; (2) to extend and to consolidate that power by the acquisition of new satellites; and (3) to oppose and to weaken any competing system of power that threatens Communist world hegemony.

These objectives are inimical to American ideals which are predicated on the concepts of freedom and dignity. . . .

It must be assumed that these concepts and objectives of American life will come under increasing attack. If they are to be protected, the nation must be determined, at whatever cost or sacrifice, to preserve at home and abroad those conditions of life in which these objectives can survive and prosper. We must seek to do this by peaceful means and with the cooperation of other like-minded peoples. But if peaceful means fail we must be willing and ready to fight.

Conceding the possibility of such a war, what are the relative capabilities of the U.S. and its probable allies, and the U.S.S.R. and its probable allies?

As a first consideration, Russia's progress in the development of atomic bombs probably means that an approximate stalement in nuclear weapons will be reached by about 1954. The United States might extend its advantage for a few years longer if the hydrogen bomb should be perfected, but success in that effort is uncertain.

While the economic and productive capacity of the U.S.S.R. is markedly below that of the West, its potential for growth is great, and the Communist nations are striving more determinedly than the West to realize full potentials for growth.

In spite of these weaknesses, the Communist military capability for conventional, or nonatomic, warfare is now substantially superior to that of the West and is continuing to improve at a more rapid rate. The imbalance can be expected to continue for at least as long as it takes to achieve the economic rehabilitation of Western Europe and the full implementation of the NATO alliance.

Could the crisis between the two great powers be reduced through negotiation and particularly by mutual arms reduction? The prospects at present are poor, given the immutability of Soviet objectives and its advantage in military power. The West cannot abandon its efforts to negotiate, particularly to neutralize the threat of a nuclear holocaust, but it must act in the realization that Stalin respects the reality of force a great deal more than he does the abstraction of peace.

Based on these premises, an indefinite period of tension and danger is foreseen for the United States and for the West—a period that should be defined less as a short-term crisis than as a permanent and fundamental alteration in the shape of international relations. To meet this new condition, four possible lines of action are open to the United States:

1. It can continue on its present course of reduced defense budgets and limited military capabilities, but without reducing its commitments to free-world security.

2. It can abandon these commitments, maintain its military capabilities at the present level, and withdraw behind the shield of a "fortress America."

3. It can attempt through "preventive war" a quick, violent but possibly more favorable redress in the world balance of power.

4. It can strike out on a bold and massive program of rebuilding the West's defensive potential to surpass that of the Soviet world, and of meeting each fresh challenge promptly and unequivocally. Such a program must have the United States at its political and material center with other free nations in variable orbits around it. The strength of such an alliance should be insurmountable as long as each of its members remains strong.

This fourth alternative is inescapably the preferred one. Its fulfillment calls for the United States to take the lead in a rapid and substantial buildup in the defensive power of the West beginning "at the center" and radiating outward. This means virtual abandonment by the United States of trying to distinguish between national and global security. It also means the end of subordinating security needs to the traditional budgeting restrictions; of asking "How much security can we afford?" In other words, security must henceforth become the dominant element in the national budget, and other elements must be accommodated to it.

The wealth potential of the country is such that as much as 20 percent of the gross national product can be devoted to security without causing national bankruptcy. This new concept of the security needs of the nation calls for annual appropriations of the order of $50 billion, or not much below the former wartime levels.[20]

While the document intentionally avoided making the assertion that the Kremlin design was an ideological commitment looking toward world hegemony, it did assume an inherent conflict of interest between the two super-powers based upon ideological differences. It also pictured a situation four years in the future in which the Soviet Union would have enough A-bombs and a sufficient capacity for delivering them so as to offset substantially the deterrent capability of American nuclear weapons. The document also noted the absence of an American capability of meeting "limited" military challenges for lack of mobile striking forces. Most momentous in the view of its implications for the Administration's budgetary thinking was the study group's conclusion that even in peacetime as much as 20 percent of Gross National Product could be directed toward national security expenditures without encountering economic bankruptcy.

Secretary of Defense Louis Johnson's first reaction to the report of the study group was hostile. He came around later. Dean Acheson explains what happened:

When the paper was completed early in April, I had it submitted to him [Johnson] so that he might sign it, if he chose to do so. To my surprise he did, and it went to the President on April 7, 1950, as a Joint Report. Johnson's signature, I learned later, did not surprise my colleagues as much as it did me, for they had submitted it to him bearing not only my signature but the concurrences of the Chiefs of Staff, the Joint Strategic Survey Committee, the Liaison Committee, and the secretaries of the three services. Johnson was not left in a strong offensive position.[21]

Surely neither Acheson nor Nitze imagined circumstances in peacetime when as much as 20 percent of GNP would go for defense spending. The figure Acheson and Nitze had in mind apparently ranged between $35 billion and $50 billion on an annual basis. This contrasts with the $13.5 billion ceiling imposed by the Truman administration in fiscal year 1950. Indeed, when costs were discussed with General Landon, he turned to General Gruenther of the Army and General Norstad of the Air Force for a larger figure. The two generals thought that a $5 billion increase, which would bring the annual Defense budget to a level of $17 or $18 billion, would probably do the trick. The policy paper, as it came from the study group, gave no indication of what its proposed program would cost. This was not an oversight, Acheson later explained. "To have attempted one would have made impossible all those concurrences and prevented any recommendation to the President." [22]

One of the men who participated in the process later told Dean Acheson that he found NSC–68 "the most ponderous expression of elementary ideas" he had ever come across. Acheson viewed NSC–68 instrumentally.

REARMING AS GLOBAL POLICEMAN

"The purpose of NSC–68," he explained years later, "was to so bludgeon the mass mind of 'top government' that not only could the President make a decision but that the decision could be carried out." [23]

The decision presumably was to rearm, for the role of global policeman.

If NSC–68 was a ponderous expression of elementary ideas, how is one to explain the passion it aroused in Kennan and Bohlen? Why were Acheson and Nitze so determined to override the criticism from Soviet experts in their own department?

Kennan, of course, was troubled that the vast and complex problems of American foreign policy could be reduced to a few elementary ideas, ponderously expressed. Crude and clumsy oversimplifications in basic documents, he felt, were partly responsible for the growing overemphasis on military factors and methods in the conduct of the nation's foreign policy. It could not have pleased him that the top leadership in the State Department provided most of the punch in this military emphasis. His own views conflicted with a growing tendency, he thought,

> to base our own plans and calculations solely on the *capabilities* of a potential adversary, assuming him to be desirous of doing anything he could to bring injury to us, and to exclude from consideration, as something unsusceptible to exact determination, the whole question of that adversary's real *intentions*.[24]

Bohlen did not carry scars from the Mr. X experience, yet he also had real objections. He did not oppose the preparation of the policy paper, but he wished to see the problem stated with precision and a degree of technical sophistication. When the study group prepared a draft listing world domination as the primary objective of Soviet policy, Bohlen challenged the assumption.

> He argued that the Kremlin had no grand design in view, that world hegemony was a tertiary goal, following the Soviet regime's primary interest in preserving and improving its internal power position and its secondary objective of consolidated control over the Soviet satellites. In his view, the Russians worried a great deal about overextending their commitments—for instance, because of the fact that they had troops stationed in Europe.[25]

Hammond tells us that the study group came to accept the force of what Bohlen was saying. Hammond also reports that before it was over Acheson had become "bored" with the dispute; the Secretary evidently thought it of little practical consequence in which order the Soviet objectives were listed so long as they were all there.

Acheson refers to the dispute among Nitze, Bohlen, and Kennan in a note appended to his memoirs:

> When the argument reached the point which President George Vincent of the University of Minnesota has described as the "you hold the sieve while I milk the barren heifer" stage, the way to peace and action required separating the chief contestants for a

cooling-off period. Accordingly, one stayed in Washington, one
went to South America, and the third to Europe.[26]

Kennan was sent to Latin America on a six-weeks' fact-finding
mission. Bohlen was assigned to our embassy in Paris. Nitze
stayed in Washington to preside over the preparation of NSC–
68. Acheson may have regarded the disagreement as insignifi-
cant. The three policy assistants did not. The problem as Nitze
viewed it has since been summarized in Hammond's analysis:

> Nitze had listed Soviet objectives in order of their importance to
> the United States, and *in such a way as to emphasize the Soviet
> threat*. Apparently, his was largely a rhetorical point. Obviously,
> he recognized that there was more to the motivations of the
> Soviet state than following Communist dogma. But since Soviet
> motivations (or those of any nation) are so much more complex
> than that, he apparently reasoned, one is entitled to select a
> dramatic and prominent theme such as world domination and
> emphasize it as the most important, or at least the most uniquely
> characteristic, of Soviet objectives. [Italics mine.] [27]

Further, Hammond advises that Nitze's ordering of objectives
was identical with that of Acheson, though "neither of them
thought it intrinsically important."

Nitze, in preparing a fundamental reassessment of United States
national security vis-à-vis the USSR, found it expedient to exaggerate the Soviet threat in order to achieve the appropriate
"persuasive impact," to borrow Hammond's felicitous concept.
Bohlen, on the other hand, was "more sensitive, both to the Soviet
viewpoint and to the possibility of drawing false conclusions
from inaccurate premises about that viewpoint." [28]

Perhaps Nitze's position is best explained by his attitude toward the document that the study group produced. Nitze had
hopes that the statement could be turned into accepted policy,
and he and his principal, the Secretary of State, held strong
views as to what that policy should be. Nitze anticipated that
the military threat would be discounted; hence, his willingness
to exaggerate the threat, "with the hope that the reaction of
opinion leaders would be commensurate with the threat—that
is to say, would be rational as measured against the actual threat,
though not against the portion of NSC–68 which purported to

describe the threat." [29] Hammond concludes that Acheson, like Nitze, "was more interested in the polemic value of NSC–68 than in its precise rationality. Evidently he saw it as a device for challenging established policies and premises which he thought needed reexamination."

Dean Acheson and Paul Nitze wanted to bring about an expanded American military effort at the beginning of the 1950s. This was their "rational" objective. Hence, the use of exaggerated notions of Soviet designs in a top policy document seemed acceptable as a means of moving national policy in the direction leading members of the policy elite believed it ought to go. The accomplishment of this "rational" objective—a substantial rearmament effort that would include development of the H-bomb —would intensify the Cold War. This, in turn, was deemed necessary in order to maintain a position of United States military superiority over the Soviet Union. There was less cynicism in this than a supreme confidence in the correctness of the elite's view. At the same time, the existence of NSC–68 gives the official United States reaction to the Korean attack in June 1950 the definite appearance of a self-fulfilling prophecy. Acheson and his colleagues within the inner circle of closed politics could only assume, consistent with their own exaggerated world view, that the North Korean military initiative was part of an overall Soviet global strategy, although, ironically, the attack came at a point that Acheson publicly had placed outside the line of vital United States interests.[30]

THE ACHESON IMPACT

Dean Acheson, we are told, was "the principal author and manager" of the nation's foreign policy during the Truman years: "He, more than any other man, suggested the courses which the President ordered for the nation during the most dangerous phase of the Cold War." [31] Dean Acheson was a man of sharply etched views and exceptional competence: prime qualities in a leader of an important policy elite. His views were fundamentally "conservative" in the sense that they were aimed at restoring "what Acheson considered to have been the nearly ideal world of the 19th century, except that *Pax Britannica* would become *Pax Anglo-American.* The beneficiaries of that world were implicitly the decent, civilized middle class of Acheson's own experience." [32] Such views were likely to appeal to an establishment, although they also had serious limits as applied to public policy.

Acheson remained largely ignorant of Asia during the first fifty years of his life; his interest in the Third World was slight; his knowledge of modern economics virtually nonexistent; his awareness of the tides of social change sweeping over Asia, Africa, and even his own country was exceedingly dim. At a minimum, his class-bound view of the world was bound to lead to difficulty in assessing the reality of the Soviet presence in world affairs.

At the time of Acheson's death, Professor Arthur Schlesinger, Jr., memorialized him for "personal bravura," noting that: "In a city of gray and anonymous men, Dean Acheson stood out like a noble monument from another and more vivid era." If, by the time of his passing, Dean Acheson stood forth as something of an anachronism, his role as a Cold Warrior was a major one, as Schlesinger also noted, in presiding over "the growing militarization and globalization of American foreign policy." [33] Acheson was the leader of a small, able group of like-minded civilian militants whose policy preferences prevailed in the policy struggles that are reflected in NSC–68 and in the Presidential directive on the H-bomb. Gaddis Smith reports that during Acheson's tenure as Secretary, "there were few occasions when his advisers challenged his accepted notions. Only Kennan directly and repeatedly opposed Acheson." If the practice might seem to encourage sycophancy, Smith finds that it was really a

> natural adaptation to an intellectual process.... Seldom did Acheson's men pause to reexamine their assumptions—a practice Acheson deplored in men of action—or to entertain the possibility that they were wrong. Acheson's confidence in the accuracy of his own view of the world was so supreme that he could dismiss alternative views as naive or irresponsible.... Acheson's advisers either thought as Acheson did from the beginning or quickly learned to do so.[34]

National security policy-making appears to be vulnerable to a high degree of elite domination. It is, therefore, not inconsequential when alternative views, *within the elite,* are readily dismissed on the grounds that they are "naive" and "irresponsible." Dean Acheson, as Secretary of State, led the way to the formulation of NSC–68 while also shaping the Presidential decision to proceed with the building of the H-bomb. It was necessary to exaggerate the Soviet threat, Acheson later explained, in order to "bludgeon the mass mind of top government." Leaving aside the point that the mass-mind concept is a curious one when used in relation to policy elites, the question of the degree of effective competition over substantive issues *within the elite* appears open in this instance. Acheson, as leader of his policy elite, faced considerable opposition to the rearmament proposal from the Secretary of Defense. Two of Acheson's experts on Russian matters held a less militant view than he did of Soviet *intentions.* Acheson was able to override the opposition from Secretary Louis Johnson, at the same time ignoring his own experts when their views differed from the assessment he wished to make. Still, NSC–68 might have been simply another policy paper marked "Top Secret," if the Korean attack had not come when it did. The point of view held by Nitze and Acheson, embodied in NSC–68, virtually guaranteed that the Secretary of State would interpret the North Korean venture as an element in a global strategy masterminded from Moscow. The official United States response to the attack meant that military spending would shortly exceed even the upper limits that Acheson and Nitze had in mind in sponsoring NSC–68.

Gaddis Smith, who concludes that Acheson represented the generation deeply affected by Munich as well as any man of his time, seems reassured that Acheson's approach to the Cold War, stressing military strength rather than negotiation, enjoyed broad public and Congressional support. Unfortunately, this leaves unanswered the question of how much the public and the Congress may have been influenced by the exaggeration of the threat upon which Acheson's Cold War policy was based. General support for the dominant elite's national security program is likely to be forthcoming in a political system that discourages the formulation of effective alternatives to the establishment's views.

The lessons derived from Munich were not necessarily without meaning as applied to Stalinist Russia in the immediate postwar era; but, even if one assumes that a firm United States policy was called for, such a policy should have been based upon a more accurate assessment of Soviet intentions, a more honest appraisal of Soviet weaknesses, a lesser reliance on sheer military preponderance, and a much greater effort to negotiate with a difficult and trying adversary.

CONCLUSION

It is possible, of course, to seek an explanation of the NSC-68 experience as part of a process by which American leaders invented and then cynically manipulated the Soviet threat in an effort, based upon capitalism's categorical imperative, to fasten economic control over the globe. Gabriel and Joyce Kolko have examined the United States' foreign policy during the Truman years in terms of this thesis; and while they show American leaders exaggerating and misrepresenting the nature of the Soviet threat, relying on military force, and spurning negotiations, they are not able to demonstrate that coherent economic motives dominated their behavior. A more promising explanation seems to lie in the way a dominant elite *perceived* the Soviet threat. Gaddis Smith summarizes this position:

> The generation of Acheson and Truman believed that it was too late to deter Hitler when he first presented himself as an unequivocal threat. Hitler ought to have been deterred long before he came to power in Germany by means of a high level of military, economic and technological preparedness. Thus, the generalized enemy of the future—conveniently embodied by Russia —had to be deterred by expensive and continuing measures. If Congress and the public needed to be frightened into paying the bills—so be it. Crises would have to be manufactured and controlled in order to prevent the ultimate catastrophe of a third world war. If business interests balked at the expense, they could be persuaded by emphasis on the secondary economic advantages which would flow from heavy foreign aid and high military budgets.
>
> Of course, Acheson and his disciples did not believe in an immediate Russian threat—an attack next month or next year, or next decade. They thought in longer terms and imagined them-

selves custodians of the great sweep of human (i.e. Anglo-European-American) civilization. Having been young men during World War I and leaders already in intermediate or high authority during World War II, they knew the answers. They worshipped military strength. They sought economic strength as an essential foundation. They believed that diplomacy except from a position of overwhelming strength was another name for appeasement and that with overwhelming strength diplomacy was unnecessary.[35]

This was the world view of Dean Acheson, the leader of the policy elite that wrote NSC–68.

The Munich syndrome is important in offering a partial explanation for the pervasive influence of the Achesonian world view, but one feels certain that there were moralistic, messianic, and pragmatic strands whose roots lie deeper in the nation's psychic past.

Chapter Four Notes

1. The analysis of NSC–68 in this chapter is based upon a defini-
    tive study by Paul Y. Hammond, "NSC–68: Prologue to Rearma-
    ment," which was published in 1962 in *Strategy, Politics, and
    Defense Budgets,* written by Warner R. Schilling, Paul Y. Ham-
    mond, and Glenn H. Snyder (New York: Columbia University
    Press, 1962). The study was sponsored by the Institute of War
    and Peace Studies of Columbia. Hammond interviewed scores
    of Washington officials including the principals involved in
    NSC–68. He was able to write about NSC–68 in an authoritative
    manner although the document itself is classified. Apparently
    NSC–68 is one of those significant documents which some
    people are allowed to write about even while it remains classi-
    fied. Gaddis Smith describes NSC–68 as "the most famous un-
    read (because still classified 'top secret' as late as 1972) paper
    of its era." Cabell Phillips, in his book *The Truman Presidency*
    (New York: Macmillan Co., 1966), presents an elaborate para-
    phrase of NSC–68. This has also proved helpful in the prepara-
    tion of this chapter.

2. See both Dean Acheson's *Present at the Creation* (New York:
    W. W. Norton, 1969) and Gaddis Smith's *Dean Acheson* (New
    York: Cooper Square, 1972) for more detail concerning Secre-
    tary Johnson's bizarre behavior on this occasion.

3. Acheson, *Present at the Creation,* p. 740.

4. Joseph M. Jones, *The Fifteen Weeks* (New York: Viking, 1955),
    p. 100.

5. Smith, *Dean Acheson,* p. 25.

6. All quotations from Hammond in this chapter are taken from his
    study of NSC–68 cited in note 1.

7. Smith, *Dean Acheson,* p. 79.

8. Ibid., p. 156.

9. Ibid., p. 162.

10. Acheson, *Present at the Creation,* p. 219.

11. Jones, *The Fifteen Weeks,* p. 140.

12. Ibid., p. 141.

13. Acheson, *Present at the Creation*, p. 219.

14. Ibid., p. 233.

15. Ibid., p. 375.

16. Hammond, "NSC–68," p. 289.

17. Ibid., p. 292.

18. Warner R. Schilling, "The H-Bomb Decision: How to Decide Without Actually Choosing," *Political Science Quarterly*, Vol. 76, No. 1 (March 1961), 38.

19. Hammond, "NSC–68," pp. 299–300.

20. Cabell Phillips, *The Truman Presidency* (New York: Macmillan, 1966), pp. 306–8.

21. Acheson, *Present at the Creation*, p. 374.

22. Ibid.

23. Ibid.

24. George F. Kennan, *Memoirs, 1925–1950*, p. 475. See also Hammond, "NSC–68," pp. 315–16.

25. Hammond, "NSC–68," p. 309.

26. Acheson, *Present at the Creation*, p. 753.

27. Hammond, p. 309.

28. Ibid., p. 310.

29. Ibid., p. 371.

30. Smith, *Dean Acheson*, p. 189. "From the beginning Acheson was convinced that the North Korean attack was part of a Soviet 'grand design' whose ultimate purpose was to weaken the West and upset the balance in the most important of all theaters— Europe.... A failure to meet this aggression ... would be incalculable defeat." See also Glenn D. Paige, *The Korean Decision* (New York: The Free Press, 1968).

31. Ibid., p. ix.

32. Ibid., p. 16.

33. *New York Times*, October 17, 1971.

34. Smith, *Dean Acheson*, pp. 399–400.

35. Gaddis Smith, in a review of Joyce and Gabriel Kolko, *The Limits of Power: The World and United States Foreign Policy, 1945–1954* (New York: Harper & Row, 1972), in the *New York Times Book Review*, February 27, 1972. *The Limits of Power* is a continuation of Gabriel Kolko's study of American policy,

1943–45, *The Politics of War* (New York: Random House, 1969). See also Kolko's *The Roots of American Foreign Policy* (Boston: Beacon Press, 1969). Kolko's intricate analysis of the American role in the outbreak of the Korean war suggests that United States policy-makers, led by Acheson, used the conflict to buttress their policy position as stated in NSC–68.

5 INDOCHINA AND CONTAINMENT, THE EARLY 1950s

It was ritualistic anti-Communism and exaggerated power politics that got us into Vietnam. These were articles of faith and were not, therefore, ever seriously debated.

Leslie H. Gelb, editor

The Pentagon Papers (1971)

This chapter examines the making of American policy toward Vietnam (Indochina) in the early 1950s. This was a time when there should have been an opportunity to debate policy alternatives within the innermost circle of national security decision-making. If pluralist forces were at work within the inner circle of closed politics, one would expect to find evidence of a profound discussion of the wisdom of extending containment principles to Southeast Asia. The year 1950 was a key one in placing the United States on a Cold War course *around the globe*. It was the year that produced NSC–68. The decision to proceed with the building of the H-bomb was made in 1950. It was the year that the Korean war broke out. It was also the year in which the United States accepted Indochina as being strategically important to American vital interests in Asia. In this fashion, containment doctrine was expanded to embrace Asia as well as Europe before the Korean attack! The policy of globalism, implied in the Truman Doctrine, was made explicit in 1950. It is our purpose in this chapter to inquire into the nature of the decision to locate Indochina as an area of vital interest to the United States and to apply the doctrine of containment to a small country in which the future of French colonialism was at issue.

FDR'S TRUSTEESHIP PROPOSAL

It has long since been established that President Franklin D. Roosevelt held strong personal views about Indochina's place in the postwar world, looking forward to the establishment of an international trusteeship in Southeast Asia. Vague as the Roosevelt concept was, it apparently assumed a commanding United States presence that presumably would override any attempt aimed at restoring French political control over the colonies. Cordell Hull related a conversation with Roosevelt early in 1944, a conversation that followed a meeting between the President and Lord Halifax, the British Ambassador. Roosevelt had explained to Lord Halifax:

> quite frankly that it was perfectly true that I [Roosevelt] had, for over a year, expressed the opinion that Indo-China should not go back to France. . . . France has had the country . . . for nearly one hundred years, and the people are worse off than they were at the beginning. . . . The case of Indo-China is perfectly clear. France has milked it for one hundred years. The people of Indo-China are entitled to something better than that.[1]

The case for Indochina may have been "perfectly clear" to Franklin D. Roosevelt in 1944, but Roosevelt's wartime burdens left little time for Indochina. France was to entertain other ideas about the future of her Southeast Asian colonies, and soon Roosevelt would be dead. In the meantime, OSS (Office of Strategic Services) forces in the area were in touch with a Viet Minh resistance group led by Ho Chi Minh, whose Communist credentials were never in doubt. Chester Cooper, who has offered us a high-level bureaucrat's view of American involvement in Vietnam (a lost crusade, as he saw it), reports it "not unlikely" that OSS agents were in contact with Ho Chi Minh before October 1944. Cooper served with the OSS in China; hence one takes seriously his observation that the OSS appears to have been in contact with the Viet Minh resistance movement while President Roosevelt was still pondering what the official United States position should be toward Ho's group. Cooper also reports that Ho probably made a series of secret visits to the OSS headquarters in Kunming, China, late in 1944 and in early 1945, seeking arms and ammunition in exchange for intelligence and other services. Admiral William Leahey obtained Roosevelt's agreement in April 1945 that American aid might be given to Ho's forces provided it involved no interference with Allied operations against Japan. Within a month, a small band of OSS personnel was parachuted into Ho Chi Minh's headquarters in Tonkin. At this time, by way of contrast, Bao Dai, whom the French were later to restore as emperor in Vietnam, was enjoying the salubrious atmosphere of the French Riviera.

Cooper has described the activities of the OSS men during the next few months:

> The Americans lived and worked closely with Ho and his follow-ers, and for several months there was a flourishing exchange of views and ideas. It was through OSS radio that Ho first con-tacted the French in Kunming with respect to the forthcoming negotiations about Vietnam's postwar future. According to one OSS officer, Ho sought his advice on framing the Viet Minh's declaration of independence. The actual declaration begins with the familiar: "All men are created equal. They are endowed by their Creator with certain unalienable rights, among these are Life, Liberty and the pursuit of Happiness." [2]

It would be easy to make too much of Roosevelt's hopes for Indochina in the postwar world and of the early American rela-tionship with Ho Chi Minh. If there ever was any even partially serious American intention of working toward a trusteeship ar-rangement in Indochina, that intention died with Franklin Roose-velt. The intelligence community's link-up with Ho Chi Minh appears to have been largely a wartime improvisation aimed at exploiting any opportunity of increasing military pressure on the fast-fading Japanese Empire. But the irony of the situation seems not to have gotten through to elite policy-makers committed to Pax Americana. The British were to liquidate their empire. The reluctant Dutch were driven from the East Indies, while the French, who had to rely on Nationalist Chinese and British troops to disarm Japanese troops in Indochina, were soon insist-ing on retention of control over their small Asian empire. After Harry Truman came to the White House, the United States government did not seriously challenge the French government's effort to reassert colonial control over Indochina. Once France and Ho Chi Minh's regime took the issue to the battlefield, the United States government faced increasing pressure from the French to support the French position in Indochina. This pressure proved effective because our official political-strategic doctrine required an effective resistance to "Communist expansion" in Southeast Asia. Ho Chi Minh was a Communist. His forces, therefore, were perceived within the policy elite as being part of a monolithic Communist expansionist movement directed from Moscow.

The precise manner in which the United States moved to a position directly supporting French colonialism in Indochina bears closer examination because it reveals the manner in which the Cold War turned global. This is also another episode in which we find Dean Acheson playing a dominant role. There are at least two basic interpretations of this experience: Acheson's version as found in his memoirs, *Present at the Creation,* and the official version, not made public until the Pentagon Papers were released. The two versions differ in fundamental ways. This brief analysis follows Acheson's account first and then reviews the assessment of United States action as it appears in the Pentagon Papers.

ACHESON'S ACCOUNT

Acheson's account has the virtues of brevity and compactness. In a book totaling nearly eight hundred pages, one of our most articulate statesmen managed to devote less than eight full pages to American early involvement in Indochina. Acheson's chapter focuses on the decisions that led to the American underwriting of the French effort in the 1950–52 period. Thus, one learns that some time during the spring of 1950[3] (roughly coinciding in time with NSC–68) the State Department, "after some hesitation," recommended aid to France and the associated states of Vietnam, the government headed by Emperor Bao Dai, which the French had established to combat Ho's insurgency. Since there was no reason to doubt Ho's Communist background and since the policy elite *assumed* that he had close ties with Moscow, it was relatively easy for the French to make the case that their client regime headed by Bao Dai was resisting part of "the international Communist movement."

The State Department's recommendation to provide aid for economic and military supplies was made with some "hesitation" because some of Acheson's colleagues (he does not identify them) believed that even with American military and financial help the French-assisted Bao Dai regime would be defeated in the field by the Viet Minh.[4] By May 1950, *a full month before Korea* and only a few weeks after the presentation of NSC–68, President Truman approved a program of economic and military support for the French effort in Vietnam. *This was the beginning of the Americanization of the war in Vietnam. It came in May 1950. The principal policy "recommender" was Dean Acheson.*

The outbreak of war in Korea a month later simply tied American aid to Indochina more closely to a global Cold War–containment policy. Acheson later recalled: "One of the first decisions announced by President Truman after the attack on South Korea was that military aid to the Philippines and Indochina would have to be intensified."[5] It should be noted that these decisions were made while Dean Rusk was serving as Assistant Secretary of State for Far Eastern Affairs and while Paul Nitze headed up State's Policy Planning staff. These decisions relating to Vietnam coincide in time with the formulation of NSC–68, as discussed in chapter 4.

The picture Acheson drew was that of a Secretary of State who was in a bind. He needed French cooperation in Europe where the Truman Doctrine–Marshall Plan–NATO complex was rapidly taking final shape. In consequence, the United States government and the government of France concluded in September 1950 that "the creation of indigenous armies in Indochina was the only way to save the situation there and preserve the French army in Europe." At the same time, Acheson reports, French officials insisted "that to raise these armies France must have our help in finance and military equipment."[6] *Thus, the creation of the South Vietnamese army was from the very beginning subject to American underwriting.* What started as an initial $10 million grant in May 1950 had swelled to a $1 billion annual contribution by the siege of Dien Bien Phu, four years later.

The military situation in Vietnam deteriorated throughout the remaining months of 1950. A memo that Livingston Merchant prepared and was forwarded to Acheson by Rusk warned that the military situation in Vietnam was "extremely serious" and recommended that military aid should receive the "highest priority." [7]

The pattern, viewed in retrospect, seems familiar, as does Secretary Acheson's reaction: "We agreed to a large increase in military aid." [8]

The reader is reminded that this occurred in the autumn of 1950.

A PERCEPTIVE WARNING

At approximately the same time, Acheson received "a perceptive warning" from John Ohly, described in the memoirs simply as "an able colleague." Mr. Ohly believed that the appearance of Chinese forces in Korea required taking a second look at where the United States was going in Indochina. Acheson notes:

> Not only was there real danger that our efforts would fail in their immediate purpose and waste valuable resources in the process, but we were moving into a position in Indochina in which "our responsibilities tend to supplant rather than complement those of the French." We could, he added, become a scapegoat for the French and be sucked into direct intervention. "These situations have a way of snowballing," he concluded. [9]

Despite the perceptive warning, Acheson was prepared to assume responsibility. He notes in his memoirs:

> The dangers to which he pointed took more than a decade to materialize in full, but materialize they did. I decided, however, that having put our hand to the plow, we would not look back. [10]

There evidently was no second look in 1950. The hand was on the plow. The policy was set. The containment policy was now a global policy, and Indochina was a "vital" area subject to American intervention.

There was, Acheson insists, a thorough review of the situation in Indochina in August 1951. This review brought a warning from the Joint Chiefs of Staff against any United States statement that would commit, or seem to the French under future eventualities to commit, United States armed forces in Indochina. Acheson reports: "We did not waver from this policy." [11] Perhaps not.

On the other hand, the United States had begun the inexorable process of underwriting the French military effort in Vietnam, and Acheson was one of the first American officials to conclude that the French could not do the job effectively on their own. By his own admission, U.S. military aid to the French in Indochina rapidly mounted to half a billion dollars in 1951.

Furthermore, as their own military situation worsened, the French authorities continued to press for an ever larger American dollar involvement in underwriting the South Vietnamese army. In June 1952, while Americans were warming up for a Presidential campaign, Secretary Acheson met with Anthony Eden and Robert Schuman to discuss four points: first, the willingness of the United States to do more about developing "an indigenous military force" in Vietnam; second, the desirability of sending a tripartite warning to Peking about the danger of "aggression" in Vietnam; third, consideration of what Peking's reaction might be; and fourth, consideration of what the three Western powers might do if the warning were ignored. The meeting of the three foreign ministers ended with the issuance of a communique that viewed the struggle in Indochina as part of a worldwide resistance to Communist attempts at "conquest and subversion." [12]

THE ACHESON LEGACY

As he prepared to leave the State Department following the Presidential election of 1952, Acheson warned that Vietnamese forces alone could not maintain the existing stalemate. The outgoing Secretary of State also received a final plea from Robert Schuman asking for relief from what he referred to as France's "solitude" in Indochina. At this point, Acheson later recalled, he lost patience with the French.[13] In the meantime, the United States continued to underwrite French colonialism in Indochina.

Acheson has left us a puzzling assessment of United States

policy in Vietnam during the period of his stewardship. On the one hand, he calls it "a muddled hodgepodge"; on the other hand, he writes: "So, while we may have tried to muddle through and certainly were not successful, I could not think then or later of a better course." [14] Was there no possibility of withholding American assistance to France in its military effort in Indochina? The result, Acheson suggests, "would, at most, have removed the colonial power."

The possibility of doing nothing to assist the French in Indochina did not appeal to Acheson: "That might have had merit, but as an attitude for the leader of a great alliance toward an important ally, indeed one essential to a critical endeavor, it had its demerits, too." [15]

As a result, Acheson's approach placed the United States squarely on a course, which, if not altered, would ultimately make the United States the successor to French colonialism in Indochina, after the British and Dutch had liquidated their empires in Asia. Eventually, this course was to lead to direct and major American military involvement in Indochina. This, in turn, would divide the American nation more deeply than it had been since the 1860s, while sowing seeds of cynicism and alienation at a time of mounting social tension. The policy of containment as applied in Southeast Asia also had demerits that are nowhere examined in Acheson's memoirs, a book that speaks of having been at the creation . . . of what? More to the point, these demerits, to use Acheson's language, appear not to have been examined very carefully in 1950, despite John Ohly's warning that "these situations have a way of snowballing." [16]

A DIFFERENT INTERPRETATION: A NEW GLOBALISM

The Pentagon Papers offer a view of American policy toward, and actions in, Vietnam which is at variance with the version Dean Acheson left us. Most significantly, the Pentagon Papers reveal that the basic course of United States policy in Southeast Asia was in the process of being firmed up in *the final months of 1949:* this course, based on a global doctrine of containment, placed Indochina as a key area within Southeast Asia, an area of vital interest to the United States. Before February 1950 was over, the National Security Council had officially adopted the containment course as basic United States policy in Asia. From that time forward, it was *never* merely a matter of the United States giving in to French pressure, as Acheson so frequently implied: to the contrary, the United States national security policy elite grew increasingly apprehensive about the French military effort in Indochina precisely because it did *not* measure up as an effective instrument for *our* containment policy. The truth is that Truman and Acheson, deeply affected politically by the "loss of China" charge, were far from being reluctant partners in trying to prevent the "loss" of Indochina to "Communism." In any event, once United States troops were engaged in fighting an increasingly unpopular war in Korea, the administration had no alternative, given the global containment policy, but to support the French military activity in Indochina. As the Kolkos have shown, United States officials, led by Acheson, had previously looked to Indochina as the most likely "trouble spot" in Southeast Asia and were surprised when the attack came in Korea.[17]

The Pentagon Papers describe three fundamental perceptions that affected elite decision-making during this early period in the Cold War. There was first an awareness of Asia's growing importance in world politics. Second, the Communist threat was seen as being worldwide in scope and monolithic in structure, with Moscow directing a global strategy. Third, Ho Chi Minh was a Communist engaged in forcing the French out of Indochina; he was, therefore, part of this universal movement. When the three perceptions were focused on Southeast Asia, they led, logically enough, to what has since been called the domino theory. Something very similar to the domino concept was adumbrated in National Security Document 48/1, discussed by the NSC on December 28, 1949, which reads in part:

> The extension of communist authority in China represents a grievous political defeat for us: if southeast Asia also is swept by communism we shall have suffered a major political rout the repercussions of which will be felt throughout the rest of the world, especially in the Middle East and in a then critically exposed Australia.[18]

This was followed by NSC–64, which was adopted as policy on February 27, 1950. NSC–64 called for "all practicable measures" being taken to prevent further Communist expansion in Southeast Asia while referring explicitly to Indochina as being a "key" area. On May 8, 1950, President Truman publicly announced that $10 million in military and economic assistance would go to support the French military effort in Vietnam. In this fashion the foot-in-the-door policy was initiated before the outbreak of the war in Korea.

The role that highly placed civilian militants performed in leading to the basic policy decisions in the winter and spring of 1950, prior to Korea, is suggested in a memo signed by Dean Rusk, as Deputy Undersecretary of State, to Major General James H. Burns, a key aide to the Secretary of Defense. The memo was sent on March 7, 1950, as a means of "facilitating" the Pentagon's consideration of NSC–64. The following excerpts faithfully represent Rusk's memo:

> The Department of State continues to hold that Southeast Asia is in grave danger of Communist domination as a consequence of aggression from Communist China and of internal subversive activities. The Department of State maintains that Indo-China, subject as it is to the most immediate danger, is the most strategically important area of Southeast Asia.
>
> The Department of State believes that within the limitations imposed by existing commitments and strategic priorities, the resources of the United States should be deployed to reserve Indo-China and Southeast Asia from further Communist encroachment. The Department of State has accordingly already engaged all its political resources to the end that this object be secured. The Department is now engaged in the process of urgently examining what additional economic resources can effectively be engaged in the same operation.
>
> It is now, in the opinion of the Department, a matter of the greatest urgency that the Department of Defense assess the strategic aspects of the situation and consider, from the military point of view, how the United States can best contribute to the prevention of further Communist encroachment in that area.[19]

There appears to be no basis, then or now, for questioning Dean Rusk's sincerity or consistency concerning the American

involvement in Vietnam. The policies with which he was identified in the 1960s coincide with the policies he advocated in
1950 while serving as an influential assistant to Secretary Acheson. Gaddis Smith feels that Acheson considerably overstated
his case in suggesting that the United States originally became
committed in Vietnam because the French virtually "blackmailed"
our government into aiding them in Southeast Asia in return for
French acceptance of American plans (very dear to Acheson's
heart) for German economic revival. As Smith sees it:

> The United States was poised in 1949 to give the French mili-
> tary aid. Acheson simply tried to get a little more leverage from
> that aid on French behavior in Europe. Before the Truman Ad-
> ministration ended, the United States was giving the French all
> the military equipment they could use and far more advice than
> they wanted.[20]

The Pentagon Papers amply support Smith's interpretation. Smith
goes further, however, in speculating that had the Truman administration been in power at the time of the French defeat at
Dien Bien Phu, the United States would have intervened militarily.

THE CONTAINMENT ELITE

Leaving speculation aside, it is obvious that the line of decision we have been tracing in this chapter relates to the formulation of NSC–68 discussed in chapter 4. NSC–68 argued the case
for a huge increase in defense spending, which the State Department under Acheson's leadership deemed necessary in order
to support *militarily* the containment doctrine that NSC–64 had
broadened to include Asia, as well as Europe. NSC–68 recommended a vast increase in military spending necessary to support a policy of containment expanded to include the globe.
   Gaddis Smith concludes that

> President Kennedy brought many of the veterans of the Truman
> years back into positions of power—most notably Dean Rusk as
> Secretary of State. They then took the opportunity to do what,
> had they been able, they might have done years before.[21]

The analysis in this book indicates that Kennedy appointed to important national security decision-making positions a significant number of civilian militants from the Truman era who were also members of the special elite group responsible for formulating the containment doctrine and then for rapidly transforming it into global dogma. These civilian militants were vitally interested in keeping the pressure on for a stronger military posture throughout the Eisenhower years, at a time when a number of them were located outside government. Our analysis supports Professor Gaddis Smith's judgment that the Truman administration marks the beginning of the American military involvement in Vietnam, an involvement deliberately entered into as part of a global policy of containment. Smith finds no villains to identify in connection with Vietnam. Rather, he sees "an entire generation of foreign policy leaders—the self-styled best that American society could produce—sharing the madness." [22]

Should we leave it this way? Who were the men representing "an entire generation"? In what sense were they the "best" this society could produce? Professor Smith reported finding the Pentagon Papers full of "lethal, self-reenforcing clichés, neatly organized in numberless, often indistinguishable cables, position papers, and 'action memoranda' flowing endlessly through the typewriters and mimeograph machines." [23] How are we to account for the potency of these foreign policy clichés, if that is what they were? They persisted, after all, with apparently irresistible force over a very long period of time—from Truman to Eisenhower to Kennedy to Johnson and into the indefinite future.

One of the curious aspects of Cold War decision-making is the way in which intelligence estimates prepared within the national security bureaucracies frequently cast doubt on basic assumptions that underlay Cold War dogma. [24] For example, a State Department estimate dated July 2, 1948, after noting that Ho Chi Minh was a Communist (a fact he never denied, so far as I have been able to discover) reported "no evidence a direct link between Ho and Moscow, but assume it exists." The same estimate was unable to evaluate the amount of pressure or guidance Moscow might have been exerting on Ho Chi Minh: it did, nevertheless, report an "impression" that Ho was being accorded a "large degree latitude." [25]

The Office of Intelligence Research, Department of State, reported in the autumn of 1948: "If there is a Moscow-directed conspiracy in Southeast Asia, Indo-China is an anomaly." [26] The most likely possibilities occurring to the intelligence estimators were either that Moscow was not issuing rigid directives to Ho or that he had worked out some special dispensation from his Kremlin masters.

The containment dogma left no room for the complex reality that Ho Chi Minh was a lifelong Communist who also led with remarkable skill and persistence an indigenous native nationalist movement in Indochina. A State Department cable to the American Consul in Hanoi, signed by Acheson and dated May 20, 1949, makes clear the official State Department mind-set on this crucial point: "Question whether Ho as much nationalist as Commie irrelevant. All Stalinists in colonial areas are nationalists." [27]

Ipso facto.

It hardly seems too much to suggest that it was this "irrelevant" distinction, which seems never to have been assessed critically when basic decisions were taken, on which the ultimate American effort in Vietnam foundered. This fundamental point appears *not* to have occasioned discussion within the inner circle of closed politics in the 1949–50 period.

There can be no doubt that the United States through decisions taken in 1950 within the national security elite broadened the containment doctrine—which had been designed with the expansion of Soviet power in Europe in view—to cover Southeast Asia. This expansion of the geography of the Cold War was substantially accomplished *before* the attack in Korea. It was also accomplished at a time when there seems to have been little firm evidence of Soviet leadership of an expansionist program in Southeast Asia. Such evidence as was available to our intelligence community tended to suggest that the Soviet role in Indochina, for example, left a wide degree of latitude to Ho Chi Minh. The principal architect of containment in Asia was Dean Acheson, the Secretary of State. Paul Nitze, his principal policy planning assistant, led the way in drafting NSC–68, which called for greatly increased military strength to make the Cold War a *global* crusade. At the same time, Dean Rusk, Acheson's principal assistant for Far Eastern affairs, was urging the Defense

Department to make the kind of military assessment of Indochina's strategic importance that the State Department civilian leadership had previously written into NSC–64.

When French authorities were tempted to exaggerate what they were pleased to present as the "Communist threat" in Indochina, they must surely have understood how ready Acheson and his colleagues were to accept the thesis, coinciding as it did with views they were advocating in national security elite circles. We now know that Acheson and Nitze were themselves involved in exaggerating the threat of Communism (that is, Soviet military power) in order to carry the day for global containment within the inner circle, and also in order to provoke the "appropriate" response in Congress and among the members of the attentive public. The Pentagon Papers establish beyond any conceivable doubt that the containment course in Asia was set in late 1949–early 1950. The domino theory is in essence the Asian corollary of the containment doctrine.

HOLDING THE LINE

The most salient fact about the Eisenhower–Dulles era in terms of this analysis is that the Republican administration managed to stay on the containment course that had been set by Truman and Acheson. Even after the French military position collapsed at Dien Bien Phu, Eisenhower and Dulles deliberately passed up the opportunity thus provided for getting the United States out of any further involvement in Indochina. If Communism was to be contained in Indochina and if the French were no longer in a position to fight Ho Chi Minh, there was only one alternative left (within the limits of our own conceptual framework): the United States would have to create and then support a regime in Saigon, which in turn would be prepared to carry on the military struggle against Ho's forces for an indefinite period of time. This decision was made entirely within the inner circle of closed politics.

Secretary Dulles's greatest fear at the time of the Geneva conference in 1954 was that the French would "sell out" to Ho Chi

Minh. Dulles personally would have preferred a form of direct American military intervention at Dien Bien Phu. The lack of British support and the unwillingness of Congressional leaders to give their sanction to a unilateral effort finally dictated Eisenhower's decision *not* to intervene militarily. It is noteworthy that all the great powers concerned, except the United States, found the Geneva accords an expedient way out of open warfare in Indochina. The French, the British, the Russians, the Communist Chinese, and a rather reluctant Ho Chi Minh, accepted the accords. Only the South Vietnamese regime and the government of the United States were openly hostile to the Geneva settlement. Thus, the Eisenhower administration in 1954 faced the question: how far was the United States prepared to go in terms of force commitments to insure that Indochina stayed out of Communist control? The question was discussed at the National Security Council level *before* the battle of Dien Bien Phu. There were discussions in January 1954 during which *State Department spokesmen urged that the United States decide to utilize its own military forces in the fighting in Southeast Asia.* By the middle of March, active discussion was under way at the NSC level as to whether the United States government should be prepared to commit American combat troops to the region. Although it had long since been decided that Indochina was of vital importance to the global containment effort, there was little enthusiasm at the highest political level for the use of American ground troops so soon after the Korean settlement. Eisenhower, of all people, did not want another Korea on his hands.

But the question persisted: what should the United States do following a French pull-out?

The Pentagon Papers offer the following assessment:

> In such a case the United States could either accept the loss of Indochina, or adopt an active policy while France gradually withdrew its troops. Should we accept the latter course, our "most positive" step offering "the greatest assurance of success" would be, NSC estimated, to join with indigenous forces in combatting the Viet Minh until they were reduced "to the status of scattered guerrilla bands." U.S. land, sea, and air forces would be involved.[28]

In this fashion the question was posed in the spring of 1954 while the siege of Dien Bien Phu was just beginning and with the Geneva conference then only six weeks away.

The Truman-Acheson administration set the basic course in Vietnam; the Eisenhower administration continued on the same course. Just a few days after the Geneva accords—one of the rare moments when the United States might have found a graceful exit from Indochina—Eisenhower's National Security Council decided that the accords were a "disaster" and approved action to prevent further Communist expansion in Vietnam. According to the Pentagon Papers this NSC decision in 1954 had a direct role in the ultimate breakdown of the Geneva settlement.[29] The National Security Council at a meeting on August 3, 1954, ordered an urgent program of American military and economic aid, including American advisers, to the new South Vietnamese government of Premier Diem. Curiously, the NSC decision followed a national intelligence estimate that stated:

> Although it is possible that the French and Vietnamese even with the firm support of the United States and other powers may be able to establish a strong regime in South Vietnam, we believe that the chances for this development are poor and moreover, that the situation is more likely to continue to deteriorate progressively over the next year.[30]

CONCLUSION

This chapter reveals a pattern of Cold War decision-making that is consistent with the findings in earlier chapters. Highly placed civilians, especially in the State Department, appear to have been most influential in extending the containment doctrine, centerpiece of the Cold War mosaic, to Southeast Asia in general and to Indochina specifically. Dean Acheson was the single most important civilian Cold War policy-shaper below the level of the President in the period 1949–52. The group around Acheson included Dean Rusk and Paul Nitze, who were destined to hold positions of still greater influence during the

Kennedy years. Both men continued to play important roles in helping shape the Johnson administration's Vietnam activity.

Daniel Bell, a sharp and early critic of Mills's power elite concept, has written:

> What powers people have, what decisions people make, how they make them, what factors they have taken into account in making them—all these enter into the question of whether position can be transferred into power.[31]

Mills would agree: those men who man the "command posts" in the modern technocracy wield enormous—even decisive—power. Mills's view is clear and unequivocal:

> The elite cannot truly be thought of as men who are merely doing their duty. They are the ones who determine their duty, as well as the duties of those beneath them. They are not merely bureaucrats: they command bureaucracies. They may try to disguise these facts from others and from themselves by appeals to traditions of which they imagine themselves the instruments, but there are many traditions, and they must choose which ones they will serve. They face decisions for which there simply are no traditions.[32]

It would be difficult to find a paragraph anywhere in the literature of social science that more accurately portrays the true role played by Dean Acheson and his closest associates in the period under examination.

Bell may have been misled by a naïve conception of how the "big decisions" are made in the modern military technology. He questioned Mills's list of "big decisions," which included the use of the A-bombs, Korea, and the Dien Bien Phu episode, arguing that these were typically Presidential decisions, hence not subject to elite determination. Bell seems not to have been curious about how a policy elite might shape and structure Presidential decision-making. After all, President Truman, in "deciding" to use the A-bombs against the two Japanese cities, ratified a decision that had been *assumed* from the very start within the inner circle of closed politics. Likewise, the Presidential role in transforming containment into global dogma appears to have been largely formal in view of the persistent effort of Acheson's elite. Although Eisenhower rejected the advice of those urging U.S. military intervention at Dien Bien Phu, he continued the policy of global containment and the direct United States involvement in Indochina. On the basis of our examination thus far of the powers people have, the decisions they make, how they make them, the factors taken into account in making them, there can be little room to doubt that *position* within the inner circle of closed politics carries unusual power in shaping national security policy. Further, when key positions within the same innermost circle are occupied over long periods of time by leading members of a reasonably coherent policy elite, it is not at all obvious where pluralism's countervailing forces might be located in the total system.

Very little evidence has been found to support the notion of a vigorous competition among autonomous elites over United States policy alternatives in Southeast Asia in 1949–50. Who within the inner circle questioned the misapplication of containment in an area where there was no direct Soviet military threat? Who questioned the reality of the Soviet "menace"? Acheson mentions only the doubts expressed by John Ohly, and then dismisses them. Kennan later reported that he had been preoccupied during these critical months in 1950 with the question of Soviet *intentions*. He further reported that he had briefed the Secretary of State and his senior advisers daily on the evidence relating to the subject. Although he was listened to thoughtfully, Kennan found that his interpretations proved "quite ineffective with relation to the development of governmental thinking." This is Kennan's view of the manner in which the Soviet threat was perceived within the policy elite at the time of the Korean attack:

> Somehow or other, the North Korean attack came soon to appear to a great many people in Washington as merely the first move in some "grand design," as the phrase then went, on the part of the Soviet leaders to extend their power to other parts of the world by the use of force. The unexpectedness of this attack— the fact that we had no forewarning of it—only stimulated the already existent preference of the military planners for drawing their conclusions only from the assessed *capabilities* of the adversary, dismissing his *intentions*, which could be safely assumed

to be hostile. All this tended to heighten the militarization of thinking about the cold war generally, and to press us into attitudes where any discriminate estimate of Soviet intentions was unwelcome and unacceptable.[33]

Kennan also noted the tendency of viewing Soviet intentions "as something existing quite independently of our own behavior. It was difficult to persuade these men that what people in Moscow decided to do might be a reaction to things we had done." [34]

The American involvement in the struggle for Indochina began in 1949–50. The decision was made within the inner circle of closed politics at a time when Dean Acheson played a "commanding" (in Mills's sense) role. The *New York Times* version of the Pentagon Papers offers this summary of the decision and its significance:

> A key point came in the winter of 1949–50 when the United States made what the account describes as a watershed decision affecting American policy in Vietnam for the next two decades: after the fall of mainland China to the Chinese Communists, the Truman Administration moved to support Emperor Bao Dai and provide military aid to the French against the Communist-led Vietminh.
>
> This decision, which was made amid growing concern in the United States over the expansion of Communism in Eastern Europe and Asia, reversed Washington's long-standing reluctance to become involved with French colonialism in Indo-China.[35]

Although the French government exerted steady pressure while seeking support for their military effort against Ho Chi Minh's forces, several documents printed in the Pentagon Papers show that the policy that viewed Indochina as vital to the United States global effort aimed at containing "Communist expansion" was formulated within the inner circle of closed politics *prior to the Korean attack*. The departure of Acheson, Nitze, and Rusk from the inner circle during the Eisenhower years did not alter the basic policy. The containment doctrine, applied to Asia as well as to Europe, provided the conceptual framework within which national security decision-making took place during the 1950s. The national security debate of the 1950s centered around the structure of military forces. While John Foster Dulles spoke of "massive retaliation" based upon an assumed American nuclear superiority, and men like Acheson and Nitze came forward as critics of what they regarded as an overreliance on our strategic air power, the Eisenhower administration continued to accept containment and all that it implied in terms of the American global mission. The established doctrine was not challenged.

In the meantime, Cold War decision-making increasingly involved the application of military technology to the "solution" of complex political, social, and economic questions. In a system in which membership in a significant elite was at least partially determined by the positions occupied and by the kinds of decisions made, it was inevitable that technocrats, often largely anonymous in a public sense, would come to play a special role. Unfortunately, their precise role in decision-making, especially when it is cloaked in official secrecy, is not easily established in the scholarly literature. For this reason alone, the Pentagon Papers become an unusually valuable source of information for political analysis. Chapter 7 examines the role of the new technocrat in national security decision-making during the 1960s.

With reference to an establishment orchestration model, it should be noted that Acheson's group would suffer no disabilities in effecting linkage with an American establishment. The civilian militants who have figured prominently in this analysis have all enjoyed close ties with the Council on Foreign Relations, the organization Domhoff pointed to as a central agency in recruiting elite figures for the nation's national security decision-making apparatus. Most of the men we have met thus far in this study have been members of the upper class. If it is assumed that the cohesiveness of an elite is based upon a community of interests and a commonly shared "ideology," a policy elite has been closely identified with the creation of the containment doctrine; leading members of this group, furthermore, kept at their task with great persistence until the doctrine had been transformed, largely through their efforts within the inner circle of closed politics, into global dogma. The containment dogma coincided with the development of a *permanent* military establishment of incredible technological sophistication. The military establishment, in turn, necessitated public expenditures on a scale that vitally affected the employment and income objectives of the so-called affluent society. In short, the level of military spending had profound domestic economic consequences.

When strategic-political doctrine manages to prevail for more than two decades and persists through a series of national administrations, a critical political science might be expected to question rather complacent pluralist assumptions about the making of national security policy. There would be little point, however, in examining the part a policy elite plays in policy-making unless an effort were made to relate this to the impact on public policy. When the American involvement in Southeast Asia is seen for what it was; that is, an increasing *military* involvement over more than twenty years—an activity in which certain leading civilian militants appear to have provided much of the effective policy leadership and continuity—it would seem to require unusual obtuseness *not* to make some intellectual effort toward linking the policy results with the people who occupied positions of special influence. Following Daniel Bell's prescription, the analysis should be curious about what powers people have, what decisions they make, how they make them, and what factors they take into account in making them. If one were to assume a pluralism-in-miniature within the elite, the effectiveness of the people we have identified with the containment dogma in having their policy preferences prevail over a long period of time would be all the more impressive.

Chapter Five Notes

1. Cordell Hull, *Memoirs* (New York: Macmillan, 1948), p. 1597.
2. Chester Cooper, *The Lost Crusade* (New York: Dodd, Mead, 1970), pp. 26–27. (In either 1947 or 1948, while preparing a graduate school paper on French colonial policy, I met and talked with a former OSS officer who said he had been parachuted to Ho Chi Minh's command post in 1945. He told me essentially the same story about the writing of the Viet Minh declaration of independence.—J.C.D.)
3. Dean Acheson, *Present at the Creation* (New York: W. W. Norton, 1969), p. 672.
4. Ibid.
5. Ibid., p. 673.
6. Ibid.
7. Ibid., p. 674.
8. Ibid.
9. Ibid.
10. Ibid.
11. Ibid., p. 675.
12. Ibid., p. 676.
13. Ibid., p. 677.
14. Ibid., p. 673.
15. Ibid.
16. (Quoted by Acheson), ibid., p. 674.
17. Gabriel and Joyce Kolko, *The Limits of Power* (New York: Harper & Row, 1972), pp. 560–62.
18. *U.S.–Vietnam Relations,* Study Prepared by Department of Defense, Committee Print, House Committee on Armed Services, 92nd Congress, 1st Session, Volume 8, p. 248. Henceforth in using this official version of the so-called Pentagon Papers, the citation will read P.P. (off.), followed by volume and page number(s).
19. Ibid., p. 288.

20. Gaddis Smith in a review of "United States–Vietnam Relations, 1945–1967" (the Pentagon Papers) in the *New York Times Book Review*, Nov. 28, 1971.

21. Ibid.

22. Ibid.

23. Ibid.

24. Daniel Ellsberg was the first to call public attention to this vital fact. See his *Papers on the War* (New York: Simon and Schuster, 1972).

25. P.P. (off.), Vol. 8, p. 127.

26. Quoted in the Pentagon Papers as published by the *New York Times* (New York: Bantam Books), p. 8. Henceforth in citing the Bantam Books edition of the Pentagon Papers, the citation will read P.P. (NYT) followed by the page number(s).

27. P.P. (off.), Vol. 8, p. 196.

28. P.P. (off.), Vol. 1, "Perceptions of the Communist Threat to Southeast Asia and the Basic U.S. Interests," p. B-9.

29. P.P. (NYT), pp. 13–15.

30. P.P. (off.), Vol. 10, p. 692.

31. Daniel Bell, *The End of Ideology* (New York: The Free Press, 1960).

32. C. Wright Mills, *The Power Elite* (New York: Oxford University Press, 1956), p. 286.

33. George F. Kennan, *Memoirs, 1925–1950* (Boston: Little, Brown, 1967), p. 497.

34. Ibid.

35. P.P. (NYT), p. 5.

6   THE GAITHER REPORT: NSC–68 REVISITED, 1957

*Common purpose can only emerge out of broadly
based policy discussion and widespread participation
in the policy-making process. It cannot be decreed
from on high.*

Samuel P. Huntington

The Common Defense (1961)

This chapter examines the process by which the Gaither report, a major Cold War policy document, was prepared in 1957. The analysis focuses again on the inner circle of closed politics, seeking to identify those who were chiefly responsible for preparing the report that called for a major rearmament effort. It is part of the purpose of this analysis to discover, if possible, why key individuals, defying Presidential judgment, deemed it important that the Gaither committee findings be made public, since the document remains to the present time highly classified, having been prepared solely for Presidential guidance. It will be a matter of some interest to see what relationship, if any, there may have been between the men who wrote the Gaither report and those men previously identified with the policy elite who proved so influential in the preparation of NSC–68. Since the findings of the Gaither report have not remained secret, the experience may also indicate something about the linkage between policy elite and attentive public when activity within the inner circle of closed politics frustrates the elite's purposes.

The Gaither report was the product of an ad hoc committee composed entirely of individuals in private life who were technically serving as consultants to the National Security Council. Although the committee was established by Presidential directive to examine the implications of a proposed massive fallout shelter program, the report soon became the vehicle for an overall review of the American defense posture vis-à-vis the Soviet

Union. In a number of its essential aspects the Gaither report bears striking resemblance to NSC–68. There is the same emphasis on the grave Soviet military threat. Indeed, the authors of the report felt an urgent need to overcome what they regarded as "complacency" at the highest levels of the Eisenhower administration with respect to Soviet military capacity. Like NSC–68, the Gaither report recommended an enormous increase in American defense spending in order to provide for a limited war capability as well as for a greatly expanded nuclear weapon-missile deterrent capacity. The committee met in secret sessions; its very existence remained a secret for several months. Nevertheless, the report rapidly became a matter of public controversy.

CIVIL DEFENSE STUDY

It was in the spring of 1957 that the Federal Civilian Defense Administration submitted a report to President Eisenhower recommending that the government spend $40 billion over a period of several years to erect shelters that would provide protection against the blast effect of nuclear weapons. Shortly thereafter, the FCDA proposal was discussed by the National Security Council, whereupon the President ordered a study to be undertaken by an ad hoc committee of private citizens.

Morton Halperin, who has written an authoritative account of the Gaither report, observes: "The FCDA proposal was too serious to be rejected out of hand and it was too expensive to be adopted." [1]

Halperin continues:

> The sense of the NSC meeting had been that before the Administration considered spending a sum equal to its annual military expenditures, it should investigate other possible uses of the $40 billion. It was argued that if the government were prepared to increase spending for defense, it should explore the advantages of increasing its active defense efforts. [2]

President Eisenhower, on the advice of Robert Cutler, a wealthy Bostonian who served as his Special Assistant for National Security Affairs, appointed a committee headed by H. Rowan Gaither, a West Coast lawyer, who combined the chair-

manship of the board of the Ford Foundation with that of the
RAND Corporation, the Air Force's strategic think-tank.[3] Neither C. Wright Mills nor William Domhoff would have been
surprised by those selected to serve on the committee: Robert
Sprague, the industrialist; William C. Foster, who had served as
Deputy Secretary of Defense; and William Webster, a utility
magnate, represented the corporate elite. They were joined by
James A. Perkins, vice-president of the Carnegie Corporation
(later president of Cornell University); Jerome Wiesner of MIT;
Robert Calkins, an economist, who was soon to head the Brook-
ings Institution; John J. Corson, a high-level bureaucrat who
moved easily from the Washington executive establishment to
various consultancies and to a peripatetic professorship at Princeton; and James Phinney Baxter, a historian of impeccable Yankee
patrician background, who was president of Williams College.
Two other members, Robert Prim, director of research for Bell
Telephone, and Hector Skifter, a radio engineer, may have been
added to the committee for reasons of presumed technical expertise.

The Gaither committee, which functioned technically in a
position subordinate to the National Security Council, met briefly
in the spring of 1957 in order to authorize a series of technical
studies by its scientific staff. These staff studies were prepared
during the summer of 1957. The committee reassembled in the
fall in Washington to devote full time to a study of defense
policy. At this point the committee appointed two "special advisers": Colonel George A. Lincoln of West Point and Paul A.
Nitze, a principal author of NSC–68. As late as the autumn of
1957 no public announcement had been made of the existence
of the committee.

The Gaither committee lost no time in broadening its mandate.
The first decision taken by the group was quite simply to broaden
the scope of its inquiry to cover the whole range of defense
problems facing the country. In view of his later handling of the
report, it is conceivable that President Eisenhower may have
been somewhat irritated that a group of private citizens presumed to alter the nature of a confidential inquiry based on
Presidential directive. There was a rationale, of course, for the
committee's prompt decision to broaden its own role.

Halperin explains:

> In this case the panel had been asked in effect how the United
> States could best spend an additional sum for continental de-
> fense. But clearly defense is only one part of the deterrence
> strategy and hinges on how well the other parts function. It
> might very well be true that the greatest payoff for continental
> defense would come, for example, by investing in ballistic mis-
> siles. In the absence of any priority plans for spending additional
> sums for various systems, the Committee was forced to study
> the whole problem.[4]

It seems improbable that the committee needed very much
"forcing." As Halperin also suggests:

> the members were so prominent and had such definite opinions
> on the problems of American military policy that it was natural
> for them to decide to use the rare opportunity of drafting a
> paper for the NSC to present their views on a wide range of
> topics.[5]

Halperin apparently assumes that it is "natural" for prominent
citizens to rewrite national defense policy across the board. This,
at any rate, is what the members of the Gaither committee intended to accomplish, if possible. Their ready agreement on this
point would seem to indicate a rather broad policy consensus in
establishment circles.

The active direction of the committee's work was assumed by
Sprague and Foster because Gaither was taken ill and was hos-
pitalized for several weeks. In addition to its own staff-directed
technical studies, the committee drew upon the abundant resources of the Defense Department, the CIA, and the Joint
Chiefs of Staff, as well as private experts and the RAND Corporation. There was also an advisory panel, appointed by the President, which met frequently with the committee members. Robert
Lovett and John J. McCloy were active members of this advisory panel, as was Frank Stanton, the president of CBS. The
committee members soon agreed that the top echelons of the
executive branch did not appreciate the extent of the Soviet
threat as fully as they did. Furthermore, just as the report was
in its final stage of preparation, the Soviet Union announced on
October 4, 1957, that it had launched Sputnik. A week later the

report was completed and presented to the President. On November 7, 1957, President Eisenhower presided over a meeting of the National Security Council where the Gaither report was discussed. An unusually large group attended this meeting. In addition to the regular NSC members, the Gaither committee, its advisory panel, the service secretaries, and the Joint Chiefs of Staff were in attendance.

SOVIET MILITARY POWER

The report presented a frightening picture of Soviet military power. The USSR was pictured as spending 25 percent of Soviet GNP for defense while the United States was investing 10 percent. The committee estimated that both countries were spending the same absolute amount; but, assuming a faster rate of economic growth in Russia, the Soviet Union would soon be devoting much larger sums to defense. The report contrasted the two and a half million men in our armed forces who were equipped and trained, so the Committee reasoned, *only* for general nuclear war, whereas the larger Soviet army was supplied with weapons for both nuclear and conventional warfare.

In the judgment of the Gaither committee, the major danger facing the United States was the vulnerability of the American strategic force. The Committee had been influenced by a classified RAND report prepared under the direction of Albert Wohlstetter.[6] The vulnerability of the Strategic Air Command was stressed. Our planes were exposed and concentrated, making it very unlikely that they could survive a nuclear attack. Hence, the ability to maintain an effective second-strike capability, so central to deterrence theory, came into question. Indeed, the Committee warned that by the early 1960s the Soviet Union, armed with an operational ICBM force, would be capable of destroying the American retaliatory force.

It was a principal argument of the report that the United States give top priority to the development of an invulnerable second-strike force. SAC should change tactics so as to be able to survive an all-out attack; our IRBM program should be accelerated; in the longer run the whole U.S. missile production program should be greatly accelerated; American missile launching sites should be hardened and dispersed.

The report reflected:

> the feeling of the Committee members that top Administration officials did not have a complete understanding of the problem of effectively deterring a Russian strategic strike. The Report stressed the need to look at the problem in terms of the vulnerability of the force rather than its initial destructive capacity. This was the problem which most bothered the Committee and gave its members the feeling that the government was dangerously underestimating the gravity of the Russian threat.[7]

But it was not merely the assumed vulnerability of the American strategic striking force that troubled the committee. The committee wanted the military to develop a capacity to fight so-called limited wars as well. The committee assumed that, once a nuclear balance had been established, there would be a tendency for the assumed adversary to move to local aggression as a likely form of warfare; and the Committee believed that the United States was not equipped to engage in limited wars. Hence, the second major recommendation was that the United States train and equip additional forces for conventional warfare. (In the Kennedy-McNamara era this was covered by the theory of "flexible response," providing a direct route to military escalation in Vietnam.)

Oddly enough, the Gaither committee, which had been called into existence by the issues raised when FCDA proposed spending $40 billion for blast shelters, did not think well of blast shelters, assigning a very low priority to such construction. In the civil defense field, the report was content with a relatively modest proposal that called for spending several hundred million dollars in the following few years for research on various aspects of shelter construction. Secondary priority was given a proposal to spend approximately $22 billion for the construction of radiation (rather than blast) shelters.

Chalmers Roberts, in his authoritative account of the Gaither committee report, adds:

> One of the recommendations in this area on which the Gaither Committee was particularly emphatic was the allocation of a

great deal more money—the exact amount was not specified—
to basic scientific research and development.[8]

The Gaither report did not give an exact estimate of the cost
of all its recommendations. It did indicate, however, the need
for rapid increases in the military budget to about $48 billion per
year in the 1960s. This contrasted with the determined effort of
the Eisenhower administration to hold defense spending on an
annual basis below $38 billion.

FIXED DEFENSE SPENDING

It was the budgetary argument that was destined to find hard
going at the higher reaches of the Eisenhower administration.
The Eisenhower administration was even more committed than
the Truman administration had once been to the notion that
there had to be a fixed upper limit on all federal spending for
fear of economic bankruptcy; hence, defense spending was fixed
at a rigid point while the armed services fought over the size of
allocation each was to receive in the budgetary-appropriations
struggle.

The role played by John J. McCloy and Robert Lovett, one-
time protégés of Colonel Stimson, in urging acceptance of the
Gaither report, has been described by Roberts:

> At that dramatic NSC meeting, with some 45 persons crowded
> into the White House broadcast room, two of the President's
> most valued friends in the financial world—John J. McCloy and
> Robert Lovett—pledged to Mr. Eisenhower the complete back-
> ing of the American financial community if he would approve
> the program proposed.
>
> McCloy and Lovett, both Republicans who held high posts in
> past Democratic administrations, expressed the conviction that
> the American public would shoulder the burden and accept the
> responsibilities of such major increases in the budget. They said
> also that the American economy was capable of carrying the
> load.[9]

The report that McCloy and Lovett felt it possible to offer the
President the complete backing of the American financial community carries unusual interest for those who are curious about

elite behavior. Neither Morton Halperin nor Samuel P. Huntington saw fit to pursue the point in their studies of this period.

The National Security Council meeting of November 7 broke
up without any sense of the meeting having been taken, although
the President followed the briefing very closely. According to
the standard procedure, the report was next sent formally to the
various departments for their information and comments. A close
student of the process advises:

> In general, with reports of this nature nothing further happens.
> The reports are either used or rejected at the department level
> and the consultants return to their civilian jobs.[10]

In this case, however, the consultants felt that they had a
clearer perception of a grave threat to national security than did
the President himself (a former five-star general) and his leading cabinet officers. In consequence,

> some of the Committee members made a determined effort to
> have their proposals implemented and at the same time they
> joined with others in seeking to have the Gaither Report made
> public.[11]

Sensing failure and frustration at the Presidential level, key
members of the ad hoc advisory committee, having taken on the
task of redirecting American defense policy, wished to take the
issue to the attentive public. The President was determined that
the Gaither report, a confidential report to the National Security
Council prepared in accordance with a Presidential directive,
was not to be made a public document, and it never has been
declassified. Its essential contents did not remain secret for long,
however.

The report was not a typical NSC document. It did not result,
as pluralist interpretations insist most policy documents do, from
a compromise of the views of a number of departments and agencies. It was not bound by previous government policy decisions,
nor was it prepared within the framework of budgetary limitations laid down by the President. In all of these important respects, the Gaither report bore a marked resemblance to NSC–68
seven years earlier. Like NSC–68, the report called for measures
deemed necessary by those elite representatives who wished to

bring about a major rearmament effort. Halperin states that the Gaither report

> ... deviated from government policy in a number of ways, but most fundamentally in the estimation of the danger facing the country and the amount of money which the United States should spend for defense.[12]

On this vital point, the report also resembled NSC–68. Unlike NSC–68, however, the Gaither report was not followed abruptly by another Korean war, and it offered advice to a President who regarded himself as a defense expert of long experience.

Even while they were preparing the report, some members of the committee were concerned that their responsibility should include a strenuous effort to obtain the implementation of their proposals. The committee members, it must be remembered, saw a glaring discrepancy between the Soviet threat being described to them by the Pentagon and the CIA and what they came to regard as "complacency" at the Presidential level. As consultants to the NSC, they were surely aware that their only real hope for success in obtaining implementation lay with the President. John Foster Dulles, the Secretary of State, was firmly committed to the doctrine of "massive retaliation." In the event any additional budgetary dollars were to be provided, Dulles preferred having them allocated for foreign aid. Dulles came to view the Gaither report as containing only a slightly veiled attack on his doctrine. At the November 7 NSC meeting Dulles spoke out strongly against the report's recommendations. He was not prepared to endorse a program calling for a sharp increase in "spending" nor to a policy that would commit the United States to local defense in peripheral areas. He worried that the shelter program might frighten our European allies. Neil McElroy, the Secretary of Defense, viewed his role as that of an administrator who did not get involved in strategic discussions or in debates about the level of defense spending. His job, as he viewed it, was to run a complex administrative organization with "efficiency." The Treasury and the Bureau of the Budget were opposed to the large increase in spending that the Gaither committee advocated.

NUCLEAR RETALIATORY FORCE

President Eisenhower's initial response offered some encouragement to the members of the Gaither committee. Speaking in Oklahoma City a week after the NSC meeting at which the report was presented, the President struck a new note in discussing the budgetary implications. He asserted:

> now, by whatever amount savings fail to equal the additional costs of security, our total expenditures will go up. Our people will rightly demand it. They will not sacrifice security to worship a balanced budget.

Eisenhower recognized that the first requirement was to maintain a nuclear retaliatory force so that an attack by the Soviets "would result, regardless of damage to us, in their own national destruction." The President also saw the need for forces to deal with any form of local aggression and for more money to accelerate the SAC dispersal and the missile programs. He declared:

> The answer does not lie in any misguided attempt to eliminate conventional forces and rely solely upon retaliation. Such a course would be self-defeating.[13]

If the Gaither committee members were pleased to find some of their ideas making their way so rapidly into a Presidential speech, they soon sensed that the President was far from having decided to implement their recommendations in his next budget, which was about to take final shape prior to presentation to the Congress early in 1958. At this point, several members of the committee, led by Foster and Sprague, turned their attention to the various operating agencies. In theory, the operating agencies might have been expected to jump at the opportunity to expand their own budgets. In reality, departmental budget officers were already involved in the final stages of the preparation of the executive budget. They knew how real the limitations were as the Budget Bureau imposed actual figures on their budget documents. The budgetary pie was not going to be much bigger in the coming fiscal year.

Other problems were encountered at the level of the operating agencies. The FCDA was not likely to enthuse over a report that rejected its major proposal for blast shelters and all but killed its hope for getting into the "big" money. The Army would naturally endorse a proposal for a limited-war force, but might find it difficult to agree that it lacked any present capacity to fight such a war. The Air Force was not likely to concede that the Strategic Air Command was vulnerable to enemy attacks. At this level, pluralist forces appear to have a certain validity.

The committee members were back to a choice of either continuing their effort to persuade the President or of taking their case to the public. The latter course was made difficult by the fact that the President regarded the report as confidential advice for his guidance, not as a document for dissemination to the public.

Finally, in mid-December a meeting was held in Foster's home in Washington. Among those present were Frank Stanton and Paul Nitze. Vice President Nixon also attended, evidently on his own initiative, although one report suggested that he had the approval of the President. In addition to briefing the Vice President, the informal group heard suggestions from Foster: first, that the group work to bring about the publication of a "sanitized" version of the Gaither report; and second, that a committee be formed to alert the American people to the grave Soviet threat. The gathering broke up without a firm decision on whether or not to form a committee for these purposes. There was a general feeling, apparently, that without the President's active support a group of private citizens could do relatively little to arouse the public on vital matters of national security. But the men who met in Foster's home did agree to work for the release of the report to the public. Part of their problem was that the committee had submitted the report to the President without Congress or the public being aware of its existence.

Nevertheless, bit by bit, the contents of the report were slowly leaked to the press. Chalmers Roberts was able to write a remarkably detailed account of the report, which appeared in the *Washington Post* on December 20. The same account was later reprinted in the *Congressional Quarterly Weekly News Service*, while Senator Joseph Clark, Democrat of Pennsylvania, inserted the Roberts article in the *Congressional Record*, assuring the readers of the *Record* that the article accurately represented the contents of the report.

The attitude of leading Congressional Democrats toward the Gaither report is instructive. They were quick to realize that the budget submitted by the President in January 1958 called for only a modest acceleration of the missile and SAC dispersal programs; even more striking was the fact that conventional forces and civilian defense were curtailed in order to provide part of the additional money for the expanded activities. Judged on the basis of his budget for fiscal year 1959, the President did not share the sense of urgency concerning the Soviet threat that consumed members of the Gaither committee.

SECRECY OF DOCUMENT

With the prospect of a Congressional election in November 1958, leading Democrats presumably saw an issue in the making: a complacent President playing Russian roulette with the nation's security. Senator Clark was clear that the "[Gaither] Report should have caused this administration to have a far greater sense of urgency than it presently gives any indication of having." [14] The editorial pages of the *Times,* the *Herald-Tribune,* and the *Washington Post* all carried demands for the release of the report. The Gaither committee members continued to press for publication of a "sanitized" version, which Foster was ready to prepare.

Still the President refused to yield. He wrote to Senator Johnson in part as follows:

> from time to time the President invites groups of specially qualified citizens to advise him on complex problems. These groups give this advice after intensive study, with the understanding that their advice will be kept confidential. Only by preserving the confidential nature of such advice is it possible to assemble such groups or for the President to avail himself of such advice. [15]

To publish the report would violate the privacy of the arrangement and also a rule that NSC documents are not made public.

The members of the Gaither committee found themselves handicapped by the secrecy that ordinarily characterizes Cold

War national security decision-making within the inner core of closed politics. It was difficult for the Gaither committee members to arouse the attentive public when the public was unaware of the committee's existence. Furthermore, private citizens such as Sprague, Foster, Nitze, McCloy, and Lovett were in the peculiar position of insisting that they saw a graver danger to the national security than did the President, the Secretaries of State and Defense, and the Joint Chiefs of Staff. Civilian militants offering advice about the Soviet menace from their private positions appear to be at a distinct disadvantage when the formal policy leadership posts are held by men holding a different view.

The theme was struck a number of times in testimony later given to Senator Henry Jackson's Senate subcommittee on National Policy Machinery. Paul Nitze, who was familiar with the advantages of being a cold war technocrat on the *inside*, put it this way:

> Those members of the executive branch who are actually responsible for carrying out policy . . . feel, perhaps rightly, that such groups (as the Gaither Committee) are out of touch with the real problems with which the officials, in the end, must always deal. In any case, it is obvious that the committee, once its report has been presented, is in a poor position to help fight its recommendations through the decision stage. Both of these difficulties characterized the reception of the Gaither Report two years ago.[16]

Robert C. Sprague explained it to the Jackson subcommittee:

> I believe . . . that the danger is more serious than the President has expressed himself to the American public. I do not know whether he feels this or whether he does not. But I do not believe that the concern that I personally feel has as yet been expressed by the President to the American public. This is a complicated matter.[17]

Indeed, the matter is complicated. Although the men who formed the nucleus of the Gaither committee seem to fit a Mills-Domhoff model of an upper-class elite with strong ties to a military-industrial-educational complex and although their views were almost predictably dominated by Cold War militancy, their specific recommendations met resistance within the highest levels of the governmental decision-making apparatus.[18] The Eisenhower administration, following an anachronistic set of economic myths, was firmly set against the level of expenditures that the Gaither report recommendations called for. The principal policy leadership positions around the Presidency may be used to restrain military expansion, when it is advocated by an elite group, as well as to support expansion, as has happened so frequently throughout the Cold War.

At the same time, it should be noted that the change of administrations from Truman to Eisenhower, which brought the departure of Acheson's coterie from the inner circle of closed politics, did not carry with it a challenge to the containment doctrine. John Foster Dulles accepted the premises on which the doctrine was built but placed a greater reliance on strategic weapons than a number of members of the original policy elite thought prudent. Especially after the launching of Sputnik, pressure mounted in elite circles for a major rearmament program.

It is odd to find members of the Cold War policy elite so concerned to see that the "real" facts about national security were brought to the attention of the public when the normal operating assumption in elite circles appears to have been that such matters are too esoteric for the "mass" mind to comprehend. Men like Foster, Sprague, and Nitze were unduly pessimistic about their influence, over the longer haul. What they were experiencing was a delay enforced by an administration bemused by its own economic myths. The Kennedy-McNamara national security program followed the main lines of the Gaither report: the building of the great missile complexes including Minuteman and Polaris (later Poseidon), thus insuring the second-strike capability; the hardening of the missile sites; the highly mobile, mechanized army for the "flexible response" so needed in "limited wars" (Vietnam being the classic example); the vast expansion of military research development; the McNamara managerial revolution transforming defense budget-making from the old "political" methods followed by Truman and Eisenhower to the more "rational" PPBs, cost-benefit-analysis techniques that have since been associated with the F-111, the C5A, and massive cost "overruns," to say nothing of inflated defense budgets.

CONCLUSION

In short, the defense policies advocated by the leading civilian militants in the 1950s, as reflected in NSC–68 and the Gaither report, found implementation in the 1960s. Equally striking is the manner in which leading members of the Cold War elite of the earlier period were located in key positions within the Kennedy administration. Two of Acheson's principal deputies were placed in positions ideally situated to carry out the policies advocated in NSC–68 and the Gaither report: Dean Rusk moved from the Rockefeller Foundation to Secretary of State, while Paul Nitze left the Foreign Service Educational Foundation to serve as Assistant Secretary of Defense for International Security Affairs, where he headed up the Pentagon's "little State Department" before moving on to even more important positions. William Bundy, Acheson's son-in-law, was to move from the CIA, where he had been serving as a Cold War technocrat for a decade, to key positions in the Defense Department and later in the State Department. McGeorge Bundy, Stimson's biographer, who had written a book explicating Dean Acheson's foreign policy views, became JFK's Special Assistant for National Security Affairs. John J. McCloy was placed in charge of disarmament negotiations, while William C. Foster became Kennedy's arms control chief. Jerome Weisner, who had served as executive director of the Gaither committee, was named Science Adviser to President Kennedy. In view of these appointments, it is not surprising that the Kennedy administration proved more amenable to the defense theories of the Cold War elite than did its predecessor. With these key positions in the executive branch policy-making machinery firmly in the hands of experienced Cold War civilian militants, it was hardly to be expected that the Kennedy administration would produce an effective critique of the Cold War or the containment dogma. And it did not.[19]

Samuel P. Huntington's detailed analysis of defense decision-making in the 1950s, which follows conventional wisdom in viewing the process in terms of consensus-building between diverse interests, agencies, and institutions within the national security "community," draws distinctions between the NSC–68 experience and that which followed the Gaither report. There is the obvious point that NSC–68 was followed by the Korean war so that a huge increase in military spending inevitably became a feature of the early 1950s. Likewise, it was probably inevitable —given our reaction to the attack in Korea—that NSC–68 should have been seized upon, as it was, by the Truman administration as a rationalization for the increased level of military spending. The Gaither report coincided with another dramatic event, the launching of Sputnik, but this was an event whose military significance was neither immediate nor direct. Although the civilian technocrats and the uniformed military readily appreciated the fact that the Soviets had demonstrated a new capacity to deliver nuclear weapons to the American heartland, the general public did not necessarily perceive the military implications. Huntington saw a difference in the nature of the catalysts:

in the one case an act of aggression, in the other a demonstration of superior scientific and possibly military capabilities. The latter was an indirect challenge rather than a direct one. As a scientific achievement, Sputnik could only be greeted with praise, an epoch-making accomplishment of the human race.[20]

In any event, Huntington concluded: "The Gaither program was adopted only in so far as it did not seriously disturb existing goals." [21] While this was an accurate conclusion when Huntington published his study early in 1961, it would hardly have been possible to arrive at the same conclusion once the Kennedy-McNamara defense programs had been put into effect.

Having studied the NSC–68 and Gaither report episodes, Huntington finds:

The Administration in power originated and decided upon major changes in the strategic balance. Public opinion, non-governmental experts, the press, and Congress played peripheral roles in determining overall strategy.[22]

Of course, Huntington's model does not include the possibility that a Cold War policy elite may have played a role in which it was able to exert disproportionate influence on national security policy over a long period of time. He makes nothing of the fact that Paul Nitze, for example, who served as Dean Acheson's principal deputy in writing NSC–68, appears to have been a remarkably active and interested "adviser" in the preparation of the Gaither report and in the campaign to implement it. Naturally, Huntington could not have foreseen that Nitze would come back to function as a significant policy-maker in the Kennedy-Johnson years. The Gaither report, based on an extreme view of the Soviet military threat (as was NSC–68), reflected the views of a group of extraordinarily influential civilian militants who appear time and again in this analysis: Dean Acheson, John J. McCloy, Robert Lovett, the Bundys, Paul Nitze, and Dean Rusk are among those elite figures whose policy-making activities have become at least partially visible; and they appear to have been effective in shaping a hard-line Cold War policy vis-à-vis the Soviet Union. Huntington's analysis (another product of the Columbia University Institute of War and Peace Studies and the Carnegie Foundation) misses the reality of this group's presence and active involvement in the making of national security policy. As a result, no attempt is made to assess the group's influence. One does not "measure" what one does not see.

Pluralist scholars will find encouragement in the differences that existed between the Eisenhower administration and those elite leaders who supported the Gaither report. They will note with pleasure that John Foster Dulles, who opposed the report's recommendations, possessed qualifications for membership in an upper-class elite that were fully as impressive as those of Dean Acheson. But pluralists are inclined to slide quickly by the fact that the struggle within elite circles throughout the Cold War has involved the level of public expenditure *in support of the containment doctrine.* While it is true that leading business and financial interests supported Eisenhower in the elections of 1952 and 1956, pluralists would do well to ponder the manner in which leading members of the Cold War elite maneuvered to go over the head of the President when he seemed reluctant to accept the elite's view of the Soviet menace and the need for heavier military spending. And in the long run, as we shall note in subsequent chapters, it was the elite's view that prevailed. The support John J. McCloy and Robert Lovett offered Eisenhower, if he were to accept the report, indicates the establishment position on these matters, and it was stated (within the inner circle of closed politics) as openly as it is likely ever to be.

The data in this chapter are quite consistent with an establishment orchestration interpretation. However much that factions *within the elite* differed over the Soviet threat and the appropriate American posture, they were *not* engaged in a fundamental reexamination of the strategic-political doctrine. Both elite factions were prepared to rely overwhelmingly on military technology in order to "contain" Soviet expansion. C. Wright Mills assumed the existence of factions within the elite; he also postulated that an internal discipline and community of interests would bind the "power elite" together.[23] In this instance political leadership at the top of the structure was prepared to resist the arguments of those within the inner circle of closed politics who urged a higher level of spending on military "defense." Some members of the elite wished to take the issue outside the inner circle of closed politics; in taking their case to the attentive public they clearly hoped that a body of opinion, previously alerted to the Soviet menace, would assist in moving the administration in the direction recommended by the Gaither committee. This, too, is consistent with an establishment orchestration approach, which assumes a fairly open relationship between the elite structure and an acquiescent public. Pluralist scholars who are impressed by the relatively pluralistic struggle, at the elite level, in the bureaucratic politics mode, are hard put to explain the persistence of the containment dogma and the steady growth of the new militarism in postwar America.

From a long-term perspective, the foreign policy decisions of the Cold War period appear to be curiously "of a piece" with one another. Our analysis in this book notes the remarkable resemblance between the recommendations set forth in the Gaither report and the defense program carried out in the early 1960s by an administration staffed in key positions by leading members of essentially the same policy elite that was chiefly responsible for NSC–68 and the Gaither report. This aspect of reality is not to be lightly dismissed.

Chapter Six Notes

1. Morton M. Halperin, "The Gaither Committee and the Policy Process," which appeared first in *World Politics,* Vol. 13, No. 3 (April 1961), 360–84, and has since been reprinted in Thomas E. Cronin and Sanford D. Greenberg, *The Presidential Advisory System* (New York: Harper & Row, 1969). The page numbers in the citations are taken from the latter, p. 187.

2. Ibid., p. 187.

3. See Joseph Kraft, "RAND: Arsenal for Ideas," *Harper's Magazine,* July 1960, pp. 71–73. Also, Bruce L. R. Smith, *The RAND Corporation* (Cambridge, Mass.: Harvard University Press, 1966).

4. Halperin, "The Gaither Committee," p. 188.

5. Ibid.

6. Wohlstetter's paper was later published as "The Delicate Balance of Terror," in *Foreign Affairs,* Vol. 37, No. 2 (January 1959).

7. Halperin, "The Gaither Committee," p. 191.

8. Article by Chalmers Roberts, *Washington Post and Times-Herald,* December 20, 1957, reprinted in *Congressional Record,* 85th Congress, 2nd Session, 1958, p. 858.

9. Ibid.

10. Halperin, "The Gaither Committee," p. 193.

11. Ibid.

12. Ibid., p. 190.

13. Reprinted in *New York Times,* November 14, 1957.

14. *Congressional Record,* 85th Congress, 2nd Session, Washington D.C., 1958, p. 860.

15. Quoted in Halperin, "The Gaither Committee," p. 203.

16. *Organizing for National Security,* Selected Materials, U.S. Senate, Subcommittee on National Policy Machinery, Commission on Government Operations, 86th Congress, 2nd Session, 1960, p. 168.

17. Ibid., p. 55.

18. See C. William Domhoff, *The Higher Circles,* chapter 5, "How

the Power Elite Make Foreign Policy" (New York: Vintage–Random House, 1971).

19. See especially Richard J. Walton, *Cold War and Counterrevolution: The Foreign Policy of John F. Kennedy* (New York: Viking, 1972).

20. Samuel P. Huntington, *The Common Defense* (New York: Columbia University Press, 1966), p. 112.

21. Ibid., p. 113.

22. Ibid.

23. C. Wright Mills, *The Power Elite* (New York: Oxford University Press, 1956), p. 283.

7 ROBERT McNAMARA: SUPER-MANAGER AS CIVILIAN MILITANT

Civilian control versus military control is a distinction without a difference if the civilians think the same way the military does.

Richard J. Walton

Cold War and Counterrevolution:
The Foreign Policy of John F. Kennedy (1972)

If Americans have the capability to go anywhere and do anything, we will always be going somewhere and doing something.

Senator Richard Russell

As quoted in Graham Allison's
Essence of Decision (1971)

The nation had been frozen in its Cold War stance for a decade and a half when John F. Kennedy was inaugurated President. Containment had long since been extended to Asia. Discussion within the inner circle of closed politics during the 1950s reflected a broad policy consensus among the elite in which primary emphasis was placed on maintaining military superiority around the globe; the only question was how this was to be accomplished. The discussion in elite circles, often spilling over into the public forum, centered around the appropriate American military posture vis-à-vis the Soviet Union (or, alternatively, the Sino-Soviet bloc), with the Eisenhower administration favoring the strategic nuclear deterrent over conventional forces. The tactical use of nuclear weapons also bemused the military planners. John F. Kennedy made the status of the nation's defense forces a major issue in the 1960 Presidential campaign, and in doing so he assisted in popularizing the so-called "missile gap" based on the notion that the nation was in danger of falling behind the Soviet Union in strategic nuclear forces.

The public debate took place within the basic conceptual framework as it was put together by the policy elite members who originally created the doctrine of containment. The doctrine assumed a nearly monolithic international Communist movement, centering in Moscow, bent on world domination by means of an inexorably expansionist policy. Containment's basic premises went unchallenged in elite circles as a cadre of Cold War technocrats assumed ever larger responsibilities in the effective functioning of a permanent military establishment closely linked with major corporations and the Congressional power structure.[1] Members of the elite and highly placed technicians joined together in discussions of the appropriate weapons-mix: nuclear weapons for deterrence, tactical nuclear weapons, and conventional military forces to fight "brush fire" wars in peripheral areas of the globe. By the early 1960s the nation's national security "problem" increasingly was seen in its technical, administrative, and managerial aspects. President Kennedy gave voice to the new spirit:

> The fact of the matter is that most of the problems or at least many of them, that we now face, are technical problems, are administrative problems. They are very sophisticated judgments which do not lend themselves to the great sort of "passionate movements" which have stirred this country so often in the past.[2]

This being the President's view and having made the rebuilding of national defense the central problem, it was to be expected that he would seek an able crisis manager to address these complex, esoteric, "administrative" problems as Secretary of Defense. Robert Strange McNamara has generally been considered to have been the most effective of all the super-technocrats who manned the command posts of the military technocracy in the second decade of the Cold War. While McNamara's record as Secretary of Defense is central to a study of national security decision-making, he also emerges as a symbolic figure, the inspirational leader of an entire cadre of Cold War technicians whose golden years came during the early and middle 1960s.

MIDDLE-CLASS BACKGROUND

Robert McNamara does not appear to fit the classical model of a policy elite figure in terms of social and family background, education, or career pattern. This is not a man who attended one of the exclusive Eastern preparatory schools en route to Harvard and Yale for college and law school training before joining the prestigious law firm or the leading Wall Street banking house from which he might then move gracefully to the higher echelons of the State Department–Pentagon–CIA complex. McNamara's family background was solidly middle class, not upper class. He was educated in a public high school in California and graduated with high honors from the University of California and the Harvard Graduate School of Business. If World War II had not provided a unique opportunity for a young man trained in statistics to pioneer in early computer technology, it is easy to imagine Robert McNamara spending a happy and useful life as a high-achieving member of the Harvard Business School faculty, where he once served as assistant professor of accounting. While still a young Air Force officer, McNamara joined a small group of statistically minded technicians in developing new methods of control useful in dealing with large numbers of units: in this case, airplanes and airplane parts. During this period, while serving as a young, middle-level technician, McNamara first came to the attention of Robert Lovett, an influential and original civilian militant who was fully qualified for membership in a national security policy elite.

In declining an offer to join the Kennedy administration as Secretary of Defense, Robert Lovett suggested Robert McNamara, who had just assumed the presidency of the Ford Motor Company after a postwar career in which mastery of the new statistical-computer-oriented control techniques had carried him from middle-level technician (cost accountant variety) through the controller's office to the presidency of the corporation. It was an impressive technical as well as personal achievement.

There is extensive technical literature on the contribution of the Program-Planning-Budgeting System (PPBS) to the formulation of public policy. Recently, Enthoven and Smith, two of McNamara's assistants in the Pentagon, themselves leading

PPBS technicians, have written an important book in which the case is made for PPBS as it was used in the Defense Department during the McNamara era.[3] Likewise, the task of examining in detail the precise steps McNamara took as Defense Secretary to strengthen the nation's military forces has been accomplished with skill and sympathetic understanding by William W. Kaufmann, whose book appeared in print in 1964, prior to military escalation in Vietnam.[4] Kaufmann's study, apparently completed immediately following the assassination of President Kennedy, might have emerged as the definitive study of McNamara, architect of a new defense strategy, *if* McNamara had resigned following the assassination. Kaufmann's assessment was completed *before* the Americanization of the war in Vietnam. The American role in Vietnam appears to Kaufmann an appropriate use of counterinsurgency techniques against guerrilla forces; McNamara, having broadened the options, is given full credit for having made it all possible.

Our examination of Robert McNamara as Defense Secretary challenges the popular legend that tends to assign McNamara the role of policy *innovator* in the 1961–68 period. A powerful Secretary, so highly regarded by the two Presidents he served, must have been a creative policy-*maker,* so the legend runs. The analysis in this chapter indicates that McNamara was not essentially a *maker* of policy, but a manager of bureaucratic structures. He did not innovate a single major policy, but accepted basic concepts derived from discussion in elite circles during the previous decade. McNamara *never* examined critically the assumptions upon which global containment was based, nor was he expected to do so by the man who appointed him. McNamara's innovations were to be managerial in nature. McNamara came upon the facts early that made it clear to him that there was no missile gap; he knew not later than February 1961 that the Soviet Union was not engaged in a major build-up of its strategic nuclear force. Later he was to discover that the official estimates of the strength of Soviet conventional military forces also had been greatly exaggerated. Nevertheless, McNamara, the advocate of "rational" defense planning, led the way to a major increase in United States defense spending. McNamara, who had had no previous public service (with the exception of

World War II experience in the Air Force, referred to above), came to the cabinet as an extraordinarily gifted technician, a statistical and computer-oriented, cost-benefit-analytical, modern corporate manager, dedicated to getting the job done. He was preeminently the super-manager fascinated by the problem of controlling the huge bureaucratic structures that dominate the postindustrial system. McNamara was, in David Halberstam's brilliant portrait, "the man from Detroit," whose job it was "to translate ideas into workable processes at Defense, accepting their assumptions without doubt or misgiving." [5] There is no evidence that McNamara ever questioned the *purposes* that the new militarism and global containment were designed to serve. Arthur M. Schlesinger, Jr., an admirer, describes McNamara as "the residuary legatee of a body of doctrine which had taken form under the Truman administration in the late forties and gained clarity and force in a series of debates within and without the Eisenhower administration through the fifties." [6]

BALANCED FORCES, FLEXIBLE RESPONSE

The established doctrine of which McNamara became legatee as Defense Secretary was global containment spelled out in terms of military forces in such basic documents as NSC–68 and the Gaither report. John F. Kennedy entered the White House with very well developed ideas about these matters. He believed in "balanced forces" with the capacity for "flexible response." If Hilsman seems to confirm the obvious in reporting that McNamara shared Kennedy's views, he also notes that McNamara had "the imagination to push those views even further down the line of their logical development." [7] Robert McNamara was the "rational," efficient, supremely self-confident Secretary of Defense whom the situation called for if the military expansion advocated in the Gaither report were to be put into effect by the new administration, even after the assumptions about Soviet military strength upon which the report had been based were found to be erroneous.

The critical issue to be faced in this analysis is: *what programs, policies, and purposes were served by the application of the new administrative techniques that McNamara installed in the Pentagon?* A principal result of McNamara's administrative reform was to install a decision-making system that had the effect of increasing the centralization of authority in and around the office of the Secretary of Defense. This was especially the case in decisions having to do with the selection and the development of weapons systems; that is, military "hardware" decisions involving judgments based on estimates of dollar costs. McNamara's administrative innovations substantially increased the influence of civilian advisers on questions relating weapons systems to matters of military strategy. Closely related to this increase in the centralized power of a group of civilian militants was a great emphasis on "efficiency" in certain aspects of national security decision-making. An alternative program (almost invariably this turned out to be an alternative weapons system) was to be preferred if it could be shown that it was more "efficient." McNamara's system, if it worked well, held out the promise of making the American war machine a more efficient and more centralized war machine—a machine guided by a new generation of civilian militants.[8]

Robert McNamara, who had helped devise the new methodology while serving in the Air Force statistical branch during World War II, went to the RAND Corporation, the Air Force's leading postwar "think-tank," for Charles Hitch and Alain Enthoven, the men he selected to provide the technical leadership in carrying out the PPBS revolution within the Pentagon. These men placed a large value on the "rationality" of their system as opposed to what they regarded as the "irrationality" of the methods employed in defense decision-making during the Truman and Eisenhower years.[9] Enthoven explained to Senator Jackson's National Security subcommittee:

> First and fundamental is the fact that since 1961 the Secretary of Defense has not operated with any predetermined budgetary ceiling. Rather, he judges each proposal on its merits, considering the need, the contribution of the proposal to increased military effectiveness, and its cost in natural resources.[10]

It should be noted, parenthetically, that Enthoven did not until much later comment publicly on the fact that this approach was *not* applied to Vietnam decisions. Nor has he ever commented on the obvious distortions in public priorities that this led to, since no Kennedy-Johnson cabinet officer on the domestic side was given a similar opportunity to shape his programs in terms of "needs" rather than predetermined budgetary ceilings.

Stewart Udall, Secretary of the Interior in the Kennedy-Johnson administrations, told a Congressional committee inquiring into the relationship between the military budget and national priorities that neither administration in which he had served had "any institutionalized way whereby there was a forum where you could intelligently argue domestic priorities versus military priorities." [11] Adam Yarmolinsky, one-time Special Assistant to Secretary McNamara, in his study of the military establishment, observed that while McNamara's approach to budgetary matters "improved the quality of the budgetary product submitted by the Secretary to the Budget Bureau and the White House, it increased the imbalance between defense spending and other governmental spending. No such presidential instructions or requirements 'without regard to arbitrary or predetermined budget ceilings' had been given to other Executive departments." [12] McNamara came to a system in which military requirements carried a higher priority than domestic needs; his managerial and budgetary methods had the effect of increasing this distortion of public priorities.

THE PRE-McNAMARA APPROACH

But the contrast Enthoven wished to make was in terms of the Truman-Eisenhower insistence on a predetermined ceiling on defense spending, a ceiling which he regarded as being not "rational." Truman, prior to Korea, and Eisenhower, after Korea, imposed a rigid ceiling on defense spending; the rigid ceiling was by no means a low ceiling inasmuch as defense spending in the 1950s customarily represented 60 to 70 percent of total federal expenditures as shown in the administrative budget. Nevertheless, a firm ceiling was enforced in both administrations; hence, the various branches of the armed services were engaged throughout the 1950s in a continuing struggle over their respective shares of a budgetary pie that tended not to grow in size. Eisenhower apparently felt that between $36 and $38 billion annually was about enough for the defense establishment. Toward the end of his second term, following Sputnik and the completion of the Gaither report, the relentless pressure of rising costs, combined with the insistence of those who thought the nation was drifting dangerously toward a position inferior to the Soviet Union, pushed the military spending level above $40 billion.

Enthoven and Smith, profound nonadmirers of this system in which the armed services bargained over the defense dollar, have described the pre-McNamara approach as follows:

> Starting with the Truman administration and continuing under Eisenhower, the President, relatively early in the budget cycle, provided guidance to the Secretary of Defense on the size of the defense budget which he thought economically and politically feasible for the next fiscal year.[13]

"The problem," Enthoven and Smith continued, "was that this figure was usually arrived at by simply estimating the government's total revenues, then deducting fixed payments . . . , the estimated costs of domestic programs, and expenditures on foreign aid. Whatever 'remained' was then allocated to the military." [14]

Enthoven nowhere explores the social consequences of Eisenhower's budgetary policy in starving domestic programs having to do with education and human welfare. Specifically, a systems analyst with less interest in weaponry than Enthoven has shown might have raised serious questions about the "rationality" of budgetary and fiscal policies that doubled unemployment among black Americans during the Eisenhower years. Enthoven also appears remarkably unconcerned that his new budgetary system, as it was installed during the Kennedy years, created a new "remainder" system; only this time what was "left over" went for urgent domestic needs. Since Kennedy held total expenditures annually below $100 billion and since he presented a military budget averaging $52 billion a year, it is obvious that vital domestic programs survived on extremely modest budgets throughout the golden One Thousand Days. There was one intense struggle when the Labor Department urged the launching of a youth employment program bearing a tentative price tag of approximately $150 million annually. Budget Bureau operatives, following White House guidance, decreed that there was no room in the budget for this $150 million item. This occurred in 1962 at a time when military spending was averaging approximately $1 billion a week. It is an interesting, important, and seldom remembered fact that vital domestic programs in the fields of health, education, manpower, and welfare expanded in significant ways only *after* Lyndon Johnson assumed the Presidency.

McNamara installed the new budgetary system with substantive changes in mind; it was a management tool to be used in effecting changes in the nation's defense posture. As previously noted, the defense debate during the Eisenhower years centered around the role of nuclear air power in deterring a future aggressor. It is not surprising that a certain disenchantment with "massive retaliation" grew as the Soviets exploded an A-bomb, followed by an H-bomb, and then demonstrated a superior missile capacity in launching Sputnik, all within less than a decade. The Army was especially unhappy with the massive retaliation doctrine that assigned United States ground forces a relatively minor role in the nuclear age. Enthoven and Smith have shown that between 1954 and 1961 defense dollar allocations remained remarkably constant at about 47 percent for the Air Force, 29 percent for the Navy, and 24 percent for the Army.[15] Under the circumstances one would expect the Air Force to experience the least difficulty in accepting the Eisenhower approach and the Army to grow increasingly restive.

TAYLOR AND THE ARMY'S CASE

The Army's case against what it regarded as a dangerous overreliance on nuclear weapons and air power was considerably strengthened by the Gaither report. Since the Gaither report was to remain classified, it finally fell to General Maxwell Taylor to make the Army's case publicly in his book *The Uncertain Trumpet,* published in 1959. The book offered a lucid summary of the argument the Army had been making within the higher levels of the national security apparatus for several years. The book includes as an appendix an article the general had written in 1956 entitled "Security Through Deterrence." General Taylor, serving at the time as Army Chief of Staff, resisted the assumption that the nation's defense effort should be directed almost exclusively toward preventing a general atomic war. The general was fearful of what might happen short of nuclear Armageddon:

> In a period when the atomic air fleets of the opposing power blocs offset one another by their countervailing threats, it would seem increasingly likely that the dynamism of Communism will become more likely than ever to seek an outlet in the form of aggression with limited objectives. If such pressures are unresisted, the Free World will be exposed to loss through piecemeal erosion; if resisted, there will be the danger of general war developing out of a local "brush fire." [16]

General Maxwell concluded that "a national military program must make early and adequate provision for responding effectively to local aggression wherever it occurs." [17]

Wherever it occurs.

The notion that the American military establishment should have a permanent built-in capacity to fight in brush-fire wars in order to resist "local aggression" *anywhere on the globe* is basic to flexible response, a doctrine articulated originally by General Maxwell and subsequently adopted as the basis of Kennedy-McNamara defense policy. General Taylor prepared his 1956 article for publication in *Foreign Affairs* magazine, where it might have been expected to have enlightened essentially the same readership that attended the Mr. X article of the previous decade. General Taylor's article did not reach *Foreign Affairs* elite readership, however, because both the State and Defense Departments opposed its publication unless it were extensively revised. Another three years passed before General Taylor made his case public with the publication of *The Uncertain Trumpet*.

In the meantime, support for the Taylor thesis continued to grow in elite circles. The year (1957) in which the Gaither report appeared also witnessed the publication of Dr. Henry A. Kissinger's book *Nuclear Weapons and Foreign Policy*,[18] following a year and a half of study and discussion on the part of a special committee of the Council on Foreign Relations. The committee included among its establishment-based members: McGeorge Bundy, Roswell Gilpatric, Paul Nitze, and James A. Perkins. Kissinger served as executive director of the study. Kissinger's book, sponsored by the CFR, accurately reflected the nature of the discussion that took place in elite circles in 1956–57. In discussing the problems of limited war, Kissinger faced the question of fighting a limited *nuclear* war.

As Kissinger viewed it:

> One of the most urgent tasks of American military policy is to create a military capability which can redress the balance in limited wars and which can translate our technological advantage into local superiority.[19]

It has since become clear that Robert McNamara was fascinated by the technical problems involved in translating American technological advantage into local superiority, and that Vietnam finally provided the unique opportunity for testing the doctrine of flexible response. There is no evidence to suggest that the elite group that assembled around Kissinger questioned the desirability of applying superior American military technology in a small country torn by civil war where aspirations for national independence were combined with a need for far-reaching social reform.

Nor did General Taylor address this basic question in his published work, although he did not hesitate to criticize the way national security decisions were being made. Taylor charged that the Basic National Security Policy, an annual statement prepared by the National Security Council, was couched in language so ambiguous as to support virtually *any* military program. At the same time, basic strategic issues often went unresolved for years while the armed services squabbled over the annual budget. The whole approach to budget-making obscured the impact of the budget on the functions being served. "In other words, the three services develop their forces more or less in isolation from each other," General Taylor asserted, "so that a force category such as the strategic retaliatory force, which consists of contributions of both the Navy and the Air Force, is never viewed in the aggregate." [20] The general was reenforcing a point emphasized a year earlier (1958) in the Rockefeller Brothers report, which Kissinger and Nitze had helped to prepare. The report had recommended that a start be made toward a budgetary system that

> corresponds more closely to a coherent strategic doctrine. It should not be too difficult to restate the presentation of the Service budgets so that instead of the present categories of "procurement," "operation and maintenance," [military personnel], etc. there would be a much better indication of how much goes, for example, to strategic air, to air defense, to anti-submarine warfare, and so on. [21]

General Taylor's argument for a stronger civilian policy leadership in weapons-system decision-making foreshadowed McNamara's managerial "revolution." Taylor wrote in *The Uncertain Trumpet*:

> There is a special group of problems which plague the Joint Chiefs of Staff, relating to the technical feasibility of new weapons systems. . . . Here is an area where the Secretary of Defense should be better able to determine the technical merits of the case than the Joint Chiefs of Staff. The questions involved are largely scientific or engineering in nature, and lend themselves to consideration by civilian experts outside of the interested military services. The Secretary of Defense could help immeasurably if he took responsibility for determining the degree of technical reliance to be placed on new weapons systems. [22]

NUCLEAR POWER BUILD-UP

The defense debate of the 1950s set the stage for the managerial system that McNamara brought to the Defense Department in the 1960s while also providing the impetus for a stepped-up military program. The Gaither report argued for a sizeable increase in defense spending in response to the growth in Soviet nuclear and missile striking power. The report stressed the need for a rapid expansion of missile programs and for an equally rapid development of mobile Army striking forces capable of fighting so-called "limited wars" in order to deter local aggression, *wherever it might occur*. Local aggression was undefined in these formulations.

McNamara and his staff of civilian technicians lost no time in building the nation's second-strike capability as they began the process of implementing the flexible response doctrine. In doing so, they concentrated first on the acceleration and expansion of missile systems developed during the Eisenhower years. The Atlas and Minuteman missile systems were rapidly expanded, as was the fleet of nuclear submarines armed with Polaris (and later with Poseidon) missiles, a weapons system also inherited from the past. Although McNamara knew no later than February 6, 1961, that the so-called missile gap did not exist, he accelerated the existing Polaris program nine or ten months; a month later he recommended adding ten more Polaris submarines to the fleet, and he doubled the production capacity for the Minuteman ICBM system. The Secretary also ordered one-half of the Strategic Air Command bombers on a quick-reaction general alert. McNamara later reported:

> In the short term, that is to say, between 1961 and 1962, we have simply taken the steps that were within our capability to increase the megatonnage as rapidly as possible in the alert force.[23]

Roswell Gilpatric, McNamara's deputy, advised the corporate elite at a meeting of the Business Council on October 10, 1961, that "the total number of our nuclear delivery vehicles, tactical as well as strategic, is in the tens of thousands; and of course, we have more than one warhead for each vehicle." [24]

William W. Kaufmann, in describing this rapid build-up of nuclear power in 1961–62, refers to McNamara's having used "the technique of the quick fix"; that is, "doing those things which would add measurably to combat strength in a relatively short period of time." [25] (The term "quick fix" also derives from General Maxwell Taylor's *The Uncertain Trumpet*.)

The quick-fix technique was also applied to increase both tactical nuclear strength and the size of the Army and to provide highly mobile forces for participation in "local" wars. Thus McNamara recommended the procurement of 129 new longer-range modern airlift aircraft to improve mobility, at the same time providing additions to the Army and Marine Corps conventional forces. McNamara's first year also brought a new interest in counterinsurgency.

> Perhaps the most spectacular change was in the size of the Army's Special Forces. These forces had been designed to act as guerrillas in a general nuclear war. McNamara reoriented them toward the counterinsurgency mission and more than doubled their numbers.[26]

The new Secretary of Defense was not satisfied, despite the quick fix, Kaufmann reports:

> Although existing conventional forces were adequate to cope with only one small-scale local action at a time, the specter of seemingly inexhaustible Communist manpower discouraged a sharp break with the heavily nuclear-dependent strategy of the past.[27]

By the summer of 1961 McNamara was increasing the rate of annual military spending by $3.5 billion, and the Army was being increased from 875,000 to about a million men. General Taylor, who was to serve President Kennedy as a personal military adviser, could feel satisfaction that the views he had advocated in the previous decade were finally being implemented. Eisenhower's final budget for fiscal 1962, which Kennedy and McNamara inherited, provided $43.685 billion for military spending. The Kennedy administration, following the quick-fix approach, amended this budget three times, raising it finally to $49.8 billion. The first completely Kennedy administration budget, presented in January 1962, proposed $51.6 billion for defense in fiscal 1963. The Army was to be increased from eleven to sixteen combat ready divisions, combined with twenty-one tactical air wings plus three Marine divisions with their air wings. McNamara at this point looked forward to something like a ten-division strategic reserve, very useful if the United States were to become engaged in fighting a "medium sized local conventional" war. Kaufmann noted: "With it, he [McNamara] could handle a Korean-sized engagement and still have several divisions left over for another emergency." [28]

In two short years, McNamara had gone a long way toward

giving the United States the military capability of fighting another Korean war. The United States would soon have the capacity to contain "Communism" anywhere on the globe, or, as
Kaufmann expressed it: "All in all, the country was obtaining a
greater number of options—achieving more flexibility—in its
military posture." [29]

PPBS CRITERIA

The "rational" methods of analysis contained in PPBS were
used almost exclusively in military hardware decisions; they were
used only slightly and tangentially in the larger policy questions
that arose during the McNamara regime. McNamara failed to examine critically the purposes for which the new flexible response
forces were to be used. There was no critique of the containment dogma as it was misapplied in Southeast Asia throughout
the 1960s. Indeed, the more one reviews the technical discussions of the PPBS experience in McNamara's Pantagon, including a full-scale defense of systems analysis by Enthoven and
Smith, two leading practitioners of the occult art, the more clearly
one sees that McNamara's use of systems analysis was limited
even when it was being applied to matters of military hardware.
PPBS was not used in the basic decision which led to the development of the F-111, for example.

Enthoven and Smith acknowledge the fact that their "shop"
played no important role in any major decisions relating to Vietnam.

> PPBS was not involved in the really crucial issues of the Vietnam
> war. Should the United States have gone into Vietnam in the
> first place? Did we go in at the right time, in the right way, and
> on the right scale? What force levels should we have had there?
> How should these troops have been used? What timetable should
> we set up for withdrawal? How can we best achieve a speedy
> and just settlement? [30]

These are crucial questions, Enthoven and Smith agree, and
yet the systems analysis office which Dr. Enthoven headed was
not used by Secretary McNamara on questions of obvious mo-

ment. Enthoven came late to Vietnam decision-making, and his role was peripheral.

"While PPBS can help," Enthoven and Smith declare, "it cannot by itself answer such questions: nobody has claimed that it could. There are obvious limits to what any management system can accomplish. Still, the contributions of PPBS to the US effort in Vietnam have been useful." [31] At this point systems analysis appears to be in need itself of further rigorous analysis. Obviously no management system is in a position to guarantee wise decisions or even to replace human judgment; nevertheless, management systems *do* claim to be of assistance in helping shape alternatives, thus facilitating the making of judgments. PPBS *does* claim to offer solid criteria for analyzing difficult problems.

Enthoven and Smith imply that McNamara employed one management system for making certain decisions about most weapons systems and that he used another system (was it no system other than intuitive judgment?) for making other decisions on questions more complex, elusive, and not easily quantified. Such a question arose in an especially urgent form between 1964 and 1965: should the Secretary of Defense join in recommending that the President commit a substantial force of U.S. ground troops and U.S. air and sea power to fighting, on one side in the prolonged Indochinese civil war so that our client regime in Saigon would not collapse of its own dead weight? The question required the best analysis it could get.

A brief examination of PPBS criteria may sharpen the question of Secretary McNamara's contribution to Cold War national security decision-making. What is it that distinguished PPBS from other approaches to decision-making within large bureaucratic organizations?

Enthoven and Smith list six criteria essential to their approach to decision-making:

1. Decisions are to be based on explicit criteria of the national interest;
2. Needs and costs are to be considered together;
3. Alternatives are to receive explicit consideration at the top decision level;
4. The analytical staff is to be used actively at the top policy-making level;

5. A plan is to be formulated combining both forces and costs in a way which projects into the future the foreseeable implications of current decisions;

6. There is always to be open and explicit analysis; that is, each analysis should be made available to all interested parties, so that they can examine the calculations, data, and assumptions and retrace the steps leading to the conclusions.

Further, Enthoven and Smith add:

Indeed, all calculations, data and assumptions *should* be described in an analysis in such a way that they can be checked, tested, criticized, debated, discussed, and possibly refuted by interested parties.[32]

The men who have thus described the essentials of the PPBS system advise that *none of this was applied systematically to the major questions growing out of the deepening American involvement in the Vietnam war.* Leaving aside political or moral issues and viewing the American military involvement in Vietnam as if it had only budgetary significance, what is to be said for a "system" that requires needs and costs to be considered together but that is not used in major decisions (military intervention in Vietnam) whose dollar costs between 1965 and 1969 totaled $100 billion? Eugene Eidenberg has shown in convincing fashion that the civilian advisers to President Johnson made no serious estimate of the costs of bombing as a means of staying in Vietnam early in 1965.[33] The Americanization of the war came about because the decision was made within the inner circle of closed politics to stay in Vietnam, *no matter what the costs might be.* President Johnson's innermost circle of national security advisers, McNamara included, was virtually unanimous in recommending action that led to the Americanization of the war in Vietnam.[34]

THE ELLSBERG CONTRIBUTION

In leading the way to the new system of defense decision-making, Robert McNamara represented a group of technocrats whose professional expertise and careers were devoted to the development and management of complex weapons systems.

Hitch and Enthoven functioned in positions that have been at least partially visible to close students of the process. Recently, men who served in lesser positions during the McNamara era have offered fresh insights into the manner in which the process worked. Daniel Ellsberg's release of the Pentagon Papers brought to public attention important new information about the milieu in which Cold War technicians operate. In a real sense, Daniel Ellsberg offers another example of the Cold War technocrat whose career flourished in McNamara's Pentagon. Ellsberg's doctoral dissertation at Harvard dealt with the theory of decision-making under uncertainty. Bearing the title, "Risk, Ambiguity, and Decision," the thesis begins: "To act reasonably one must judge actions by their consequences. But what if their consequences are uncertain? One must still, no doubt, act reasonably: the problem is to decide what this may mean." [35]

It was a problem Daniel Ellsberg was to struggle with long after the thesis was completed. While still a Junior Fellow at Harvard, he was invited to spend the summer of 1958 as a consultant to the RAND Corporation; he joined RAND's Economics Department on a full-time basis in 1959. This led to a study of "command and control" problems at the Presidential level. As a RAND staff member, as a member of the CINCPAC Command and Controls Study, 1959–60, and as a member of the General Partridge Task Force on Command and Control, 1961, Ellsberg examined the question of protecting and assuring the President's control of nuclear forces and the prevention of "unauthorized actions" (the "Strangelove/Fail-Safe" problem). He participated in both the Defense and State Departments' working groups serving the executive committee of the National Security Council during the Cuban missile crisis of 1962. Ellsberg was sole researcher in 1964 on a project sponsored by Walt W. Rostow, then Chairman of State's Policy Planning Staff, which studied patterns in high level decision-making in crisis. Ellsberg later reported that this assignment gave him "unprecedented access to data and studies in all agencies on past episodes, such as the missile crisis, Suez, the Skybolt decision, Berlin, and the U-2 incident." [36]

In mid-1964 Ellsberg joined the inner circle of closed politics when he became special assistant to John McNaughton, who served as Robert McNamara's close confidant and adviser on all matters having to do with Vietnam. Ellsberg first visited Saigon in the autumn of 1961, shortly before the famous Taylor-Rostow mission. Late in 1965, a key moment in the history of escalation, Ellsberg returned to Vietnam, this time as a member of the team headed by General Edward G. Lansdale. Ellsberg returned to the RAND Corporation in 1967, joining his friend and fellow technician, Leslie Gelb, who had agreed to edit Secretary McNamara's study of U.S. decision-making in Vietnam, later to be called the Pentagon Papers. Ellsberg joined the Center for International Studies at MIT as a Senior Research Associate in April 1970. The following September he presented his paper "The Quagmire Myth and the Stalemate Machine" at the annual meeting of the American Political Science Association. At that time, Ellsberg was one of two people—Gelb being the other—who had read the seven thousand pages of the study entitled, "United States Decision-making in Vietnam, 1945–1967." [37]

Daniel Ellsberg, the student of risk and ambiguity in decision-making, had come to doubt the "rationality" of national security decision-making prior to joining the MIT center in April 1970. The center provided academic freedom so that those doubts might be shared with the public and with other political analysts who had not been "inside" McNamara's Pentagon. Ellsberg's revelation that he had not read the history of Vietnam in the 1945–54 period until August-September 1969 is suggestive concerning the conceptual limits within which vital decisions were made in the 1960s. His ignorance of the struggle between Ho Chi Minh and the French prior to Dien Bien Phu appears to have been total, by his own admission. Hoang Van Chi, a Vietnamese friend who served as a RAND consultant, told Ellsberg in the spring of 1969: "You must understand that in the eyes of all Vietnamese, we gained our independence in March, 1945, and the French set out to *reconquer* us in the North almost two years later."

Ellsberg has reported his own reaction: "I scarcely knew, then, what he was talking about; nor would, I suspect, almost any U.S. official I had worked with." [38]

Ellsberg's account indicates that he was associated with McNamara, McNaughton, Rostow, Lansdale, Vance, Komer, Wil-

liam Bundy, and Gelb, among the scores of Cold War technocrats who were involved in Vietnam decision-making in these
fateful years.

Subsequent chapters will examine in closer detail the manner
in which Robert McNamara approached Vietnam decision-making. If he did not utilize his own rigorously analytical methods
in the decisions that led to the Americanization of the war, this
may be partially explained by the way in which the Kennedy
administration uncritically accepted the basic assumptions deeply
carved in containment dogma. General Maxwell Taylor, whose
views on many vital military questions foreshadowed McNamara's, does not appear to have questioned containment as an
overall doctrine. In October 1956 General Taylor outlined his
program for carrying out national security policy in a document
that presented "the first coherent statement of the new strategy
of Flexible Response." In the first paragraph, Taylor states the
"central aim" of U.S. national security policy: "... the deterrence
of Communist expansion in whatever form it may take." He further
stipulates that the nation should seek "by any and all means
acceptable to the American people to alter the international
Communist movement to the end that it will no longer constitute
a threat to the national security of the United States." [39]

The second paragraph of the document suggests the manner
in which the United States should proceed in "altering" the international Communist movement:

2. Objectives of the National Military Program

The National Military Program must be integrated with all the
other national programs and have as its basic objective the
maintenance of military strength which is capable of dealing
with both general war and aggression under conditions short of
general war. The military strength of the U. S. and her allies
must be so constituted as to prevent war if possible, limit war if
it occurs, and successfully defeat any aggression that may
threaten the national interest.[40]

General Taylor used several concepts that systematic analysis
should have probed and apparently did not:

1. "the international Communist movement"
2. "aggression"
3. "deterrence of Communist expansion"

General Taylor was an authoritative spokesman for the flexible response doctrine before the Kennedy administration made it its own. In the absence of firm evidence to the contrary, it seems reasonable to assume that the doctrine *in practice* included assumptions similar to those expressed by Taylor in 1956. Testifying before the Senate Foreign Relations committee on June 14, 1961, Secretary McNamara spoke of "the double threat" countries; that is, "those nations contiguous to or near the Sino-Soviet bloc that face a direct threat from without and an indirect threat from within." He pointed to Vietnam as "a classical example" of a double threat country and then discussed the American role:

> The two-fold threat requires dual-purpose forces in terms of arms, equipment and personnel. Our military assistance programs play an essential role in furnishing arms and equipment and in teaching troops to operate, maintain and use them. Because of this two-fold threat the military aid we plan to give them is proportionately high. We recognize the inadequacy of their forces to cope with an outright Communist invasion, yet with our assistance we count on their courage and ability to deal with large-scale guerrilla warfare. Should they suffer an open attack across their borders, we look for local forces to resist the initial thrust *until such time as Free World forces may come to their support. In these areas the capability of our own forces to deploy quickly against aggression* is heavily dependent upon the development and maintenance of base facilities or military infrastructure on the spot or in the vicinity. [Italics mine.] [41]

Secretary McNamara candidly explained that he was restructuring the American military machine so that it would be able to deploy quickly against "local" forms of "aggression."

CONCLUSION

It is difficult to locate McNamara with precision in relation to a policy elite featuring the men we have met in earlier chapters, although Robert Lovett, a leading member of the elite, recommended him for the cabinet post. McNamara appears to have been a super-technocrat who occupied a major civilian "command post" in the Cold War decision-making apparatus during a crucial period in the recent past. In this role he was chiefly responsible for installing methods and techniques that proved highly useful in altering the balance of military forces, but the programs, on examination, bear striking similarity to proposals brought forth earlier within elite circles. Roswell L. Gilpatric and Cyrus R. Vance, two of his principal deputies in the Pentagon, had careers that mesh well with those of policy elite figures identified in previous chapters. Paul Nitze and William Bundy became close McNamara associates, indicating that the concepts presented in NSC–68 and the Gaither report were to receive thoughtful attention. With Dean Rusk heading the State Department and General Taylor serving as White House military adviser, it is obvious that President Kennedy was prepared to carry out the policy of global containment. McNamara's prime task was to organize the military forces to support the doctrine.

Writing in 1965 before the Americanization of the Vietnam war had fully accelerated, Professor Schlesinger offered the following assessment of Robert McNamara as super-manager:

> McNamara brought striking gifts to his new responsibility—an inquiring and incisive mind, a limitless capacity for work, and a personality which lacked pretense and detested it in others. But, more than this, he brought new techniques of large-scale management. American social prophets—Bellamy, Veblen, Howard Scott, Adolf Berle, James Burnham—had long tried to prepare the nation for the coming of the managers. But none had predicted anything quite like this tough, courteous and humane technocrat, for whom scientific management was not an end in itself but a means to the rationality of democratic government.[42]

So it seemed to Professor Schlesinger in 1965 at a time when he and McNamara were supporting an active American military policy in Indochina designed to deter "local aggression"; the purpose, presumably, was to "contain" an expansionist Communist movement. Robert McNamara has been judged a "courteous" and "humane" person by a number of people who were associated with him during his Pentagon career. It would be fatuous, after all, to assume that this able leader and super-technocrat should have been discourteous and inhumane. In the light of the Vietnam obsession the question persists, however, whether Robert McNamara as manager of the military establishment applied his exceptional technical skills to advance the cause of "the rationality of democratic government." He appears to have achieved his greatest effectiveness in building a military capability that made a major, direct American military participation in the Vietnamese struggle possible, an accomplishment entirely consistent with the principles of the flexible response and containment doctrines—creations of the national security policy elite.

McNamara has published his "reflections in office" bearing the title *The Essence of Security.* While the book has little to say about Vietnam, it does offer McNamara's philosophy of management:

> God—the Communist commentators to the contrary—is clearly democratic. He distributes brain power universally, but He quite justifiably expects us to do something efficient and constructive with that priceless gift. That is what management is all about. Its medium is human capacity, and its most fundamental task is to deal with change. It is the gate through which social, political, economic, technological change, indeed change in every dimension, is rationally spread through society.
>
> Vital decision-making, particularly in policy matters, must remain at the top. This is partly, though not completely, what the top is for. But rational decision-making depends upon having a full range of rational options from which to choose, and successful management organizes the enterprise so that process can best take place. It is a mechanism whereby free men can most efficiently exercise their reason, initiative, creativity and personal responsibility. The adventurous and immensely satisfying task of an efficient organization is to formulate and analyze the options.[43]

This study now turns to the making of United States national security policy in its various manifestations as related to Vietnam during the 1960s. We shall be interested in examining how the full range of rational options was formulated and analyzed so that wise decisions might be made.

Chapter Seven Notes

1. See John C. Donovan, *The Policy Makers* (New York: Pegasus, 1970), chapter 7, for a more detailed analysis of the Congressional role in the military-industrial complex.

2. President Kennedy speaking at White House Conference on National Economic Issues, May 1962.

3. Alain C. Enthoven and K. Wayne Smith, *How Much Is Enough?* (New York: Harper & Row, 1971).

4. William W. Kaufmann, *The McNamara Strategy* (New York: Harper & Row, 1964).

5. David Halberstam, "The Programming of Robert McNamara," *Harper's Magazine*, February 1971, p. 38.

6. Arthur M. Schlesinger, Jr., *A Thousand Days* (Boston: Houghton Mifflin, 1965), p. 306.

7. Roger Hilsman, *To Move a Nation* (New York: Delta Book, Dell Publishing, 1964), p. 55.

8. See chapter 5 as well as pp. 138–140 in my book *The Policy Makers*.

9. For more detail on the contrast between defense decision-making before and after McNamara and for a more complete presentation of the theory behind PPBS by one of its principal architects, see Charles Hitch, *Decision Making for Defense* (Berkeley: University of California Press, 1965).

10. Subcommittee on National Security and International Organizations, Government Operations Committee, U.S. Senate, 90th Congress, 1st Session, *Hearings PPBS Selected Comment,* Part II, p. 69.

11. A. P. Dispatch, *Portland* (Maine) *Press Herald,* June 7, 1969.

12. Adam Yarmolinsky, *The Military Establishment* (New York: Harper Colophon, 1971), p. 87.

13. Enthoven and Smith, *How Much Is Enough?,* p. 13.

14. Ibid.

15. Ibid.

16. Maxwell Taylor, *The Uncertain Trumpet* (New York: Harper, 1959), p. 185.

17. Ibid., p. 186.
18. Henry A. Kissinger, *Nuclear Weapons and Foreign Policy* (New York: Harper, 1957).
19. Ibid., p. 155.
20. Taylor, *The Uncertain Trumpet*, p. 123.
21. Rockefeller Brothers Fund, *International Security: The Military Aspect* (Garden City, N.Y.: Doubleday, 1958), pp. 58–59.
22. Taylor, *The Uncertain Trumpet*, pp. 118–20.
23. Quoted in Kaufmann, *The McNamara Strategy*, p. 54.
24. Quoted ibid., pp. 65–66.
25. Ibid.
26. Ibid., p. 58.
27. Ibid., p. 59.
28. Ibid., p. 79.
29. Ibid., p 72.
30. Enthoven and Smith, *How Much Is Enough?*, p. 267.
31. Ibid.
32. Ibid., p. 45.
33. See Eugene Eidenberg, "The Presidency: Americanizing the War in Vietnam," in *American Political Institutions and Public Policy*, ed. Allan P. Sindler (Boston: Little, Brown, 1969).
34. George Ball, the Undersecretary of State, seems to have been the sole exception within the inner circle of closed politics. See "Top Secret: The Prophecy the President Rejected," a memo prepared by George Ball on October 5, 1964, as published in *The Atlantic Monthly*, July 1972, pp. 36–49.
35. Quoted in Daniel Ellsberg, *Papers on the War* (New York: Simon and Schuster, 1972), p. 14.
36. Ibid., p. 15.
37. Ellsberg's APSA paper, somewhat revised, and other essays appear in his *Papers on the War*.
38. Ibid., p. 29.
39. Taylor, *The Uncertain Trumpet*, pp. 30–31.
40. Ibid., p. 31.
41. Quoted in Kaufmann, *The McNamara Strategy*, pp. 62–63.
42. Schlesinger, *A Thousand Days*, p. 312.
43. Robert S. McNamara, *The Essence of Decision* (New York: Harper & Row, 1968), pp. 109–10.

8 KENNEDY AND VIETNAM: FLEXIBLE RESPONSE IN ACTION

The great enemy of the truth is very often not the lie—deliberate, contrived and dishonest—but the myth—persistent, persuasive and unrealistic. Too often we hold fast to the clichés of our forebears. We subject all facts to a predetermined set of interpretations. We enjoy the comfort of opinion without the discomfort of thought.

President John F. Kennedy

at Yale University, June 11, 1962

China is so large, looms so high just beyond the frontiers, that if South Vietnam went, it would not only give them an improved geographic position for a guerrilla assault on Malaya but would also give the impression that the wave of the future in Southeast Asia was China and the Communists.

President John F. Kennedy

on NBC, September 9, 1963, responding to a question about the domino theory

John F. Kennedy came to the White House partly on the basis of his critique of Eisenhower's national security program. Kennedy and his principal advisers, following the line laid down in the Gaither report, advocated an expansion and a modernization of the nation's military establishment, now grown both nuclear and permanent, at the same time advocating the doctrine of "flexible response" as a means of restoring sagging American prestige. The soaring rhetoric of Kennedy's inaugural address announced that we were prepared to "pay any price, bear any burden, meet any hardship, support any friend, oppose any foe," thus suggesting the activism that was to mark the next one thousand days. In retrospect, it is not clear, however, that American freedom was close to its hour of "maximum danger" in January 1961. In any event, Kennedy and McNamara seized upon flexible response, a concept born in the midst of the discussion that took place in elite circles during the 1950s, as the symbol of a new American military posture. At issue was the search for an alternative to nuclear Armageddon: how to continue the policy of containing "Communist expansion" (as it was viewed) without limiting United States tactical options to those flowing from a military posture almost exclusively devoted to the deterrence of an all-out nuclear exchange between the super-powers.

The manner in which the Kennedy administration faced up to this question (and to the implications of the Presidential rhetoric)—and the general direction in which the administration was to move—were largely determined by the men Kennedy appointed to the principal positions in the national security apparatus (C. Wright Mills would have seen them as civilian "command posts"). Chapter 7 examined the revolution in managerial techniques that Robert McNamara brought to this undertaking, his most important contribution since the ideas he sponsored originated elsewhere. Kennedy appointed a man that he scarcely knew as his Secretary of State; in Dean Rusk he had an original "true believer" in the containment dogma especially as applied in the Far East. Paul Nitze, fresh from his labors in behalf of the Gaither report, was appointed Assistant Secretary of Defense in charge of what was to become the Pentagon's little State Department, a subsystem in the civilian military bureaucracy that housed (at one time or another) William Bundy, John McNaughton, Townsend Hoopes, and Paul Warneke and, as middle-level technicians, Leslie Gelb, Daniel Ellsberg, and Morton Halperin. McGeorge Bundy, whose scholarly writings include accounts of the stewardships of Henry L. Stimson and Dean Acheson, took leave of his position as provost of Harvard in order to serve as the President's Special Assistant for National Security Affairs.

William Bundy, his brother and Acheson's son-in-law—already an experienced Cold War crisis manager positioned in the higher reaches of the CIA—was subsequently to hold key positions in the Pentagon and in the State Department that made him an influential shaper of the ever-deepening American involvement in Vietnam. John J. McCloy, unofficial head of the American establishment, served as President Kennedy's special disarmament adviser, presumably on the theory that disarmament requires the special knowledge of those who have always favored rearmament. William Foster, a Gaither report principal, was appointed head of the disarmament agency. Jerome Weisner, who had served as executive director of the Gaither committee, served as the President's Science Adviser. General Maxwell Taylor, the author of *Flexible Response,* was brought to the White House as the President's personal military representative.

BAY OF PIGS EPISODE

Richard J. Barnet has suggested that the President "probably exerts his greatest influence over future policy when he recruits his leading advisers." The reason is clear enough: it is in the nature of the Presidential office that "most of his decisions be affirmations, or at most modifications, of proposals from below." [1]

The Kennedy administration continued the Cold War, accepted the containment dogma uncritically as applied in Asia, and looked essentially toward a greatly strengthened military posture as a means of advancing United States vital interests around the world.[2] This general position was to have a special and specific application in Vietnam.

Kennedy's initial foreign policy experience came with the Bay of Pigs fiasco. It was, as the saying goes, a sobering experience. Although President Kennedy later wondered privately why he had not been more skeptical of the "experts" on this occasion, there was no point at which he elected to stop the invasion. He was concerned, of course, that the American involvement in the invasion plan remain secret, which would seem to indicate that the usual detached realism for which he was famous did not function in this case. Kennedy was for the plan so long as it "worked." Theodore Sorenson, in his account, insists that it was "bureaucratic momentum" that kept the Bay of Pigs plan moving toward its ignominious conclusion. As Sorenson later viewed it, the project "seemed to move inexorably toward execution without the President's being able either to obtain a firm grip on it or reverse it." [3] Not everyone will think that the President tried as hard as he might have to obtain a firm grip. Nevertheless, the Bay of Pigs episode, as described by Sorenson and Schlesinger, unsettles the comfortable notion that since the so-called "big decisions" are located at the Presidential level, the President *makes* these decisions.

The Bay of Pigs episode, coming so early in the new administration, added a profoundly cautionary dimension to the activities of an administration that preferred working well within the established limits of political orthodoxy at home and abroad. Arthur M. Schlesinger, Jr., one of the few White House political assistants who participated in the decisions that led to the Bay of Pigs (Sorenson did not participate), noted shortly thereafter "a general predisposition against boldness in all fields." [4] The Bay of Pigs disaster was "a clear consequence of the surrender of the presidential government to the permanent government." [5] If so, the surrender came early and without much of a fight.

With respect to the United States policy in Southeast Asia, the Kennedy administration placed the established national security bureaucracies in State, Defense, and the CIA (the permanent government in Schlesinger's view) under the leadership of a team of senior civilian officials who were deeply committed to containment in Asia, as well as in Europe; moreover, Kennedy's appointees came armed with a new military concept aimed at giving the United States the capacity to use American troops and weapons in a "local" or "limited war." Vietnam provided the opportunity of testing flexible response as it found expression in General Maxwell Taylor's *The Uncertain Trumpet*. Since General Taylor became a special member of the Kennedy team while establishing close personal ties to Attorney General Robert Kennedy, his views on how the United States might carry on its long-standing involvement in Indochina more effectively were bound to carry extra weight in the White House. Before the first year was over, President Kennedy was to send General Taylor to Vietnam to find a way of carrying on a more effective *military* effort.

Although we now know that Vietnam did not loom large in Kennedy's early view of the global struggle, this is not to suggest that Indochina and Southeast Asia were out of sight. Kennedy had been briefed by President Eisenhower, who called attention especially to the increasingly critical situation in Laos. In consequence, most of Kennedy's effort in Indochina during that first year, following the Bay of Pigs, was devoted to achieving a negotiated, compromise settlement in Laos. Indeed, it may be that Kennedy's more bellicose response in Vietnam is partly attributable to his unwillingness to assume political responsibility for seeking still another compromise settlement in that part of the world.[6] Be this as it may, the first display of a substantial interest in Vietnam on Kennedy's part was shown on April 20, 1961, the day after the collapse of the Bay of Pigs invasion. Kennedy established a special task force headed by Deputy Undersecretary of Defense Roswell Gilpatric to make a quick study of the situation in Vietnam. Gilpatric, a graduate of Hotchkiss and Yale, whose private career featured a partnership in Cravath, Swain and Moore, an affluent New York law firm, and whose clients included General Dynamics Corporation (of F-111 fame) reported a week later saying: "Come what may, the United States intends to *win* this battle." [7] The tone suggests that there was nothing for the President to decide, the ultimate decision to win the battle having been made. With Laos boiling on the front burner, the President apparently put the question of the Saigon regime's future aside until early autumn of 1961. At that point the situation in Saigon could no longer be ignored.

VIETNAM FACT-FINDING MISSION

The time had arrived for the first in an almost endless series of high-level fact-finding missions, a review in the field conducted by senior officials who would observe directly for the President and would report directly to him. Such a mission was expected to return with a program of action for Presidential implementation. In selecting General Taylor and Walt W. Rostow for this mission in October 1961, the President, one assumes, chose his two agents knowing that their personal predilections ran strongly in favor of a substantially increased United States military effort in Vietnam. Taylor and Rostow were not alone in holding distinct views about the United States' interest in Vietnam. As a United States senator during the 1950s, John F. Kennedy had been considered a knowledgeable student of Vietnam, one of the few in the Senate in those days. Joseph Kennedy, his father, had met and admired Diem, one of whose principal American sponsors, Justice William O. Douglas, was an old Kennedy family friend. Speaking at a meeting of the American Friends of Vietnam in Washington on June 1, 1956, Senator John F. Kennedy had referred to Diem's regime as "the cornerstone of the Free World in Southeast Asia, the keystone in the arch, the finger in the dike." Vietnam represented "a proving ground of democracy in Asia...the alternative to Communist dictatorship." This was a test of American responsibility. "The key position of Vietnam in Southeast Asia makes inevitable the involvement of this nation's security in any new outbreak of trouble." [8] The young senator might have been reading from NSC–64.

Professor Schlesinger has observed: "The very composition of the mission, headed by a general, with a White House aide as deputy and no figure of comparable rank from the State Department was significant." [9] More significant, one would have thought, was the fact that Maxwell Taylor was not "a" general but the former Army Chief of Staff and author of *The Uncertain Trumpet* who was accompanied on this mission by an articulate, Cold War ideologue whose views were familiar to the President.[10] Schlesinger suggests that the mission reflected Secretary Rusk's conscious desire to turn the Vietnam problem over to the Secretary of Defense. According to this interpretation, "Rusk doubtless decided to do so because the military situation seemed to him the most urgent, and Kennedy doubtless acquiesced because he had more confidence in McNamara and Taylor than in State." [11] Although it is to be doubted that Kennedy "acquiesced" in the selection of Taylor and Rostow, Schlesinger is correct in concluding that the effect of the Taylor-Rostow mission "was to order future thinking about Vietnam in both Saigon and Washington with the unavowed assumption that Vietnam was primarily a military rather than a political problem." [12] This is the major Indochina development of the Kennedy years; henceforth, Vietnam was viewed as being essentially a military problem.

General Taylor, whose doctrine of flexible response was now being implemented by Secretary McNamara, aware that the

Secretary intended giving the Army the capacity to send mobile striking forces into Southeast Asia (a capacity it lacked at the time of Dien Bien Phu) experienced no great difficulty in recommending to President Kennedy the introduction of a United States military force into South Vietnam. General Taylor saw this as "an essential action if we are to reverse the present downward trend of events in spite of full recognition of the disadvantages." [13] The disadvantages as Taylor listed them hardly seem trivial:

1. a weakness of the strategic reserve of United States forces;
2. a more definite involvement of United States prestige;
3. a recognition that the first contingent might not be sufficient and that the pressure to reenforce would mount;
4. the introduction of United States forces may increase tensions and risk escalation into a major war in Asia.

Taylor added: "If the ultimate result sought is the closing of the frontiers and the cleanup of the insurgents within SVN [South Vietnam], there is no limit to our possible commitment (unless we attack the source in Hanoi)." [14]

Kennedy understood the recommendations, Schlesinger reports:

> "They want a force of American troops," he told me early in November. "They say it's necessary in order to restore confidence and maintain morale. But it will be just like Berlin. The troops will march in; the bands will play; the crowds will cheer; and in four days everyone will have forgotten. Then we will be told we have to send in more troops. It's like taking a drink. The effect wears off, and you have to take another." The war in Vietnam, he added, could be won only so long as it was *their* war. If it were ever converted into a white man's war, we would lose as the French had lost a decade earlier. [15]

Kennedy was perceptive in recognizing the direction in which the Taylor-Rostow report pointed, and he appears to have been reluctant to follow it all the way. Did he choose to overlook that portion of reality that had already made the struggle in Vietnam *our* war, as well as theirs? "The need-not-to-know" factor perhaps helps in explaining why Kennedy was able to think in terms of Vietnam as *their* war while taking further steps in implementing the containment doctrine in Southeast Asia, thus solidifying the policy that had long since made it "our" war. After all, the United States had a full decade of involvement in Indochina before Kennedy reached the White House. Kennedy had been an interested and concerned Senator. NSC–64, adopted as national policy in 1950, made the struggle in Vietnam a vital part of the overall American program aimed at containing Communist expansion in Southeast Asia. Kennedy never initiated a critique of that policy either as senator or President. At best, the Kennedy administration's approach to South Vietnam appears to have been based on the hope that the issue would remain only a "little bit pregnant."

BEGINNINGS OF ESCALATION

The Taylor-Rostow recommendations offered in late 1961 bear a striking resemblance to the formula urged upon and finally accepted by President Johnson in 1965. Taylor and Rostow not only recommended an initial contingent of American troops to do battle in Vietnam; they also called for a program of "retaliation" if infiltration from the North did not halt. Indeed, it was Kennedy's rejection of these specifics that later caused controversy. Schlesinger painted the picture that tended to prevail prior to the publication of the Pentagon Papers. This is his version of the quagmire thesis:

> Each step in the deepening American military commitment was reasonably regarded at the time as the last that would be necessary. Yet, in retrospect, each step led only to the next, until we find ourselves entrapped in that nightmare of American strategists, a land war in Asia.[16]

Even before the Pentagon Papers appeared in public print, Daniel Ellsberg had published a long essay in a scholarly journal insisting that this was a false interpretation. American actions in Vietnam were typically taken as acts of desperation, because no alternative was seen, and not because officials saw much hope that the next step would be the last. After all, Taylor and Rostow reported that infiltration from the North was expected to continue. To stop this, in their view, would require a substantial United States military force in Vietnam *and the bombing of the North!* This is where Kennedy balked. He did not accept their two principal recommendations. Instead, he decided to increase the number of United States military advisers in Vietnam. (Kennedy's special legion, the Green Berets, was to show the way in counterinsurgency.)

Ellsberg commented as follows:

> There is no basis whatever for describing the President in this instance as taking a "small step" because he was promised success with it, or because it was "reasonably regarded as the last that would be necessary." What he was told was the contrary, and that from virtually every source. His decisions, he was assured, held out the almost certain prospect that new, larger steps, or else retreat, would present themselves as hard choices in the not-distant future.[17]

Kennedy took short, partial steps in November and December 1961; they may be thought of as Presidential-political steps aimed at keeping a stalemate in Vietnam from deteriorating into a "victory" for Hanoi. Kennedy, still smarting from painful lessons learned during the Bay of Pigs indoctrination, moved with extreme caution in Vietnam. Although Kennedy stopped short of a basic decision to commit American ground troops, his willingness to increase the number of American military advisers from 685 to 16,000 indicated that the military aspects of the problem had attained a priority ahead of political reform in Saigon, a point evidently not lost on Diem.

When a reporter asked President Kennedy at a press conference a few months later (this was in April 1962): "Sir, what are you going to do about the American soldiers getting killed in Vietnam?" Kennedy replied: "We are attempting to help Vietnam maintain its independence and not fall under the domination of the Communists. . . . We cannot desist in Vietnam." [18]

Still, Kennedy was far too intelligent, and too instinctively the activist, to let it go at that. The New Frontier was ablaze with schemes for winning the struggle in Vietnam by means of counterinsurgency. The President's brother, Robert, led the new movement. Roger Hilsman, a gallant guerrilla fighter in World War

II, served as unofficial chief-of-staff. This effort, in turn, led to direct participation in a complex pattern of internal intrigue in Saigon that culminated in Diem's murder and a change of regime. This was part of the legacy bequeathed to Lyndon B. Johnson in November 1963.

Kennedy faced a complex dilemma in Vietnam during his final year. The Diem government, stubbornly resisting its role as American puppet, pursuing its own devices, seemed destined to draw away from its people. If the United States applied pressure on Diem for reform, there was the danger of increasing the instability of a regime engaged in fighting off a military coup. If the United States were to see its way clear to direct military intervention using its own troops, the war would rapidly become a white man's war, a war we could not win, in Kennedy's view. Diem's strength lay in his considerable credentials as an authentic patriot; the viability of his position as leader of an "independent" regime would be greatly compromised by overt American intervention. Yet Diem was building a tighter and tighter bush-league dictatorship.

THE CRISIS MANAGERS

The most serious limitation on Kennedy's freedom of maneuver was his uncritical acceptance of the containment dogma as applied in Southeast Asia. How could he fail to support a regime dedicated to resisting Communist expansion in an area long ago declared of vital interest to the United States? This we know: Kennedy reaffirmed his belief in the domino theory only a few weeks before the fateful trip to Dallas. Furthermore, Kennedy had embraced flexible response with enthusiasm as the rationale for his administration's transformation of American defense policy, a transformation on which his own political future was based. Since Kennedy sponsored a defense policy that featured an American capacity for fighting local and limited wars against nefarious schemes for expanding Communist power, there was a powerful logic pushing his administration toward direct intervention in Vietnam. He had staffed the highest levels of the national security agencies with men who came to believe that *only* direct American intervention could achieve the objectives of global containment in Southeast Asia. How long Kennedy might have succeeded in avoiding the logic of his own position must remain a matter of conjecture.

There is nothing conjectural about the nature of the advice Kennedy was receiving in these matters, toward the end of his life. As we have seen, Kennedy, an experienced and knowledge-able Washington politician, had surrounded himself with a circle of national security advisers most of whom had invested a size-able portion of their professional careers in the Cold War. No recent administration has had so many professional Cold War crisis managers in so many key positions. James C. Thomson, Jr., a young technician (never apparently on the first team) who joined the inner circle in the Kennedy era, tells us that these Cold War technocrats really believed they were ushering in a new era: PAX AMERICANA TECHNOCRATICA.[19] This is certain: Kennedy filled the key positions in his administration with men who prided themselves on being effective crisis managers. On the na-tional security side, these men especially wished to apply their talents and a whole set of new techniques to *managing* the Cold War. It was in keeping with the style of Kennedy's administration that able men vie with one another in order to demonstrate how skillful they were in managing crises. Vietnam was an ideal ob-ject. Like Mount Everest, it was there.

In retrospect, it seems clear that there was no possibility that Kennedy would drastically alter the course in Vietnam, which had been set originally in the Truman administration. Kennedy accepted as an axiom of official policy the requirement that there should be a non-Communist regime in Saigon prepared to carry on effectively *as an instrument of United States containment policy in Southeast Asia.* By the summer of 1963 apprehension mounted within the inner circle concerning Diem's viability; his regime, having grown repressive and paranoiac, was rapidly los-ing any value it may have had as an instrument for United States official purposes. Diem was marked for extinction not so much because he headed a repressive regime, but rather because he had failed as an agent of American policy. United States policy demanded a puppet regime in Saigon capable of performing those functions that best met United States interests in Southeast Asia, although it was soon to become quite unclear just what those "interests" were.

It is not essential in this analysis to engage in a detailed review of the events that mark the tortuous trail to the murder of Diem in November 1963. The Pentagon Papers document the extent of the official American involvement in the sorry episode. The President of the United States, our ambassador in Saigon, and scores of officials at the policy level were aware of the generals' plot against Diem. Ambassador Lodge actively encouraged the coup. CIA agents in Saigon assisted the Vietnamese generals in planning the coup in which Diem and Nhu were deposed and then murdered. The last White House message from McGeorge Bundy to Lodge just prior to the coup left it up to the ambassador to decide whether the coup was likely to succeed. Lodge was reminded that once the coup was under way "it is in the interest of the United States that it succeed." [20] Memories of the Bay of Pigs debacle were still vivid.

The successful coup removed any doubt about United States purposes in Vietnam. Decisions taken in secret within the inner circle of closed politics cleared the way for bringing down the Diem regime, which had been our client after the French removed themselves from the scene in 1954. Henceforth it would be obvious that a new regime in Saigon, replacing Diem, was to serve as the instrument of official United States policy. Any regime following Diem would obviously be an American puppet to be manipulated for purposes of carrying on the struggle in which the United States had deliberately raised the stakes. The long weeks of backing and filling while prospects for the coup wavered reveal a good deal about bureaucratic decisions taken in secret. The Pentagon Papers describe the period as one in which "the United States inadvertently deepened its involvement. The inadvertence is the key factor." [21]

This seems a charitable interpretation. Henry Cabot Lodge was selected by President Kennedy upon the advice of Dean Rusk to succeed an ambassador who had invested two and a half years in trying to persuade Diem to function as a more effective instrument of United States purposes. Frederick Nolting, Ambassador Lodge's immediate predecessor, could not possibly have encouraged those who wished to overthrow Diem. Lodge, the very epitome of a latter-day Roman proconsul, was the ideal choice *if* the objective was to make over the Saigon regime in the "image" United States policy demanded. Lodge put the case with simple arrogance:

> My general view is that the United States is trying to bring this medieval country into the 20th century and that we have made considerable progress in military and economic ways but to gain victory we must also bring them into the 20th century politically and that can only be done by either a thoroughgoing change in the behavior of the present government or by another government.[22]

The balance of evidence indicates that the Kennedy administration, while indecisive, preferred a change of government in Saigon; and this was achieved in November 1963, not exactly inadvertently, although the murder of Diem came as a shock to Kennedy. History moves in ironic twists. Before the month was out, another assassination effected a change of government in Washington as well.

LBJ AND VIETNAM POLICY

The Johnson administration lost no time in reaffirming the traditional American position in Vietnam. This had been restated in a report dated October 2, 1963, which Secretary McNamara and General Taylor submitted to President Kennedy following a so-called fact-finding visit to Vietnam. To the end, the Kennedy administration remained wedded to the proposition that "the security of South Vietnam remains vital to United States security," to quote directly from the McNamara-Taylor report.[23] A special National Security Action Memorandum, drafted four days after Kennedy's assassination, declared that the purpose of the United States involvement was "to assist the people and Government of that country to win their contest against the externally directed and supported Communist conspiracy."[24] The same Action Memo repeated recommendations McNamara and Taylor had presented in October: the withdrawal of a thousand

United States troops by the end of 1963, the ending of the Vietcong insurgency in the I, II and III Corps area by the end of 1964, and in the Delta by 1965.

In choosing to keep intact the group of national security advisers he had inherited from Kennedy, President Johnson signaled his intention of working within the framework of existing policy. Johnson as Vice President had been an active participant in National Security Council discussions relating to Vietnam. Visiting the country early in 1961 at Kennedy's suggestion, he praised Diem as an Asian Churchill. Lyndon Johnson presumably understood better than most men that decisions at the level of the NSC are essentially group decisions as they make their way to formal assent by the President. Assuming that the "big" decisions in national security matters are Presidential, Johnson of all of our contemporary Presidents (prior to Nixon) had had an unparalleled opportunity of seeing how the "big" Cold War decisions were structured long before they reached the Presidential desk.

Johnson might, for example, have recalled a meeting that took place following an earlier plot against Diem, a plot that was *not* put into action. The time was August 31, 1963, and those who attended the meeting at the State Department, in addition to Vice President Johnson, included: Secretary Rusk; Secretary McNamara; Roswell L. Gilpatric; McGeorge Bundy; General Taylor; Edward R. Murrow; Major General Victor H. Krulak, a counterinsurgency specialist; Lt. General Marshall S. Carter, Deputy Director of the CIA; Richard Helms and William E. Colby of the CIA; Frederick E. Nolting, Jr., former U.S. Ambassador in Vietnam; Assistant Secretary of State Roger Hilsman; and Paul M. Kattenburg of the State Department, who headed an Interdepartmental Working Group on Vietnam. The President did *not* attend this meeting. Vice President Johnson was the highest ranking official present. Kattenburg was one of the two or three lowest ranking, a career officer at the technical level with special knowledge about Vietnam. Hilsman had been promoted to Assistant Secretary for Far Eastern Affairs in the spring of 1963. According to his own account, he was advised by the White House that he had been moved to this position because he had stood up to the Defense Department in past discussions.

The meeting has been thoroughly documented. Hilsman's account appears in some detail in his book *To Move a Nation*. The Pentagon Papers include General Krulak's detailed memorandum of what took place. The following is a rather lengthy excerpt from Krulak's memorandum:

Mr. Hilsman undertook to present four basic factors which bear directly on the problem facing the U.S. now. They are, in his view:

(a) The mood of the people, particularly the middle level officers, non-commissioned officers, and middle level bureaucrats, who are most restive.
Mr. McNamara interrupted to state that he had seen no evidence of this and General Taylor commented that he had seen none either, but he would like to see such evidence as Hilsman could produce.
Mr. Kattenburg commented that the middle level officers and bureaucrats are uniformly critical of the government, to which Mr. McNamara commented that if this indeed be fact we should know about it.

(b) The second basic factor, as outlined by Hilsman, was what effect will be felt on our programs elsewhere in Asia if we acquiesce to a strong Nhu-dominated government. In this connection, he reported that there is a Korean study now underway on just how much repression the United States will tolerate before pulling out her aid. Mr. McNamara stated that he had not seen this study and would be anxious to have it.

(c) The third basic factor is Mr. Nhu, his personality and his policy. Hilsman recalled that Nhu has once already launched an effort aimed at withdrawal of our province advisors and stated that he is sure he is in conversation with the French. He gave as supporting evidence, the content of an intercepted message which Mr. Bundy asked to see. Ambassador Nolting expressed the opinion that Nhu will not make a deal with Ho Chi Minh on Ho's terms.

(d) The fourth point is the matter of U.S. and world opinion. Hilsman stated that this problem was moving to a political and diplomatic plane. . . .
Mr. Kattenburg stated that as recently as last Thursday it was the belief of Ambassador Lodge that, if we undertake to live

with this repressive regime . . . we are going to be thrown out of the country in six months. He stated that at this juncture it would be better for us to make the decision to get out honorably. He went on to say that, having been acquainted with Diem for ten years, he was deeply disappointed in him, saying that he will not separate from his brother. It was Kattenburg's view that Diem will get very little support from the military, and, as time goes on, he will get less and less support and the country will go steadily down hill.

General Taylor asked what Kattenburg meant when he said that we would be forced out of Vietnam within six months. Kattenburg replied that in from six months to a year, as the people see we are losing the war, they will gradually go to the other side and we will be obliged to leave. Ambassador Nolting expressed general disagreement with Mr. Kattenburg. . . .

Secretary Rusk commented that Kattenburg's recital was largely speculative; that it would be far better for us to start on the firm basis of two things—that we will not pull out of Vietnam until the war is won, and that we will not run a coup. Mr. McNamara expressed agreement with this view.

Mr. Rusk then said that we should present questions to Lodge which fall within these parameters. He added that he believes we have good proof that we have been winning the war, particularly the contrast between the first six months of 1962 and the first six months of 1963. He then asked the Vice President if he had any contribution to make.

The Vice President said that he agreed with Secretary Rusk's conclusions completely; that he had great reservations himself with respect to a coup, particularly so because he had never really seen a genuine alternative to Diem. He stated that from both a practical and a political viewpoint, it would be a disaster to pull out; that we should stop playing cops and robbers and get back to talking straight to the GVN, and that we should once again go about winning the war. He stated that after our communications with them are genuinely reestablished, it may be necessary for someone to talk rough with them—perhaps General Taylor. He said further that he had been greatly impressed with Ambassador Nolting's views and agreed with Mr. McNamara's conclusions.[25]

Clearly, the Vice President identified himself with the "in-group" at the highest levels of national security decision-making.

The senior advisers appear to have developed a policy climate in which unfavorable estimates, inconvenient data, and unorthodox views were easily put aside. Kattenburg, a career specialist, was the only man present who had the audacity to suggest that the United States was on a course in Vietnam leading to disaster. His views were dismissed as being "speculative" by his own cabinet officer. Hilsman had the advantage of being a sub-cabinet officer who also was well regarded by the Kennedys; nevertheless, his rather unexceptional views about middle-level disenchantment in Saigon were treated with icy skepticism by his superiors. Lyndon Johnson was not among the dissidents or the skeptics in the autumn of 1963. The prevailing bias within the inner circle of closed politics is perfectly obvious.

PLURALIST-CONSENSUS MODEL

Roger Hilsman has presented one of the fullest accounts we have by a high-level participant in the Kennedy administration's Vietnam activities. His account is explicit in declaring that policy-making conforms to the pluralist-consensus model. He had written scholarly articles placing him in this school of political analysis before he became a member of the Kennedy advisory team.[26] As Hilsman sees it, the making of national security policy is a political process. Policy, as he perceived it in the early 1960s, was the result of a struggle between conflicting groups, interests, and institutions. That portion of the struggle in which Hilsman participated took place in what he calls "the arena of 'closed politics.'" As a participant in bureaucratic politics at this level, Hilsman perceived the process as a kind of pluralistic political jungle in which diverse groups and factions struggled to dominate American Cold War policy. At the same time, Hilsman accepted uncritically the *fact* that our Cold War policy has shown a remarkable coherence over a long period of time; his pluralistic struggle has not altered this stubborn reality. It seems not to have occurred to Hilsman that the aspect of the policy struggle in which he was engaged had only to do with the effective *implementation* of global containment as an established doctrine. In these circumstances, a scholarly observer not committed to the pluralist vision might have experienced some difficulty in seeing the push and pull of conflicting "interests" as they bore upon the purposes and objectives of national security policy. For example, in the case of the U-2 flights over Cuba, Hilsman found "conflicting interests" among the State Department, the Defense Department, and the CIA. The kind of pluralism Hilsman found at work within the inner circle was extremely limited when it came to the formulation of policy alternatives, as his own discussion of Vietnam decision-making in the Kennedy years reveals.

According to Hilsman, there were, in the summer of 1963, two groups of advisers disagreeing one with the other as to what the United States should do next in Vietnam. The group with which Hilsman identified apparently included Averill Harriman; Michael Forrestal of the White House NSC staff; George Ball, the Undersecretary of State; and Robert Kennedy. In Hilsman's view, his group was seeking a "political" approach to the Vietnam problem; Hilsman's group placed its reliance mainly on counterinsurgency methods and especially the strategic hamlet program. Since it was the strategic hamlet program, more than any other, which Nhu, Diem's brother-in-law, was exploiting as a means of building a personal dictatorship in the countryside, Hilsman's group took the initiative in pushing for the overthrow of the Diem regime in 1963. The other group, which included Rusk, McNamara, Taylor, Vice President Johnson, and the regular military establishment, was inclined to stay with more orthodox methods, including a patient effort aimed at trying to bring Diem "along."

By the summer of 1963 a fairly sharp division existed between those whose inclination was to continue support of Diem and those who felt with increasing intensity that Diem must be replaced. Hilsman views this struggle within the policy elite (a term he never uses, incidentally) as a conflict between "political" and "military" approaches to the Vietnam problem. There is no reason to doubt Hilsman's sincerity on the point; after all, he left early on this issue when the "military" side (that is, those who favored the infusion of U.S. ground troops and retaliatory bombing) appeared to be winning the debate. But one can, and should, question the accuracy of the distinction Hilsman draws between "political" and "military" in this instance. This is not mere quibbling over words, but gets to the nature of the policy struggle within the inner circle. A careful reading of the available data on the Kennedy years (including the Pentagon Papers and Hilsman's book) reveals that the discussion within the inner circle of closed politics had to do with two different *military* approaches to Vietnam: counterinsurgency versus a military partnership arrangement. There was no question of the purpose of our involvement; there was no critique of United States experience in Southeast Asia during the previous decade; no questioning of the meaning containment might have in Asia, especially in Indochina where there was *not* a Chinese military force in operation. One finds no evidence of any fundamental questioning of why Vietnam was thought to be of vital interest to United States security. Very little serious consideration was given to the feasibility of getting out of Vietnam once Diem appeared as a liability in terms of official United States purposes.

At a meeting of the National Security Council on September 6, 1963, Attorney General Robert Kennedy raised the question (heaven knows it was pertinent!) whether *any* government in Saigon, under Diem or anyone else, could successfully resist a Communist takeover. If not, the President's brother thought this was the time to get out of Vietnam. Although those attending the meeting were not able to offer an affirmative reply, the consensus was that it was necessary to resist the Vietcong with another government. Even this question from the President's closest political adviser did *not* lead to a searching reappraisal of United States policy in that beleaguered land. Even the successful coup on November 1 did not effect a reconsideration of the United States involvement. This was a time when Washington might have decided to disengage, if there had been an alternative to the established doctrine.[27] Indeed, the Kennedy administration had no clear view of what was to follow a successful coup in Saigon.

THE "FRONT MEN"

Hilsman's complete acceptance of pluralist-consensus assumptions evidently excludes any examination of the role a policy elite may play in shaping national security policy, although Gabriel Almond—whose work Hilsman admires—recognizes the presence of elite structures. The closest Hilsman comes, as we noted in chapter 1, is to describe the men who occupy the key posts within what he calls "the arena of closed politics" as "front men." Who are they? Hilsman suggests that they come from "diverse" backgrounds, but the only backgrounds he mentions are Wall Street, prestigious law firms, major corporations, the multiversities, and the military. At one point Hilsman lists about forty "front men." None is a Jew. (Hilsman's list does not include Walt Rostow or Henry Kissinger.) There are no blacks and, of course, no females on Hilsman's list. Only six of the approximately forty individuals mentioned by Hilsman appear to have had previous significant experience in electoral politics, where one would ordinarily expect to develop some sensitivity to the push and pull of pluralist politics. With perhaps two exceptions, Hilsman's front men are (or were) actively associated with the Council on Foreign Relations.[28]

Hilsman ignores the point that Kennedy was surrounded in the arena of closed politics by a group of like-minded men (many with close personal and social ties) who were deeply committed to the containment dogma and who entertained few, if any, doubts about its applicability in Southeast Asia. Hilsman's "innermost circle" pioneered in devising a new *military* approach based upon the doctrine of flexible response as a means of transforming the American role to one of active leadership of non-Communist forces in the Indochina war, a war that Ho Chi Minh's forces had been fighting since 1946. Schlesinger argues that Kennedy had no alternative but to honor Eisenhower's commitment in Vietnam. The "commitment" (so-called) predated Eisenhower and it was a commitment to ourselves, as NSC–64 shows. NSC–64 was adopted as national policy in the Truman-Acheson era before Eisenhower entered the national political arena. Schlesinger would be closer to reality if he were to suggest that Kennedy had no alternative in Vietnam because he and his team of national security advisers accepted the premises of global containment. The Kennedy administration pursued the course set in the previous decade; there was no inclination to challenge the established doctrine.

Richard Walton's recent interpretation of Kennedy's foreign policy argues that President Kennedy, operating well within the limits of conventional politics, functioned as an authentic Cold Warrior leading a global counterrevolution. Walton's book serves as a healthy corrective to the gloss put upon Kennedy foreign policy by men who were part of the Kennedy experience, most notably Schlesinger and Sorenson. But Walton oversimplifies the nature and the history of the Cold War and national security decision-making when he asserts that Kennedy "started" the American war in Vietnam. "The Vietnam war, and all its terrible consequences, are Kennedy's responsibility, for he launched America on the course of war. Johnson is responsible for escalating the war and Nixon for widening it, but it was John Kennedy who started it," Walton maintains.[29]

The analysis in this book suggests how serious a distortion of history Walton is engaged in. Kennedy, as we have seen, did nothing to bring about a fundamental reexamination of inherited Cold War assumptions, and he stayed well within the conventional limits of the containment dogma as it had been *misapplied* in Southeast Asia. But Kennedy in Vietnam is intelligible only as he fits into a quarter-century of Cold War decision-making in which an elite group of professional civilian-militants dominated the making of national-security policy-making. Walton has only a few words to say about Kennedy's advisory group; his book is based on the premise "that a President is responsible for all that takes place in his administration."[30] Still he believes there is something to be learned about a man from those he chooses to be close to, and so toward the end of his book Walton offers a group profile of Kennedy's foreign policy advisers.

> They were youngish but wedded to the old Cold War visions. They were intellectuals but understood the new world no better than the old businessmen of the Eisenhower years. They were liberal—by self definition—but prosecuted the Cold War more vigorously than had the Eisenhower conservatives.[31]

David Halberstam, in his profiles of Robert McNamara and McGeorge Bundy, states that in foreign affairs the Kennedy administration was "a deliberately structured group." It seems a useful concept. Our analysis is directed toward this deliberately structured group, and how they in turn structured policy. We have been examining the decisions relating to the United States involvement in Vietnam, 1961–63, as they were influentially shaped by this small group of key advisers just below the level of the President.

CONCLUSION

The Kennedy administration, even in the eyes of its friendliest participant-observers, altered the American role in Vietnam from limited participation to one that made us active partners with Saigon in a hot war against Ho Chi Minh's forces. Although Kennedy's own sense of cool detachment helped considerably in keeping Vietnam from becoming an official obsession, he was nonetheless responsible finally for seeking a change of government in Saigon. In doing so, the Kennedy administration cleared the stage for a new regime in Saigon, which was destined to become an overt American puppet. During his first year in the White House, Kennedy turned for advice more and more to those men who held personal views as to how the *military* effort in Vietnam might be strengthened. Kennedy looked with enthusiasm to counterinsurgency as a means of winning the war. The Kennedy administration did not question (even privately) the *purposes* of the American involvement in Vietnam. Kennedy and his advisers went along with the inherited assumption that the perpetuation of a non-Communist regime in Saigon was vital to United States interests; they were worried that Diem might seek a settlement with Hanoi. Most importantly, there was no probing of what our vital interests in Vietnam might be, nor was there any analysis of what the costs (financial, psychic, or political) might be in pursuing those interests, despite Robert McNamara's devotion to cost-benefit analysis.

Some Kennedy admirers and former associates find it hard to believe that their fallen hero would have pursued a course of military escalation in Vietnam in 1965. Kenneth O'Donnell has reported that Kennedy was prepared, during an assumed second term, to take risks for peace that he did not find politically feasible to initiate during his first three years in the White

House.[32] The point remains highly speculative at best since fate did not decree Kennedy a second term. There is no way of knowing how Kennedy would have reacted in 1964 during the months of political turmoil that followed Diem's downfall, but it is evident that the Kennedy administration did not give serious attention to the long-term consequences of Diem's disappearance from the scene.

> President Kennedy apparently assumed as he deepened American involvement that the United States, with its enormous power, would be able to control the situation; that the generals would be more malleable as instruments of American policy than Diem had been; and that, with the military in control, the war would continue and there would be no danger of a secret deal with Hanoi.[33]

Furthermore, there is no evidence that Kennedy was prepared to challenge the containment dogma; it is difficult to imagine the circumstances in which he would have questioned flexible response and the use of United States counterinsurgency forces including his own Green Berets. Leading members of the Cold War policy elite occupied key roles in national security decision-making during the Kennedy years, as they did throughout the Johnson era. It does not seem probable that the nature of the advice offered Kennedy, had he held the Presidency in 1964–65, concerning the appropriate American response to events in Vietnam, would have differed significantly from that which President Johnson received.

The election of John F. Kennedy in 1960 offered an opportunity for a searching reappraisal of our foreign and defense policies. It was one of those rare moments when an alternative to containment might have been constructed. In a pluralistic policy climate, one assumes that such an alternative would have been posed. In fact, the Kennedy administration, perhaps partly caught up in its own campaign rhetoric featuring the "missile gap," remained firmly wedded to containment, adopted flexible response as a means of broadening the military aspects of the Cold War, fuzzed the evidence showing that there was no missile gap, overreacted to Khrushchev's reference to "wars of national liberation," and proceeded to feature as its star performer a Secretary of Defense who was to see the annual level of military spending rise from $50 billion to nearly $80 billion during his seven years in office.

During Kennedy's short tenure the United States involvement in Vietnam became more military and less political. The United States government encouraged the unseating of a mandarin grown repressive by a military clique because we hoped to find a better instrument for our official purposes in Southeast Asia. Kennedy's new defense team gave the United States the military capacity to fight a so-called "local" and "limited war," with or without the use of tactical nuclear weapons. Kennedy's men operated well within the limits of Cold War doctrine as written in the early 1950s; indeed, a number of his key men had helped in writing the original doctrine.

The Kennedy years also marked the transition to a new phase in national security decision-making, as a cadre of civilian militant technocrats assumed increasing responsibilities in managing the permanent Cold War military establishment. Barnet notes the change:

> Stimson's recruits and their colleagues in FDR's wartime government became the key architects of American national security policy during the Cold War. Their assistants and proteges in turn became the technicians and managers of that policy.[34]

Whereas the earlier generation of Cold Warriors—Acheson, Lovett, McCloy, et al.—built the "structures" (Barnet defines these as "the intellectual concepts, the rhetoric, the alliances, the military networks"), the men who held the command posts during the Kennedy years were involved chiefly in maintaining, managing, and, of course, extending the structures of global containment. They were the inheritors of an established doctrine created by a national security policy elite.

Lyndon Johnson, a former leader of the bipartisan Congressional coalition and a veteran participant in Cold War decision-making, came to the White House when the situation in Saigon required clear-cut decisions as to just how far the United States was prepared to go in denying Ho Chi Minh the southern half of Indochina. The established doctrine enjoyed the firm support of the coalition in control of the Congress and an acquiescent public that had been carefully indoctrinated for more than a decade concerning the menace of Communist expansion. If there was a countervailing force—or set of forces—within the American society capable of challenging global containment, the established dogma, no political analyst has demonstrated its effective presence during the Kennedy years.[35]

Chapter Eight Notes

1. Richard J. Barnet, *Roots of War* (New York: Atheneum, 1972), p. 77.

2. See Richard J. Walton, *Cold War and Counterrevolution: The Foreign Policy of John F. Kennedy* (New York: Viking, 1972), for an interpretation of Kennedy as the leader of a global counter-revolutionary policy.

3. Theodore Sorenson, *Kennedy* (New York: Harper & Row, 1965), pp. 301–2.

4. Arthur M. Schlesinger, Jr., *A Thousand Days* (Boston: Houghton Mifflin, 1965), p. 682.

5. Ibid., p. 681.

6. John Kenneth Galbraith, NBC White Paper, "Vietnam Hindsight," August 25, 1972, Act III, p. 11; written and produced by Fred Freed. Professor Galbraith said on this occasion: "I heard him say many times, a number of times, now, there are just so many concessions that one can make to the Communists in one year and survive politically. In 1961, he liquidated the Cuban, the Bay of Pigs thing, very quickly and on terms which invited criticism. The Military wanted to go ahead as usual. He had called off the hawks in Laos and gone for the negotiations in Geneva and I remember his saying, 'we just can't have another defeat this year in Vietnam.'"

7. P.P. (NYT), p. 89.

8. P.P. (Off.), Vol. 12, "Failure of Geneva Settlement," p. 31.

9. Schlesinger, *A Thousand Days*, p. 545.

10. See Barnet, *Roots of War*, pp. 311–12. (Barnet states that it was Rostow who suggested the theme for JFK's 1960 campaign.)

11. Schlesinger, *A Thousand Days*, p. 545.

12. Ibid.

13. P.P. (NYT), pp. 141–42.

14. Ibid., p. 141.

15. Schlesinger, *A Thousand Days*, p. 547.

16. Arthur M. Schlesinger, Jr., *The Bitter Heritage*, rev. ed. (New York: Fawcett World, 1968), p. 47.

17. Daniel Ellsberg, "The Quagmire Myth and the Stalemate Machine," *Public Policy*, Vol. XIX, No. 2 (Spring 1971), 230.

18. P.P. (NYT), p. 110.

19. See James C. Thomson, Jr., "How Could Vietnam Happen? An Autopsy," *The Atlantic Monthly*, April 1968, for an elaboration of this theme. Thomson's essay was one of the first public statements by a former participant in the inner circle of closed politics to call attention to the growing influence of Cold War ideologues within the bureaucratic structures during the Kennedy-Johnson years. Barnet, who finds a national security elite of remarkable consistency, cohesiveness, and persistence, has an excellent chapter (3) in *Roots of War*, in which he examines the ideologue's mind-set.

20. P.P. (NYT), p. 231.

21. Ibid., p. 159.

22. Ibid., p. 227.

23. Ibid., p. 213.

24. Ibid., pp. 232–33.

25. Ibid., pp. 204–5.

26. Roger Hilsman, "Congressional-Executive Relations in the Foreign Policy Consensus," *American Political Science Review*, Vol. 52, No. 3 (September 1958), 725–44; and "The Foreign Policy Consensus: An Interim Research Report," *Journal of Conflict Resolution*, Vol. 3 (December 1959), 361–82.

27. P.P. (NYT), pp. 158 and 175.

28. Barnet, *Roots of War*, pp. 48–50.

29. Walton, *Cold War and Counterrevolution*, p. 182.

30. Ibid., p. 229.

31. Ibid.

32. Kenneth O'Donnell, "LBJ and the Kennedys," *Life*, August 7, 1970, pp. 44–48. The thesis is developed further in Kenneth O'Donnell, David Powers, and Joe McCarthy, *Johnny, We Hardly Knew Ye: Memories of John Fitzgerald Kennedy* (Boston: Little, Brown, 1972), which reports that Kennedy ordered an initial reduction of U.S. forces in October 1963. This order, Kennedy's former aides point out, was not rescinded by Kennedy following Diem's assassination, although it was quietly rescinded following Kennedy's assassination. Thus, the reader is asked to believe that Kennedy *would* have taken the United States completely out of Vietnam sometime following the 1964 Presidential election, since

this was his intention as expressed privately to O'Donnell and Powers.

33. Louise FitzSimons, *The Kennedy Doctrine* (New York: Random House, 1972), p. 212.

34. Barnet, *Roots of War,* p. 53.

35. Walter Lafeber, *America, Russia, and the Cold War* (New York: John Wiley and Sons, 1967). Lafeber writes (p. 229): ". . . the Kennedy administration could not lessen the Cold War tensions but only intensify them. These policies differed in no important essential from the Eisenhower policies after 1954. The new administration was only more efficient in carrying them out." The Kennedy administration does appear to have carried out the containment policy with more determination and efficiency than its predecessor; but the change from a few hundred special forces advisers in Vietnam to a counterinsurgency effort involving thousands of special American troops, the encouragement of the coup against Diem, the willingness to invade Cuba, and the showdown during the Cuban missile crisis indicate a greater reliance on military force. (One wonders what Lafeber thinks flexible response connoted if not an important departure from Eisenhower policy.)

9 THE AMERICANIZATION OF THE WAR IN VIETNAM, 1964–65

One wonders how much the American commitment to Vietnamese freedom is also a commitment to American pride—the two seem to have become part of the same package.

Senator J. William Fulbright (1966)

If the Kennedy administration is to bear the responsibility for shifting the balance in Vietnam toward a military emphasis, the Johnson administration made the decisions that led to military escalation and the rapid Americanization of the war. Faced with a steady turnover of Saigon "governments" (if they may be dignified by use of the word) following the coup against Diem, United States officials came to the conclusion during 1964 that the official American purpose—presumably to prevent a Communist takeover in South Vietnam—could be accomplished only if the U.S. government were prepared to assume the role of active combatant using United States ground troops and air power against the Vietcong forces supplemented by regular military units from Hanoi. It is a matter of conjecture whether the Johnson administration might have made the decision to enter the battle as active military combatant earlier in the absence of a Presidential campaign and election, but it is clear that the fundamental decisions to escalate and Americanize, which were taken first in February 1965, had been developed as contingency plans months earlier in the midst of the 1964 election campaign.

After the initial decisions were made, the incremental nature of group decision-making, which appears to be the characteristic mode when bureaucracies are functioning within an accepted policy consensus, led to further additions to United States military forces in Vietnam. Cold War technicians structured the specific decisions as they did during the Kennedy administration. The process moved with remarkable speed during the rest of

1965; so much so, in fact, that an original force of some 34,000 American military advisers and service forces in South Vietnam was expanded to some 170,000 men by December 1965. In subsequent years American military forces in Vietnam were to grow until they exceeded half a million men.

MANSFIELD STUDY GROUP

Senator Mike Mansfield, Democrat of Montana, the Senate majority leader, headed a five-man Senate group that visited Vietnam in December 1965 at the request of President Johnson. (The other Senators were George D. Aiken, Republican of Vermont; J. Caleb Boggs, Republican of Delaware; Daniel K. Inouye, Democrat of Hawaii; and Edmund S. Muskie, Democrat of Maine.) The following paragraphs are taken from the report that Senator Mansfield's group submitted on January 6, 1968.

The augmented U.S. ground forces were composed of two Army divisions, the 1st Infantry Division, and the 1st Air Cavalry Division, and two separate brigades, the First Brigade, 101st Airborne Division, and the 173rd Airborne Brigade.... A full U.S. Marine Division reinforced by a separate regiment was in Vietnam with the support of six Marine fighter-bomber squadrons.

The small Vietnamese coastal force was augmented by a number of U.S. naval ships and Coast Guard vessels. The United States 7th Fleet was off the Vietnamese coast. Planes from its carriers were active in the air campaign against North Vietnam. They were also reinforcing the U.S. Air Force and Vietnamese fighter-bomber squadrons in operations in South Vietnam.

Ten U.S. Air Force and Marine fighter-bomber squadrons were operating from five jet airfields in Vietnam; a sixth field was under construction. B-52 bombers from Guam were providing additional air strength, concentrating on more remote Vietcong bases which had previously been immune to harassment or attack.

The magnitude of the expanded U.S. military effort has required a vastly enlarged support complex. Starting almost from scratch in May of 1965, a logistics system has been built. There are four logistic support areas.[1]

Thus, the doctrine of flexible response applied to a "local" or "limited" war in Southeast Asia effected an impressive fighting capacity that was placed on the line in Vietnam with astonishing speed in a period of some six or seven months in 1965. It is also important to bear in mind that the force which the Mansfield group saw in December of that year represented only about a third of what was later to become the peak American military component in Vietnam.

Mansfield's committee report repeated U.S. military estimates that placed Vietcong strength in December 1965 at 230,000, including 14,000 army troops from North Vietnam. Mansfield estimated that 1500 men were being infiltrated each month from the North through Laos into South Vietnam; it was expected that this rate would soon increase threefold.

The Mansfield report also accepted the notion that this was a Vietnamese war with American troops assisting a "sovereign nation" as it resisted "aggression."

> From the point of view of American policy and practice, the war itself remains a Vietnamese war. The American command emphasizes that U.S. forces in Vietnam are there to support the Vietnamese and their Armed Forces in the effort to resist aggression by infiltration from the north and terrorism and subversion from within. Vietnamese sovereignty and the paramount role of the Vietnamese are meticulously respected and the supporting nature of the U.S. role is stressed.[2]

Senator Mansfield and his colleagues further reported:

> By November 1965, American troops were directly involved in battle to a much greater degree than at any other time in the history of the Vietnamese conflict. At the same time, the intensity of the war itself reached a new high. . . . In the month of November 1965, alone, 469 Americans were killed in action, a figure representing about 35% of all Americans killed in action in the war until that date. In addition, 1,470 Americans were listed as wounded and 33 as missing.[3]

The final months of 1965 found the United States deeply, even tragically, involved as an active belligerent in the war between two Vietnamese regimes, one based in Hanoi, the other in Saigon. Eugene Eidenberg published a case-study analysis of the process of decision-making by which the national security managers escalated the war in Vietnam. Although Eidenberg's essay appeared in print two years before the appearance of the Pentagon Papers, he was able, nevertheless, to present a picture of national security decision-making at the level just below the President, which is sustained by the Pentagon Papers. Eidenberg relied heavily on interviews with many of the key participants within the inner circle of closed politics, including McGeorge and William Bundy and Walt W. Rostow. Eidenberg writes of "the typically incremental nature of governmental decision-making" in which "the current stage was reached by successive steps, each of which seemed at the time a reasonable extension of the previous level of activity and an appropriate response to changing events." [4] He reasons further that President Johnson was "particularly committed" to the incremental approach during 1964 "because he was anxious to establish links of continuity to the policies of John F. Kennedy." [5] Actually, the links of continuity were best effected by the simple expedient of keeping intact the key group of civilian militants previously identified. The military escalation, once initiated, moved incrementally—also relentlessly—because the Johnson administration was no more prepared than its predecessor had been to challenge the established tenets of global containment.

Eugene Eidenberg has shown how influential that key civilian advisers within the national security apparatus were in shaping the specific decisions to escalate in 1964–65. The same group of men was deeply involved in structuring the President's decision made early in 1964 to hold the line in Vietnam as well as the subsequent decisions normally taken within the bureaucracy by way of implementing the essentially Presidential decision. The so-called "big decision" in this case was followed by a series of "smaller" decisions whose cumulative impact was momentous. A series of decisions was entered into in 1964 and 1965, which committed the United States to assume the major share of the fighting and to do whatever else was necessary to support the shaky military, political, and economic foundations of the Saigon regime. While the Congress willingly went along with the so-called Tonkin Gulf resolution in August 1964, the basic decisions were made within the inner circle of closed politics, without public debate, and they involved technicians as well as political officials. The alternatives posed for the President were essentially tactical and military in nature; they were influentially shaped by a coherent group of civilian militants who manned the key posts in the national security decision-making apparatus just below the level of the President.

As in the case of the Kennedy administration, one of the most important foreign policy decisions President Johnson made was in the choice of the national security managers who would structure all subsequent decisions taken within the inner circle of closed politics. After the decisions had been made, Congress and public opinion were manipulated into positions of agreement with, and acquiescence in, a course of action already decided upon. President Johnson was also to be given a larger opportunity than John F. Kennedy had for testing the flexible response concept in combat. In doing so, the Johnson administration offered substantiation to a point developed by Richard Barnet:

> The very flexibility and multiplicity of options which the national security managers constantly seek are responsible for some of their most monumental errors. The broader the canvas, the wider the discretion, the more remote the objects of one's plans, and the freer one is of outside restraint, the greater the risks of error. Advancing the national interest is no guide at all, since it means whatever the policymaker wants it to mean.[6]

In this case, the policy-makers often were technocrats hopelessly isolated from the currents of domestic politics.

GETTING READY TO GO NORTH

The most obvious factor influencing United States decisions in 1964 and 1965 was the situation in Saigon following Diem's murder. Eidenberg summarizes the situation:

> The optimism of some in the Administration that Diem's departure would create the conditions for a viable non-Communist national coalition seems, with hindsight, to have been badly misplaced. . . . In the twelve months between Diem's fall and the end of 1964 there were ten major political upheavals within

South Vietnam. Coups, counter coups, and reorganization became the order of the day. It is hard to imagine a more chaotic
political and social climate than that which gripped South Vietnam from the end of 1963 to 1965; in that same period major
presidential decisions had to be made on America's commitment
and role in Vietnam. Inevitably the instability within South
Vietnam became a major issue itself in the administration's calculations.[7]

The situation was so precarious in South Vietnam in the early
months of 1964 that the Vietcong apparently made the decision
to step up their military effort in the hope of bringing down the
Saigon regime. It was in this context that President Johnson,
speaking in Los Angeles on February 24, indirectly forewarned
Hanoi:

> The contest in which South Vietnam is now engaged is first and
> foremost a contest to be won by the government of the people
> of that country for themselves. But those engaged in external di-
> rection and supply would do well to be reminded and to remem-
> ber that this type of aggression is a deeply dangerous game.[8]

How dangerous the game might become was suggested when
several leading newspapers the next morning carried speculation
credited to "highly reliable sources" concerning possible American air raids against North Vietnam.[9]

The possibility that the United States might soon choose to
"go North," a policy recommendation originally advanced by
General Taylor and Walt W. Rostow following their Saigon visit
of October 1961, was given credence by certain personnel changes
at the sub-cabinet level in February 1964. Roger Hilsman, Assistant Secretary of State for Far Eastern Affairs, a leading figure
in the Kennedy counterinsurgency policy, resigned to be replaced by William Bundy. Bundy had been serving as Assistant
Secretary of Defense for International Security Affairs; this position was now filled by John McNaughton, who was to become
Robert McNamara's principal assistant for Vietnam matters. In
a sense, Hilsman's departure resulted in a game of musical
chairs, since no new faces were added to the small group of
civilian militants just below the level of the President. On the
other hand, those who advocated a stronger military pressure

on Hanoi found their position strengthened relatively by Hilsman's departure. The publication of the Pentagon Papers in 1971
sheds light on the significant roles William Bundy and John
McNaughton played in urging a policy of military escalation in
1964 and 1965. The same papers also revealed for the first time
the kind of thinking (if "thinking" is an adequate word) that
found its way into the documents Bundy and McNaughton prepared for their senior colleagues.

Speaking of this period early in 1964, one of the President's
chief foreign policy advisers, who evidently preferred remaining
anonymous, later told Eidenberg in an interview:

> It was clear that unless there was a wholly unexpected shift in
> the internal coherence and capability of South Vietnam, they
> were going to lose. It was a clear and general view *below the
> President* that the United States ought to take steps to prevent
> this loss. . . . President Johnson made the strategic decision to
> hold Vietnam early in 1964. He necessarily deferred the specifics
> of that strategic decision until, one, the election was over; two,
> the Gulf of Tonkin action had occurred; and, three, a more
> proximate nationally understood rationale for commitment could
> be generated. [Italics mine.][10]

The explanation may be improved upon in the light of the
Pentagon Papers. The level "below the President" was in favor
of hanging on in Vietnam *regardless of the costs.* In the level
just below the President, the only senior adviser who was clearly
disposed *against* escalation in 1964–65 was George Ball, Undersecretary of State and an ardent Pan-European.[11] The election
year setting profoundly influenced thinking and decision-making
at the Presidential level. The Gulf of Tonkin action did not "occur"; it was *engineered* as part of a scenario William Bundy and
John McNaughton wrote and rewrote over a period of several
months. The "more proximate nationally understood rationale"
may perhaps be translated more freely as the *generating* of a
plausible case that might get by an acquiescent general public.[12]

The thinking within the small circle of Presidential national
security advisers in the early weeks of 1965 was narrowing on
the retaliatory bombing tactic and the continuous bombing of
military targets in the North. The President's principal civilian

national security advisers reasoned in this fashion, according to Eidenberg, because this option seemed to them a less direct way of Americanizing the war than the alternative of adding a large force of ground troops.

> The Administration was still not seriously thinking about American troops taking over the war, although that alternative was being discussed more frequently. There remained the hope that airpower would coerce Hanoi to cease their infiltration of the South, and perhaps would even bring them to the negotiating table.[13]

Writing in 1968 Eidenberg observed:

> Either no one close to the President considered the implications of the graduated response should North Vietnam and the Vietcong refuse to yield, or American intelligence about North Vietnam's capacity and will to resist was sadly in error.[14]

EXPECTATIONS OF BOMBING

The Pentagon Papers have shown that the problem did not lie with faulty intelligence. The intelligence community held forth no expectation that bombing in the North would bring Hanoi to the bargaining table. The President's national security advisers chose bombing *in desperation* because they were not ready to face the reality of making this (as with the French) a white man's war on the ground. It was a Vietcong attack on American installations in the Pleiku area on February 6, 1965, that provided the pretext for launching retaliatory U.S. air strikes against the North. The public announcement that the President had decided to open continuous air strikes against North Vietnam in order to stem the flow of men and materials south and to bring about a negotiated settlement came three weeks later. Even then the United States government took the official position that there had been no shift in policy. During a news conference on March 13 the President said:

> the incidents have changed, in some instances the equipment has changed, in some instances the tactics and perhaps the strategy in a decision or two have changed . . . [but] our policy is still the same.[15]

Nonetheless, the President's advisers who participated in the February decisions understood that "we had once and for all cast our lot in favor of major action." Eidenberg put it simply enough: "For the President's national security team, 'the war began in February of 1965.'" [16]

It was May, however, before the decisions were taken to send U.S. ground troops to fight against the Vietcong. This followed a report from a CIA official who reported to McGeorge Bundy that same month, "the atmosphere of defeat in South Vietnam is palpable. Unless there is a major increase in the size of the army in the field, there will be a complete military collapse in the South." [17]

In short, national security managers advised the President in May 1965 to send substantial U.S. ground forces into battle in Vietnam against the Vietcong and regular North Vietnam army units *because the pursuit of official American objectives could no longer be safely entrusted to the Saigon regime.* More than thirty thousand American military advisers and special forces units, combined with the use of United States air power against limited targets in the North, had proved insufficient to keep the South Vietnamese armed forces from imminent military defeat. Although it is probable that the technical decisions to send American troops were taken late in the spring of 1965, the first public announcement did not come until midsummer. It seems all the more remarkable, therefore, that the Mansfield ad hoc committee found 170,000 United States troops in Vietnam by December of the same year. Later William Bundy was to tell Eugene Eidenberg: "By June it was clear to all the President's senior advisers that we would have to up the level of American troops. . . . This is the fork in the road when we crossed into another kind of commitment." [18]

The difficulty was that this particular fork in the road led to a kind of commitment that might prove to have no ending. Thus Senator Mansfield reported in December:

> Insofar as the military situation is concerned, the large scale introduction of U.S. forces and their entry into combat has blunted but not turned back the drive of the Vietcong. The latter have responded to the increased American role with a further strengthening of their forces by local recruitment in the south

and reinforcements from the north and a general stepping up of military activity.[19]

The report continued:

Despite the great increase in American military commitment, it is doubtful in view of the acceleration of Vietcong efforts that the constricted position now held in Vietnam by the Saigon government can continue to be held for the indefinite future, let alone extended, *without a further augmentation of American forces on the ground.* [Italics mine.] [20]

Mansfield offered no assurance as to what the ultimate increase in those American forces might be, since we were pressing against a military situation "which is, in effect, open ended.' Indeed, it was so open ended that Mansfield felt that "all of mainland southeast Asia" could not be ruled out as a potential battlefield. He noted that the war had expanded significantly into Laos and was beginning to lap over the Cambodian border while pressures increased in northeast Thailand.

Referring to the "sovereign" government in Saigon, the Mansfield committee reported:

. . . the fact is that they are, as other Vietnamese Governments have been over the past decade, at the beginning of a beginning in dealing with the problems of popular mobilization in support of the Government.[21]

The Mansfield group did not offer a fresh alternative; indeed the only visible alternative the Mansfield group saw was "the indefinite expansion and intensification of the war which will require the continuous introduction of additional U.S. forces." The grim course based upon the doctrine of flexible response had been set by December 1965. The report closed with the following sentence:

The situation, as it now appears, offers only the very slim prospect of a just settlement by negotiations or the alternative prospect of a continuance of the conflict in the direction of a general war on the Asian mainland.[22]

One wonders whether this was "the more proximate nationally understood rationale" for which the Johnson administration hoped public support could be generated.

The report of Senator Mansfield's ad hoc committee following its December 1965 on-the-spot examination of the new American military effort indicates the extent to which the Senate leadership was prepared to go along with the policy drift toward an open-ended process of adding more and more United States military forces in Vietnam ad infinitum.

THE LEVEL BELOW THE PRESIDENT

The analysis needs to be taken a further step. The Pentagon Papers offer an unusual opportunity of examining the *official thinking* of the leading civilian militants just below the level of the President, the level where a large portion of national security policy *and activity* is shaped.

The matter of carrying the war North to Hanoi—first by way of tit-for-tat retaliatory air strikes and then by continuous air warfare against selected targets—is a case where the views of key Presidential advisers are known to have been influential. While air warfare was to become a reality in 1965, the tactic had been recommended as early as the Maxwell Taylor–Walt Rostow report to President Kennedy in November 1961. Furthermore, Rostow and Taylor in the same report made the basic assumptions that eventually were to prevail, according to the *New York Times* version of the Pentagon Papers: South Vietnam's problems "could be cured if enough dedicated Americans could provide" the natives "with the elan and style needed to win"; and secondly, that, "if worst comes to worst, the United States could probably save its position in Vietnam by bombing the North." [23] Although these basic assumptions were sorely tested in the period after 1965, there is no reason to suppose that men like Taylor and Rostow were anything other than persistently sincere in urging a larger direct American military effort in the Vietnam struggle.

Technical advisers invariably come bearing conceptual gifts that contain their own distinct policy biases. Maxwell Taylor had an enormous ego involvement in the doctrine of flexible response as a means of defeating Communist-inspired wars of "national liberation." He literally wrote the book. Vietnam was obviously the best case he was likely to find for testing his ideas. (General Taylor replaced Henry Cabot Lodge as United States Ambassador in Saigon on July 23, 1964. By August the new ambassador was reporting the necessity of using United States air power to stave off the collapse of the regime in South Vietnam.)

It seems impossible to read the Pentagon Papers and not see how very seriously Walt W. Rostow took himself as a strategic thinker. Thus we find Rostow writing in February 1964, a year before escalation: "[Ho Chi Minh] has an industrial complex to protect: he is no longer a guerrilla fighter with nothing to lose." [24] Rostow, of course, did not examine the question of whether Ho Chi Minh, after 1945, was ever merely a guerrilla fighter who had nothing to lose. As the *New York Times* account of the Pentagon Papers shows, Rostow had enunciated the theory that

> a credible threat to bomb the industry Hanoi had so painstakingly constructed out of the ruins of the French Indo-China War would be enough to frighten the country's leaders into ordering the Vietcong to halt their activities in the South. [25]

Rostow was no newcomer to the idea of bombing Hanoi. In a speech delivered at Fort Bragg, North Carolina, in 1961, Rostow argued that a revolution such as the one the Vietcong were engaged in could be dried up by cutting off external sources of support and supply. The viewpoint Rostow advanced with persistence runs counter to the Strategic Survey of the effect of Allied bombing on German industrial production during World War II. Oddly enough, this study, in which both Rostow and Paul Nitze participated, showed that bombing can have the unintended result of *raising* the enemy's morale while marginally reducing his productive capacity.

Townsend Hoopes described Rostow as

> the closest thing we had near the top of the U.S. government to a genuine, all-wool, anti-Communist ideologue and true believer. An inductive thinker, he constructed theories—often with perception and ingenuity—but once the pattern of his belief was established, some automatic mental filter thereafter accepted only reinforcing data, while systematically and totally rejecting all contrary evidence no matter how compelling. In debate he showed a rare capacity for "instant rationalization" (as one col-

league put it), which amounted to a compulsion for buttressing his views by a rapid culling of the evidence immediately at hand; it did not matter whether the support that such evidence could provide was frail or nonexistent. His insensitivity to the opinions of others was legendary.[26]

Taylor and Rostow were destined to become public-policy celebrities in the sense C. Wright Mills intended. Men like William Bundy and John McNaughton, on the other hand, were little known to the attentive public until the Pentagon Papers in 1971 revealed the extent of their participation in the line of decision that led to the Americanization of the war in 1964–65. Bundy's career in the CIA and as Assistant Secretary for International Security Affairs in the Defense Department before he succeeded Hilsman as Assistant Secretary of State for Far Eastern Affairs, as well as his family background and personal relationship with Dean Acheson, would mark him as a candidate for a position within the national security elite. McNaughton became a major participant through his institutional position as a key civilian assistant to Secretary Robert McNamara. Hoopes, who became McNaughton's principal deputy in 1965, has reported that McNaughton was closer to McNamara on matters affecting Vietnam than was any other subordinate official.

William Bundy's views on Vietnam are largely derived from an examination of the Pentagon Papers. McNaughton's views are also indicated in the Pentagon Papers, and they are further clarified in Hoopes's book *The Limits of Intervention.*

Thus William Bundy, in a memo to Secretary Rusk dated January 6, 1965, prior to a meeting the Secretary was to have with President Johnson the same day, said in part:

In specific terms, the kinds of action we might take in the near future would be:

a. an early occasion for reprisal action against the D.R.V. [North Vietnam]
b. possibly beginning low-level reconnaissance of the D.R.V. at once

Concurrently with a. or b., an early orderly withdrawal of our dependents [from Saigon, but only if] stronger action [is] contemplated. If we are to clear our decks in this way—and we are more and more inclined to think we should—it simply must be, for this reason alone, in the context of some stronger action. . . .

Introduction of limited U.S. ground forces into the northern area of South Vietnam still has great appeal to many of us, concurrently with the first air attacks into the D.R.V. [Italics mine.] [27]

McNaughton had given Secretary McNamara a similar memorandum three days earlier, thus indicating that the civilian Assistant Secretaries in State and Defense shared a policy consensus. McNaughton sent another memo to McNamara on January 27 in which McNaughton stated and the Secretary agreed that the United States objective in South Vietnam was "not to 'help friend' but to contain China";—"both favored initiating strikes against North Vietnam," so reports the Pentagon Papers' anonymous analyst.[28]

Further from the *New York Times* account of these events:

Paraphrasing the memorandum and McNamara's comments, the writer says, "At first they believed these [air attacks] should take the form of reprisals; beyond that, the Administration would have to "feel its way" into stronger graduated pressures.[29]

The extent to which McNaughton was feeling his way is suggested in the *Times* account, which states that, though he doubted that the air strikes would actually help the situation in South Vietnam, he thought "they should be carried out anyway." McNamara, on the other hand, believed the air strikes probably would help, in addition to having a broader impact on the U.S. position in Southeast Asia.

THE DRIFT TOWARD ESCALATION

In January and February 1965 the President's civilian national security advisers were *drifting* into air warfare and gradual escalation of the American military effort in Indochina. Although the policy drift was connected in the minds of key participants to containment and the domino theory, it is clear that an essentially mindless quality marked this movement toward "bureaucratic homicide."

The drift toward bombing and direct military participation may be traced in some detail. Secretary McNamara made two trips to Vietnam that are pertinent to the analysis at this point. The first came in December 1963, the second in March 1964. After the first trip, McNamara offered the President a gloomy report noting that the Vietcong controlled much of the rice and people-rich Mekong Delta, south and west of Saigon, that portion which the French had been most reluctant to turn over to Ho Chi Minh nearly two decades earlier. At the same time, the President was offered the following not entirely unambiguous advice: "We should watch the situation very carefully, running scared, hoping for the best, but preparing for more forceful moves if the situation does not show early signs of improvement." [30]

Four months later, in March 1964 (ironically the month in which Johnson launched his war-against-poverty campaign in the Congress), McNamara returned from another Saigon visit reporting that "the situation has unquestionably been growing worse." McNamara also recommended planning for two programs of "new and significant pressures upon North Vietnam." The first would call for assaults against the Ho Chi Minh trail, through southeastern Laos, "hot pursuit" of guerrillas into Cambodia, "retaliatory bombing strikes" into North Vietnam on a "tit-for-tat" basis, and aerial mining of major North Vietnamese ports. All of these operations would be conducted by South Vietnam nationals, including the bombing strikes. The materiel, the logistics, and, of course, the plan itself were to be supplied by the Americans. The second program "would go beyond reacting on a tit-for-tat basis," McNamara explained to the President: "It would include air attacks against military and possibly industrial targets." The raids were to be conducted by the South Vietnamese air force *with the assistance of an American air-commando squadron (Farmgate) operating in planes with South Vietnamese markings. The air strikes would also be conducted by three squadrons of U.S. Air Force B-57 jet bombers flown in from Japan.* [Italics mine.] [31]

McNamara's proposals were adopted by the President at an NSC meeting on March 17, 1964. The President directed that planning should proceed energetically.

In the same memorandum Secretary McNamara expressed concern about the growth of "neutralist sentiment" in Saigon; his fear was that a coup might bring to power forces prepared to enter into a coalition government with the Vietcong forces *and invite the United States to leave!* It needs to be emphasized that both the President and his advisory circle were opposed to a political settlement between Saigon and the local Communists. Thus, President Johnson cabled Ambassador Lodge on March 20, 1964, that he wished to knock down "the idea of neutralization wherever it rears its ugly head, and on this point I think nothing is more important than to stop neutralist talk wherever we can by whatever means we can." [32]

In the middle of May 1964 the practice of the Johnson administration in moving slowly, deliberately, cautiously into escalation was altered to one of crisis management by the success of the Pathet Lao offensive on the Plaine des Jarres, an offensive that threatened the collapse of the pro-American government of Premier Souvanna Phouma in Laos. At this point the administration stepped up the T-28 strikes and on May 21 authorized low-altitude level reconnaissance by U.S. Navy and Air Force jets over areas held by the Pathet Lao and the North Vietnamese.

Meantime in Washington, William Bundy, John McNaughton, and William Sullivan, a State Department career officer who headed the interagency committee on Vietnam, were developing a thirty-day scenario culminating in full-scale bombing of the North. The plan was discussed at a meeting of the executive committee of the NSC on May 23. The President did not act in accordance with the Bundy scenario's proposal of air war until February 1965. Nevertheless, the *Times* exposé of the Pentagon Papers correctly points to the significance of the scenario in showing how far the Johnson national security advisory team had come in making the war in Vietnam an American enterprise months before Johnson's landslide victory at the polls.

> . . . the document is important because it reveals how far the Administration had progressed in its planning by this point and because a number of steps in the scenario were carried out piecemeal through June and July and then very rapidly during the political climate of the Tonkin Gulf clash.[33]

Bundy's scenario called for a joint Congressional resolution; the memo covering the scenario pointed out that military action would not begin until after favorable action on the joint resolution. William Bundy prepared a draft of the Tonkin Gulf resolution on May 25, more than two months before the North Vietnamese PT boats attacked the USS *Maddox* in the Bay of Tonkin.

After meetings on May 24 and 25 the executive committee of NSC, which included Rusk, McNamara, McCone, and McGeorge Bundy, decided to recommend to the President only piecemeal elements of the scenario, such as the sending of a Canadian emissary to Hanoi and the move for a joint resolution.

What was the United States objective in Vietnam in 1964? What purpose lay behind the elaborate scenario-building approach to air war and the use of United States ground troops?

The official position is perhaps best revealed in an excerpt taken from the opening paragraphs of the memo Secretary McNamara prepared for the President on March 16, 1964: "We seek an independent non-Communist Vietnam.... Unless we can achieve this objective in South Vietnam, almost all of Southeast Asia will probably fall under Communist dominance." [34]

The Secretary's memo went on to say that "the South Vietnam conflict is regarded as a test case of a U.S. capacity to help a nation meet a Communist 'war of liberation.' " [35]

One should not lose sight of McNamara's personal involvement in "proving" that the United States had the military capacity to help South Vietnam as it resisted this "war of liberation."

Townsend Hoopes summarizes the McNamara achievement:

U.S. "general purpose" forces were now organized to intervene swiftly and with modern equipment in conflicts of limited scope, well below the nuclear threshold.... This significant new military capability had been designed precisely to arrest or restore those deteriorating situations in the world where important or vital U.S. interests were judged to be engaged, to deal with ambiguous subversion-aggression characterized by little warning and low silhouette, to blunt national-liberation wars. *It was now ready.* To a rational activist like McNamara, with a very thin background in foreign affairs, it seemed entirely logical to employ a portion of this immense U.S. air power if that could arrest the spreading erosion in South Vietnam. [Italics mine.] [36]

It is virtually impossible to pinpoint the exact moment when the men within the inner circle of closed politics finally decided that United States "vital interests" in South Vietnam required direct military intervention on a large scale. But a careful reading of the documents they left behind suggests that the Vietcong mortar attack on the Bien Hoa air base on November 3, 1964, just two days before the U.S. Presidential election, had an unusually strong impact on their thinking. Ambassador Taylor urgently recommended air reprisals against the North. Hoopes believes that the Bien Hoa attack "crystallized" official U.S. determination to intervene.

CRISIS MANAGERS IN ACTION

It was at this precise moment in November 1964 that William Bundy and John McNaughton were drafting scenarios that bear a remarkable resemblance to certain events in 1965.

The following excerpts from a draft paper by William Bundy, dated November 5, suggest the way in which a modern crisis manager might approach the problem of managing other elements in the decision-making process:

1. Bien Hoa may be repeated at any time. This would tend to force our hand, but would also give us a good springboard for stronger action. The President is clearly thinking in terms of maximum use of a Gulf of Tonkin rationale.

2. Congress must be consulted before any major action, perhaps only by notification if we do a reprisal against another Bien Hoa, but preferably by careful talks with . . . key leaders. . . .

[The President] probably should wait until his mind is moving clearly in one direction before such a consultation, which would point to some time next week. Query if it should be combined with other topics (budget) to lessen the heat.

3. We probably do not need additional Congressional authority, even if we decide on very strong action. . . .

4. We are on the verge of intelligence agreement that infiltration has in fact mounted, and Saigon is urging that we surface

this by the end of the week or early next week. Query how loud we want to make this sound. . . .

5. A Presidential statement with the rationale for action is high on any check list. An intervening fairly strong President noise to prepare a climate for an action statement is probably indicated and would be important in any event to counter any SVN fears of a softening in our policy.[37]

John McNaughton's second draft of a paper, "Action for South Vietnam," dated November 6, listed U.S. aims as follows:

(a) To protect U.S. reputation as a counter-subversion guarantor;
(b) To avoid domino effect especially in Southeast Asia;
(c) To keep South Vietnam territory from Red hands;
(d) To emerge from crisis without unacceptable taint from methods.[38]

Inevitably McNaughton's memo found the situation in Vietnam "deteriorating."

Unless new actions are taken, the new government will probably be unstable and ineffectual, and the VC will probably continue to extend their hold over the population and the territory.[39]

The urgency which McNaughton felt is described as follows:

"Bien Hoa" having passed, no urgent decision is required regarding military action against the DRV, but (a) such a decision . . . should be made soon, and (b) in the event of another VC or DRV "spectacular," a decision (for at least a reprisal) would be urgently needed.[40]

There can be little doubt, in view of the Bundy and McNaughton drafts of November 5 and 6, that the national security managers in the level below the President were prepared, once the U.S. election was behind them, not to let another Bien Hoa go without an appropriate American military response, if they could help it.

McNaughton's November 6 draft memo listed three options, specifically noting that each of the three envisioned "reprisals" for any future VC-DRV "spectacular" against South Vietnam or against what the draft referred to as "U.S. assets" in South Vietnam.

The options McNaughton posed were (a) to continue present policies; (b) fast full squeeze; and (c) progressive squeeze-and-talk.

The following excerpts, taken from McNaughton's draft of November 6, help to explain the options:

Option A. Continue present policies. Maximum assistance within SVN and limited external actions in Laos and by the GVN covertly against North Vietnam. The aim of any reprisal actions would be to deter and punish large VC actions in the South, but not to the extent that would create strong international negotiating pressures. *Basic to this option is the continued rejection of negotiating in the hope that the situation will improve.*

Option B. Fast full squeeze. Present policies plus a systematic program of military pressures against the north, meshing at some point with negotiation, but with pressure actions to be continued at a fairly rapid pace and without interruption until we achieve our central present objectives.

Option C. Progressive squeeze-and-talk. Present policies plus an orchestration of communications with Hanoi and a crescendo of additional military moves against infiltration targets, first in Laos and then in the DRV, and then against other targets in North Vietnam. The scenario would be designed to give the U.S. the option at any point to proceed or not, to escalate or not, and to quicken the pace or not. The decision in these regards would be made from time to time in view of all relevant factors. [Italics mine.] [41]

The third option, Option C, carries obvious semantic advantages: communications are "orchestrated" while military moves rise in a "crescendo." Best of all, the options are viewed as being in U.S. hands while decisions are to be made in view of *all* relevant factors.

In point of fact, the United States position had been sharply narrowed by January 1965. Increasingly, the thinking within the inner circle turned toward the desirability of United States military action as a means of demonstrating a "strong" United States hand in Vietnam. The reason is clear: key members of the Presidential advisory team feared that the shaky Saigon regime was drifting toward an accommodation with the other side. A negotiated settlement was perceived as being antithetical to United States interests. William Bundy expressed the feeling in a January 6 memo that he sent to Secretary Rusk prior to a meeting the Secretary was to have with President Johnson the same day.

> I think we must accept that Saigon morale in all quarters is now very shaky indeed and that this relates directly to a widespread feeling that the United States is not ready for a stronger action and indeed is possibly looking for a way out,

Bundy observed. Bundy went on to express the view that American "weakness" was having a deleterious effect on Laos, Cambodia, and Thailand. The result, he warned, was the likelihood that the situation in Vietnam was "to come apart more rapidly than we had anticipated in November." [42] (Bundy's memo included the views of Michael Forrestal of the NSC Staff and Ambassador Unger, who had just been transferred back to Washington from Vientiane.) There was no question as to what "coming apart" might mean in this context.

> We would stick to the estimate that the most likely form of coming apart would be a government of key groups starting to negotiate covertly with the Liberation Front or Hanoi, perhaps not asking in the first instance that we get out, but with that necessarily following at a fairly early stage, [43]

the memo continued.

William Bundy did not see this as providing a desirable solution to the problem:

> In one sense this would be a "Vietnam solution," with some hope that it would produce a Communist Vietnam that would assert its own degree of independence from Peiping and that would produce a pause in Communist pressure in Southeast Asia,

he continued. Bundy also reasoned that under these hypothetical circumstances Laos would become "untenable" while Cambodia "would accommodate in some way." There was also "a grave question whether Thailand . . . would retain any confidence at all in our continued support." The "Vietnam solution," so-called, was to be opposed because "the outcome would be regarded in Asia, and particularly among friends, as just as humiliating a defeat as any other form." At this point Bundy appeared not so concerned about public opinion at home. In his words: "... the American public would probably not be too sharply critical, but the real question would be whether Thailand and other nations were weakened and taken over thereafter." [44]

PSYCHOLOGICAL DOMINO EFFECT

The line of policy that led to the Americanization of the war in 1965 was based on the assumption that an accommodation between Saigon and the other side could only have at least a psychological domino effect on Laos, Cambodia, and Thailand; this, in turn, would be "humiliating" in terms of American prestige.

The alternative was "stronger action," and "stronger action" meant a direct United States military "input" in the fighting in Vietnam. The grave difficulties this posed for the United States seem obvious. Thus, Bundy recognized that stronger action "commits the United States more deeply, at a time when the picture of South Vietnamese will is extremely weak." More than this, stronger action that included actions against North Vietnam would be disapproved by such major Asian nations as India and Japan. The probable effects on Saigon were also negative and minimal:

> Most basically, its stiffening effect on the Saigon political situation would not be at all sure to bring about a more effective government, nor would limited actions against the southern DRV in fact sharply reduce infiltration or, in the present circumstances, be at all likely to induce Hanoi to call it off.[45]

Why then did Bundy and his colleagues within the inner circle recommend an American military involvement? "Nonetheless, on balance we believe that such action would have some faint hope of really improving the Vietnamese situation." [46]

This is the faint hope which led to Rolling Thunder a month later.

Bundy's sentence quoted above has another clause: "... and,

above all, would put us in a much stronger position to hold the next line of defense, namely Thailand." [47]

South Vietnam was part of a line of defense connected to Thailand; both were connected to the doctrine of containment —and a faint hope!

The full flavor of Bundy's reasoning is revealed in the paragraph following the sentence just quoted:

> Accepting the present situation—or any negotiation on the basis of it—would be far weaker from this latter key standpoint. If we moved into stronger actions, we should have in mind that negotiations would be likely to emerge from some quarter in any event, and that under existing circumstances, even with the additional element of pressure, we could not get an outcome that would really secure an independent South Vietnam. Yet even [with] an outcome that produced a progressive deterioration in South Vietnam and an eventual Communist takeover, we would still have appeared to Asians to have done a lot more about it.[48]

It seems impossible to read the Pentagon Papers and not agree with Hannah Arendt's view that the decisions which led to military escalation and the Americanization of the war in Vietnam were formulated within the inner circle of closed politics *not* to protect vital American interests but out of an obsessive concern for the nation's "image." Arendt suggests that:

> The ultimate aim was neither power nor profit. Nor was it even influence in the world order to serve particular, tangible interests for the sake of which prestige, an image of the "greatest power in the world," was needed and purposefully used. The goal was now the image itself, as is manifest in the very language of the problem-solvers, with their "scenarios" and "audiences" borrowed from the theater. For this ultimate aim, all policies became short-term interchangeable means, until finally, when all signs pointed to defeat in the war of attrition, the goal was no longer one of avoiding humiliating defeat but of finding ways and means to avoid admitting it and "save face." [49]

The Vietcong attack on Pleiku, February 6, 1965, provided the opportunity for a response that would be in terms of stronger American action, with all the risks and disadvantages William

Bundy had recognized, as well as a number he did not discuss in his January 6 memo. In a situation filled with irony, the Vietcong attack came at a moment when McGeorge Bundy and John McNaughton were visiting in Vietnam. They were quick to recommend air warfare against the North in line with the William Bundy–John McNaughton scenario of May 1964, as well as the Taylor–Rostow report of November 1961.

The Presidential decision was taken presumably on the faint hope that it might improve the rapidly deteriorating situation in Saigon, and that it would perhaps demonstrate to our "friends" in Laos, Cambodia, and Thailand the United States determination to resist a "humiliating defeat" in Southeast Asia.

The specific steps taken were as follows. The initial blow was a Vietcong attack on a United States military advisers' compound at Pleiku in the central highlands on Saturday, February 6. This was combined with an attack on an Army helicopter base at Camp Holloway, four miles away. Nine Americans were killed; seventy-six were wounded. Less than fourteen hours later on Sunday, February 7, U.S. Navy jets from two 7th Fleet carriers delivered bombs and rockets upon North Vietnamese barracks and staging areas at Donghoi, a guerrilla training base forty miles north of the 17th parallel. Tit-for-tat.

The *New York Times* version of the Pentagon Papers comments:

> Though conceived and executed as a limited one-shot tit-for-tat reprisal, the drastic U.S. action, long on the military planners' drawing boards, under the operational code name Flaming Dart, precipitated a rapidly moving sequence of events that transformed the character of the Vietnam war and the United States role in it.[50]

Since the Vietcong were also prepared to play tit-for-tat, this was followed by a guerrilla attack on American barracks at Quinhon on the central coast. On February 11 the President launched a second and heavier reprisal raid, Flaming Dart II. Two days later, on February 13, 1965, the President decided to begin Operation Rolling Thunder, the sustained air war against North Vietnam. The President's public announcement came on February 28.

CONCLUSION

Eugene Eidenberg, one of the first scholars to examine the role of inner-circle civilian advisers in the Presidential decision to escalate in 1965, believes that our Vietnam policy during this period was the result of a "process" rather than the consequence of a single major choice. We have seen something of this incremental group decision-making process at work in this chapter. This is the mode of bureaucratic decision-making. But we have also seen the extent to which the "process" was influenced over time by certain key figures in the inner circle located institutionally just below the President and how they perceived the struggle in Vietnam. William Bundy and John McNaughton, for example, saw only a faint hope that bombing would strengthen a rapidly deteriorating political and military situation in Vietnam; but as 1964 gave way to 1965, they were apparently driven in desperation, more than in hope, to recommend direct American military action; to do less, they reasoned, would likely lead to a compromise political settlement between Saigon and the NLF (National Liberation Front). This was to be avoided because, in time, the dominoes in Laos, Cambodia, and Thailand would fall, and then the United States would have suffered a "humiliating defeat." The fact that the President evidently shared this viewpoint does not diminish the importance of the role these civilian crisis managers played in structuring the policy of escalation and Americanization of the war in Vietnam, 1964–65.

Professor Charles Lindblom, the prime author of the theory of incremental decision-making as it relates to public policy, reminds us:

> Policy making . . . is what it is because participants in the policy-making process behave as they do. Men make policy; it is not made for them. They also make the policy-making machinery. Much of what might be called the "irrationality" of the policy-making system is, therefore, the consequence of the irrationality of the participants in it. It may be serious—even disastrous. But it represents the quality of man's control over policy making, not the absence of it.[51]

We have not been examining men *in general*, but individual men who were members of a coherent and persistent national security policy elite. The judgments they made relating to Vietnam in 1964–65 effectively determined the United States role in Southeast Asia. Townsend Hoopes, an original Cold War professional in the days of Truman and Acheson who returned to the Pentagon in January 1965, on the eve of escalation, has said of "the men closest to President Johnson" that "the tenets of the Cold War were bred in the bone." [52] They accepted uncritically the established doctrine.

Thus, Secretary McNamara in his annual statement on the nation's military posture told the House Armed Services committee on February 18, a date virtually coinciding with the launching of Rolling Thunder: "The choice is not simply whether to continue our efforts to keep Vietnam free and independent, but rather, whether to continue our struggle to halt Communist expansion in Asia." [53]

Speaking of early 1965 and the atmosphere in which these decisions were made, Hoopes later observed: "Consultation, even knowledge of the basic facts, was confined to a tight circle of Presidential advisers, and there appears to have been little systematic debate outside that group." [54]

Hoopes was also to become a helpful guide through the period when members of the policy elite, as well as technocrats, lost confidence in their own program as applied in Southeast Asia. The next chapter examines Vietnam decision-making, 1967–68.

In the meantime, we have seen the crisis managers and problem-solvers at work. The United States activity in Vietnam became a testing of our new military capacity developed within the framework of flexible response, a corollary to containment that did not question the ends of the strategic doctrine. We picked the case to test our own notions about our military role in so-called "wars of national liberation." Vietnam was the object, and our crisis managers were the prime maneuverers. The thing most dreaded was a "Vietnamese solution"—what President Johnson called "neutralism"—because a settlement between the parties would bring the war of national liberation to an end without fully testing our new "theory."

Chapter Nine Notes

1. "The Vietnam Conflict: The Substance and the Shadow." Report of ad hoc Senate committee led by Senator Mike Mansfield. A report to the Committee on Foreign Relations, U.S. Senate, dated January 6, 1966. 89th Congress; 2nd Session.

2. Ibid, pp. 2–3.

3. Ibid, p. 3.

4. Eugene Eidenberg, "The Presidency: Americanizing the War in Vietnam," in *American Political Institutions and Public Policy,* ed. Allan P. Sindler (Boston: Little, Brown, 1969), p. 120.

5. Ibid.

6. Richard J. Barnet, *Roots of War* (New York: Atheneum, 1972), p. 67.

7. Eidenberg, "The Presidency," p. 82.

8. *New York Times,* February 25, 1965.

9. Ibid.

10. Eidenberg, "The Presidency," p. 94. The language used suggests that the adviser was probably Walt W. Rostow.

11. See George Ball's memo reprinted as "Top Secret: The Prophecy the President Rejected," in *The Atlantic Monthly,* July 1972, pp. 36–49.

12. Barnet has called attention to the manner in which the national security policy elite has manipulated the public in recent years; see especially his chapter 5, "The Operational Code of the National Security Managers," in *Roots of War.*

13. Eidenberg, "The Presidency," p. 108.

14. Ibid.

15. See *New York Times,* March 14, 1965.

16. Eidenberg, "The Presidency," p. 110.

17. Quoted ibid., p. 111.

18. Ibid., p. 113.

19. Mansfield committee report, p. 11.

20. Ibid.

21. Ibid., p. 12.

22. Ibid.

23. P.P. (NYT), p. 104.

24. P.P. (NYT), p. 241

25. Ibid.

26. Townsend Hoopes, *The Limits of Intervention* (New York: David McKay, 1969), pp. 20–21.

27. P.P. (NYT), p. 342.

28. Ibid.

29. Ibid.

30. P.P. (NYT), p. 242.

31. All the quotations in this paragraph are taken from P.P. (NYT), pp. 242–43.

32. Ibid., p. 244.

33. P.P. (NYT), p. 247.

34. P.P. (NYT), p. 278.

35. Ibid.

36. Hoopes, *The Limits of Intervention*, p. 18.

37. P.P. (NYT), pp. 363–64. (It is curious that William Bundy with no political-legislative background thought it necessary to offer guidance to LBJ on the matter of dealing with the Congress.)

38. Ibid., p. 365.

39. Ibid.

40. Ibid.

41. P.P. (NYT), p. 366.

42. P.P. (NYT), pp. 340–41.

43. Ibid.

44. All the quotations in this paragraph are taken from Bundy's memo in P.P. (NYT), p. 341.

45. Ibid.

46. Ibid.

47. Ibid.

48. Ibid.

49. Hannah Arendt, *Crises of the Republic* (New York: Harcourt Brace Jovanovich, 1972), pp. 17–18.

50. P.P. (NYT), p. 343.

51. Charles Lindblom, *The Policy Making Process* (Englewood Cliffs, N.J.: Prentice Hall), p. 108.

52. Hoopes, *The Limits of Intervention*, p. 12.
53. Annual Military Posture Statement by Secretary of Defense Robert McNamara to Armed Services committee, House of Representatives, February 18, 1965, as quoted in Department of State Foreign Policy Briefs, March 1, 1965.
54. Hoopes, *The Limits of Intervention*, p. 7.

10   DEMORALIZATION OF AN ELITE, 1967–68

*A feeling is widely and strongly held that "the
Establishment" is out of its mind. The feeling is that
we are trying to impose some U.S. image on distant
peoples we cannot understand (anymore than we can
the younger generation here at home), and that we
are carrying the thing to absurd lengths. Related to this
feeling is the increased polarization that is taking place
in the United States with seeds of the worst split in
our people in more than a century. The King, Galbraith,
etc., positions illustrate one near-pole; the Hebert and
Rivers statement on May 5 about the need to disregard
the First Amendment illustrates the other. In this
connection, I fear that "natural selection" in this environment will lead the Administration itself to become
more and more homogenized—McBundy, George Ball,
Bill Moyers are gone. Who next?*

John McNaughton (May 6, 1967)

The Pentagon Papers

The quotation above is taken from a memorandum that Assistant Secretary of Defense John McNaughton sent to Secretary
Robert McNamara on May 6, 1967. McNaughton had been serving as Robert McNamara's principal deputy on Vietnam matters
for nearly three years when he wrote these words. He had been
a leading figure in preparing the scenario that led to the launching of the Rolling Thunder campaign in 1965. By the spring of
1967 disenchantment with the results of United States participation in the war was beginning to take its toll within the ranks
of the inner circle of civilian cold-war decision-shapers. Several
leading members of the national security policy elite had left
government, returning to privileged positions in the academic,
foundation, and legal establishment. McGeorge Bundy was named
president of the Ford Foundation. Carl Kaysen and Francis Ba-
tor, two of his principal deputies in the White House, moved,

respectively, to Princeton and to MIT. George Ball returned to the private practice of law. Michael Forrestal rejoined his Wall Street law firm. Cyrus Vance was about to return to his. None of these gifted men, including Ball, who was already publicly identified as a critic of the United States role in Vietnam, expressed any public criticism of the policy on the occasion of leaving government service.

As these men abandoned their positions in the decision-making apparatus, there was a marked tendency for the balance to shift within the inner circle of closed politics toward the "hard liners," the most notable case being the growing influence of Walt Rostow after he succeeded McGeorge Bundy as Special Presidential Assistant for National Security Affairs. At the same time, pressure mounted on those who entertained doubts about the wisdom and effectiveness of increasing the level of direct American military participation in the Vietnam war. McNaughton became a key figure among the new skeptics because his doubts were shared with McNamara, and McNamara carried exceptional influence at the Presidential level. In the spring of 1967, McNaughton, badly shaken by his experience and near exhaustion, wished to return to civilian life, as the others were doing; but McNamara urged him to stay on, arranging for McNaughton to move to the position of Secretary of the Navy, replacing Paul Nitze, who in turn was succeeding Cyrus Vance as Deputy Secretary. Vance was leaving the Pentagon for reasons of health.

In this complicated game of musical chairs, Paul Warneke replaced McNaughton as Assistant Secretary for International Security Affairs. (Warneke, a Washington attorney, was educated, appropriately enough, at Yale and Columbia Law School.) It was during this period of transition within the policy elite that Robert McNamara commissioned the study that ultimately produced the Pentagon Papers. This action was taken in the middle of June. John McNaughton, his wife, and their eleven-year-old son were killed in the crash of a commercial airliner on July 19, 1967. Less than a month later Robert McNamara courageously broke away from the administration's fixed position on bombing at a public hearing conducted by Senator Stennis's Preparedness subcommittee.

FATAL FLAW OF STRATEGY

The extent of McNaughton's disillusionment with the course of events in Vietnam was revealed publicly for the first time in Townsend Hoopes's *The Limits of Intervention*, published in 1969. The accuracy of the portrait drawn by Hoopes is further substantiated in documents now available in the Pentagon Papers.

The following excerpts are taken from the same May 6 memo written by John McNaughton previously referred to at the beginning of this chapter; he was commenting on a May 5 "rough draft" memo that was being prepared for the President:

> I am afraid there is a fatal flaw in the strategy in the draft [memo]. It is that the strategy falls into the trap that has ensnared us for the past three years. It actually *gives* the troops while only *praying* for their proper use and for constructive diplomatic action.
>
> It follows that the "philosophy" of the war should be fought out now so everyone will not be proceeding on their own major premises and getting us in deeper and deeper.[1]

Hoopes reports that McNaughton at this point was both "physically exhausted" and "deeply disenchanted" with the administration's Vietnam policy. This is one of the rare occasions when we find reasonably firm evidence indicating that certain members of the national security policy advisory group were affected by considerations of the internal, domestic consequences of United States military activity in Southeast Asia. Further, McNaughton's plea for a discussion of the "philosophy" of the war is notable in that it came as late as it did in the sequence of events. His plea also suggests how far the decision-makers had gone in taking the nation into a war that was very imperfectly understood, *even within elite circles!*

McNaughton was at work on a Presidential draft memo, "Future Actions in Vietnam" dated May 19, aimed at hitting the President where it would hurt most.

> Most Americans do not know how we got where we are, and most, without knowing why, but taking advantage of hindsight, are convinced somehow we should not have gotten this deeply

in. All want the war ended and expect their President to end it. Successfully, or else.[2]

After one White House session, McNaughton returned to the Pentagon complaining to Hoopes: "We seem to be proceeding . . . on the assumption that the way to eradicate Viet Cong is to destroy all the village structures, defoliate all the jungles, and then cover the entire surface of South Vietnam with asphalt." [3]

These were hardly the words of a true believer. McNaughton's disillusionment, shared with McNamara, must be seen in relation to where the United States stood in Vietnam as the summer of 1967 approached. Although General Westmoreland had 470,000 United States troops, he was about to ask for an additional 200,000 men; such a request, in turn, would necessitate a decision to call up the Reserves. At the same time the effectiveness of the sustained bombing of North Vietnam had come into serious question. The bombing had been designed, so the theory ran, to lift the morale of the people in the South, to add pressure on Hanoi to end the war by way of negotiation, and to reduce the flow of men and materiel from the North. Intelligence reports had cast doubt about the extent to which any of these three objectives was being served by the bombing campaign.

Once again McNaughton had written strong words to his superiors about the domestic implications.

"There may be a limit beyond which many Americans and much of the world will not permit the United States to go," he observed in the same May 19 memo. "The picture of the world's greatest super-power killing or seriously injuring 1,000 non-combatants a week while trying to pound a tiny backward nation into submission on an issue whose merits are hotly disputed, is not a pretty one." [4]

Although McNaughton's untimely and tragic death means that his version of the critical decisions relating to Vietnam will never be available, Hoopes's book fortunately helps in filling the gap. Hoopes's thesis is that the change in policy announced by President Johnson on March 31, 1968, reflected a growing disenchantment among technicians serving at the level just below the President. Their position was not based on grounds of morality, but rather on the conviction that the series of military actions taken between February 1965 and the summer of 1967 simply had "not worked." The Americanization of the war had not produced the political results aimed for in official United States policy.

HOOPES BACKGROUND

Hoopes is an appropriate figure to guide the way through the labyrinth of Vietnam policy-making, 1967–68, as key decisions took shape within the inner circle. Like so many of the leading civilian militants we have met in this analysis, Hoopes was educated at an exclusive private school (Hotchkiss) and Yale. (Other Yale alumni who have appeared in the course of this analysis: Acheson, the Bundys, Gilpatric, Harriman, Lovett, Nitze, Rostow, Stimson, Warneke, and Hilsman, if his Ph.D. counts.) After serving as a young Marine officer in World War II, Hoopes became a first-generation Cold War technician serving first as assistant to the chairman of the House Armed Services committee, 1947–48. He was then selected by James Forrestal, the first Secretary of Defense, as one of his staff assistants. Hoopes served as assistant to Forrestal, Louis Johnson, General George Marshall, and Robert Lovett during the formative years of the Cold War, 1948–53.

Hoopes was actively involved in the preparation of NSC–68 in 1950. He is an admirer of Paul Nitze, whom he has described as follows:

> Basically a hardliner in his attitudes toward Russia, China, and Communism, he [Nitze] was however noted for his sense of proportion, knowledge, and sound judgment on matters of both policy and technique. He was that rare combination of intellectual and manager, as well as a man of unquestioned loyalty and integrity. To those seriously concerned with the effective management of defense affairs, he was a pearl of great price.[5]

Like Nitze, Hoopes left government service during the Eisenhower years. He was to return, curiously enough, in January 1965, just a few short weeks before the Rolling Thunder bombing campaign was launched. Since Hoopes had served in 1957 as executive secretary to the military panel of the Rockefeller Brothers' Special Study Project that produced the Rockefeller Report on defense policy and strategy, his acceptance of a position in McNamara's Pentagon presumably reflected a general professional-philosophic agreement with the new defense program based, as it was, upon concepts derived from both the Gaither and Rockefeller reports. The position Hoopes accepted was Deputy Assistant Secretary of Defense for International Security Affairs. As the Number 2 man in the Pentagon's "Little State Department," Hoopes functioned as principal deputy to John McNaughton, the Assistant Secretary, who, in turn, was serving as Robert McNamara's principal civilian assistant on Vietnam. In time Hoopes was to become McNaughton's friend and admirer, as well as his deputy. It was the perceived effect of the war on McNaughton from which Hoopes apparently drew much of the substance to support the thesis of his book *The Limits of Intervention.* As Hoopes saw it, a small group of civilian technocrats who helped shape the decisions to escalate and to Americanize the war in 1964–65 were actively seeking ways of reversing official policy in 1967–68. This group finally made its case with Clark Clifford, who replaced McNamara as Defense Secretary on March 1, 1968. President Johnson announced a partial bombing halt as part of his startling "abdication" speech on March 31.

Hoopes noted that McNamara's Pentagon lacked a policy-planning approach to national security decision-making comparable to that which had been established in the late 1940s. The White House appeared as a center of "action and reaction"; it was "not an ideal place for reflective thought on difficult, longer-term problems." [6] The result, as Hoopes perceived it shortly after his return to Washington in 1965, was "a notable absence of the kind of comprehensive policy analysis (and its lucid documentation) that had constituted our national policy guidance in the Truman-Acheson period." [7] National security decision-making was proceeding in the mid-1960s on the basis of concepts and assumptions drawn from the earlier period. Containment was the accepted dogma, unexamined and uncriticized in official circles. The President's advisers continued to function as "children of the Cold War" at a time when "many of the majoɪ

elements of the Cold War mosaic had undergone drastic transformation or had ceased to exist." [8]

Although his basic assignment as McNaughton's deputy did
not relate directly to Vietnam, Hoopes nevertheless grew increasingly concerned about the course of events in that beleaguered
country. Finally, he decided to offer his views to John McNaughton in a lengthy memorandum dated December 30, 1965. The
memo said in part:

> bombing of the North has been singularly inconclusive. The
> basic simplicity of the North Vietnamese transport system, com-
> bined with oriental resignation, ingenuity and abundant coolie
> labor have neutralized the bombing effect. Infiltration of the
> South has not diminished, but has in fact increased; moreover,
> the bombing has served to stiffen North Vietnamese resistance,
> both directly and by giving the Chinese an added argument for
> a policy of no concessions. At the same time it has made it more
> difficult for the Soviets to play a moderating role.[9]

Hoopes's memo to McNaughton was prepared at approximately the same time Senator Mansfield offered his pessimistic
report to the President. The Americanization of the war was less
than a year old. There were 170,000 United States troops in Vietnam. We were in the midst of a thirty-seven-day bombing halt
and a Presidential peace initiative. After arguing that an enlarged bombing program would tend to unify, rather than to split,
the Communist world and increase United States isolation in
the so-called Free World, Hoopes continued:

> Similarly, I see no rewards or gains to be reaped by a further
> infusion of US manpower; this likewise looks to be inconclusive.
> Even a doubling—from 170,000 to 350,000 men—could be
> matched without great difficulty by North Vietnamese man-
> power and Chicom-Russian equipment. . . . The best we could
> hope to gain would be a further stalemate at a higher level of
> effort, human sacrifice and risks.[10]

Hoopes's sense of proportion was offended by what he saw
in Vietnam; he was concerned about the "unbalancing" of the
United States' global position "by giving too much emphasis—
and too many resources—to Vietnam." [11] McNaughton agreed
with the general thrust of the memorandum, Hoopes later re-

ported, and even admitted readily enough the evidence of an emerging stalemate: yet he remained at this time a staunch supporter of official policy. Hoopes reasons:

> Like others who had participated in shaping the decisions of February, he was not yet prepared to acknowledge that the judgment of senior officials whom he respected, or his own judgment, had been mistaken in fundamental respects.[12]

McNAMARA REEVALUATION OF POLICY

The evidence available does not permit an exact pinpointing of the date when Robert McNamara realized that United States action in Vietnam had resulted in a military stalemate. The process of disenchantment was probably gradual, as it was for McNaughton. McNaughton appears to have been one of the very few colleagues with whom McNamara shared any doubts he may have had about the course of the war, and a number of documents published in the Pentagon Papers reveal that McNaughton increasingly expressed his concern to McNamara. Indeed, in the case of McNaughton the cumulative growth of doubt, disenchantment, and disillusionment shines through clearly in the documents. Although he has not written about his role in Vietnam, the first important *public* expression of Robert McNamara's doubt came in his statement before the Stennis Committee (the Preparedness Investigating subcommittee of the Senate Armed Services committee) August 25, 1967, on the issue of the air war against North Vietnam. The committee members shared in the frustration widely felt in executive inner circles that the Americanization of the war was producing an apparently endless and inconclusive stalemate. From the uniformed military came the charge that it was "civilian"-imposed restrictions that stood in the way of "victory." Hence the Stennis committee decided to ventilate the bombing issue by hearing testimony from ten high ranking military officers and the Secretary of Defense. The military leaders, to no one's great surprise, advocated a program of wider and heavier bombing. Secretary McNamara was placed in the unenviable position of defending a course that had led to a military stalemate while justifying its continuation. It may even be that McNamara did not know whether the President was prepared for further intensification of the military effort. In any event, McNamara had read the intelligence reports, and he knew that the bombing effort was of dubious value.

McNamara's statement to the committee made it clear that unless the United States were to shift to a program of indiscriminate bombing aimed at annihilating the people of North Vietnam the air war could accomplish nothing more than to continue putting "a high price tag on North Vietnam's continued aggression." [13] McNamara saw nothing in the record which would indicate that Ho Chi Minh's regime could be bombed to the negotiating table. His conclusion, therefore, was that an intensified campaign from the air against Hanoi was destined to be counterproductive. Such an approach, he told the committee, however tempting, would surely prove to be "completely illusory." "To pursue this objective would not only be futile, but would involve risks to our personnel and to our nation that I am unable to recommend," [14] McNamara concluded.

Hoopes summarizes the situation in late August after McNamara had drawn the line:

> The statement rang with intellectual authority, and courage. It was also a personal testimonial, for McNamara had not cleared it with either Rusk or the White House. Probably beyond his intention, it had the effect of polarizing opinion on the bombing.[15]

It had still another effect of numbering McNamara's days as Secretary of Defense. Since the Secretary's statement before the Stennis committee represents almost the only public statement by a leading member of the inner circle reflecting doubt on our military course in Southeast Asia, its significance should not be minimized. Although McNamara's courageous move did nothing to improve his effectiveness as a Presidential adviser, it did encourage other members of the inner circle and their technical assistants to continue their efforts at turning around the official course of action in Vietnam. It was a long time coming.

Actually, McNamara personally favored stopping the bombing as early as October 1966, according to the Pentagon Papers. The same study suggests that he was ready to accept the possibility of a coalition government, including the NLF, by May 1967. The extent of McNamara's deviation from the Johnson administration's official line is indicated by the fact that he commissioned the study which produced the Pentagon Papers, an action initiated on June 17, 1967, almost six months before President Johnson nominated McNamara for the presidency of the World Bank. McNamara was himself the recipient of a steady diet of pessimism from John McNaughton throughout 1966; this continued until McNaughton's tragic death in mid-July 1967. In a memo dated January 18, 1966, McNaughton warned his chieftain: "We are in an escalating military stalemate. The present United States objective in Vietnam is to avoid humiliation," [16] he continued.

None of this is to suggest that McNamara had taken George Ball's place as the official dissenter. Six days after receiving McNaughton's memo, quoted above, McNamara ordered more bombing strikes, although he did not see that they would help very much. The Secretary also recommended raising the troop level above 400,000 men before the end of 1966. Operationally, he was recommending more of the same in an escalating military stalemate. At the same time, McNamara was reporting to the President his assessment that "the odds are about even that, even with the recommended deployments, we will be faced in early 1967 with a military standoff at a much higher level, with pacification still stalled, and with any prospect of military success marred by the chances of an active Chinese intervention and with the requirement for the deployment of still more U.S. forces." [17]

ELECTRONIC BARRIER

McNamara and his closest associates, seeking a solution short of endless escalation, turned in desperation during the summer of 1966 to a group of leading military scientists. The scientists met in a secret seminar amidst the peaceful charms of Wellesley, Massachusetts. By the end of August they had produced a truly bizarre notion: namely, that an anti-infiltration barrier should be built across the northern border separating North from South

Vietnam. The recommendations of the group were placed in Secretary McNamara's hands in September. The Pentagon Papers report that the thinking of this group of eminent scientists had "a powerful and perhaps decisive influence in McNamara's mind." [18]

With respect to the Rolling Thunder air bombardment campaign, the scientists offered the following observation: "As of July 1966, the U.S. bombing of North Vietnam has had no measurable direct effect on Hanoi's ability to mount and support military operations in the South at the current level." [19]

North Vietnam was basically a subsistence agricultural country with little industry and a transport system both primitive and flexible; hence, the scientists found it "quite unlikely" that any expansion of the bombing activity would reduce the infiltration rate. More troublesome was the manner in which the scientists demolished the assumption which underlay the bombing: that bombing reduces a country's will to resist. To a man such as McNamara who believed in the efficacy of measurement, there must have been special discomfort in being advised that this problem defied measurement. The report stated:

> It must be concluded that there is currently no adequate basis for predicting the levels of U.S. military effort that would be required to achieve the stated objective—indeed, that there is no firm basis for determining if there is any feasible level of effort that would achieve these objectives. [20]

So the scientists, ingenious to the end, offered their own proposal, the building of an electronic barrier across the Demilitarized Zone. There would be an anti-troop system made up of small mines (gravel mines) and an anti-vehicle system composed of acoustic sensors capable of guiding aircraft to the target. Most of the equipment would be dropped by planes; ground troops would be used periodically to check the condition of the equipment. The estimated original cost of installation was $800 million. It would take a year to build.

The Rube Goldberg nature of the proposal is apparent in the description that the scientists included in their report to Secretary McNamara, who was "apparently strongly and favorably impressed." [21] (One has to assume, it seems to me, that McNamara was exhausted and that he had run out of options.)

> The anti-troop infiltration system (which would also function against supply porters) would operate as follows. There would be a constantly renewed mine field of non-sterilizing Gravel (and possibly button bomblets), distributed in patterns covering interconnected valleys and slopes (suitable for alternate trails) over the entire barrier region. The actual mined area would encompass the equivalent of a strip about 100 by 5 kilometers. There would also be a pattern of acoustic detectors to listen for mine explosions indicating an attempted penetration. The mine field is intended to deny opening of alternate routes for troop infiltrators and should be emplaced first. On the trails and bivouacs currently used, from which mines may—we tentatively assume—be cleared without great difficulty, a more dense pattern of sensors would be designed to locate groups of infiltrators. Air strikes using Gravel and SADEYES would then be called against these targets. The sensor pattern would be monitored 24 hours a day by patrol aircraft. The struck area would be reseeded with new mines.[22]

If there was to be a system to keep out people, there had also to be one to keep out vehicles.

> The anti-vehicle system would consist of acoustic detectors distributed every mile or so along all truckable roads in the interdicted area, monitored 24 hours a day by patrol aircraft, with vectored strike aircraft using SADEYE to respond to signals that trucks or truck convoys are moving. The patrol aircraft would distribute self-sterilizing Gravel over parts of the road net at dusk. The self-sterilizing feature is needed so that road-watching and mine-planting teams could be used in this area. Photo-reconnaissance aircraft would cover the entire area each few days to look for the development of new truckable roads, to see if the transport of supplies is being switched to porters, and to identify any other change in the infiltration system. It may also be desirable to use ground teams to plant larger anti-truck mines along the roads, as an interim measure pending the development of effective air-dropped anti-vehicle mines.[23]

The fact that Robert McNamara and John McNaughton viewed the mechanical barrier proposal with favor indicates the extremes to which otherwise "rational" men were driven in seeking a technological solution to the problem of keeping Ho Chi Minh's forces out of South Vietnam. There seems little reason to doubt that McNamara and McNaughton, after the summer of 1966, would advance any further recommendations to increase the level of military escalation only out of sheer desperation and surely not with any real hope of achieving a political settlement. The record bears out Daniel Ellsberg on this vital point.

NEW AIR OFFENSIVE

In the meantime, however, the President, acceding to pressure from the Joint Chiefs of Staff, had approved an extensive air war against North Vietnam's fuel system. The objective was nothing less than the "strangulation" of that system with the intelligence community reporting to McNamara in July 1966 that 70 percent of Hanoi's oil storage capacity had been destroyed. Still the flow of men and materiel from the North continued undiminished. The Pentagon Papers report the air attacks against the oil system an abject failure. As usual, North Vietnam's "adaptability and resourcefulness had been greatly underestimated." [24]

> McNamara, for his part, made no effort to conceal his dissatisfaction and disappointment at the failure of the . . . strikes. He pointed out to the Air Force and the Navy the glaring discrepancy between the optimistic estimates of the results . . . and the actual failure of the raids to significantly decrease infiltration.[25]

The study also notes that the attack on Hanoi's oil system was "the last major escalation of the air war recommended by Secretary McNamara." [26]

In the autumn of 1966 McNamara, increasingly aware that United States actions in Vietnam were not working, continued the process of recommending more troop increments. Upon his return from a trip to Vietnam in October, the Defense Secretary advised the President that "pacification has if anything gone backward." The air war had not "either significantly affected infiltration or cracked the morale of Hanoi." [27] In November

McNamara approved giving the Joint Chiefs new troop authorizations that would take the total to 469,000 by the following June. He did this while advising the President he saw no evidence that the addition of more troops would substantially change the situation; the bombing was yielding only "very small marginal returns" with "no significant impact" on the war in the South.[28] Three months later the President approved a new air offensive, this one to include attacks on power plants, the mining of rivers, and the relaxation of restrictions on air raids near Hanoi and Haiphong. Although McNamara's influence with the President appears to have declined steadily throughout 1967, the Secretary nevertheless fought a skillful rearguard action against General Westmoreland's persistent effort to obtain authorization for an additional 200,000 men. McNamara was still resisting the large troop increase, which would have taken the American force level above 700,000 men, as he left the government service at the end of February 1968.

McNaughton's tragic death in July 1967 and the White House announcement in November that McNamara was to be nominated for the presidency of the World Bank meant that two of the most highly placed Pentagon skeptics were to be replaced by men who might undertake a fresh assessment of the escalating military stalemate. Paul C. Warneke was McNaughton's successor in charge of the Pentagon's "little State Department," a unit where doubts ran deep among the technicians. Clark Clifford officially assumed his duties as Defense Secretary on March 1, 1968. Clifford, who had helped shape the original containment policy in Truman's White House, was thought to be an authentic "hawk" on Vietnam.[29] Yet he had been in office only one month when the President announced a sharp reversal of the official United States posture in Vietnam. Clifford, of course, assumed his position at a time when the mood of disenchantment was strongly felt within the inner circle of closed politics. When General Wheeler returned from Saigon in February 1968 requesting a 40 percent increase in the force level already set at 510,000, Hoopes reports that a number of key civilians in the Pentagon felt that at last a way was open for them "to assert their strong anti-escalation position in a favorable psychological and managerial climate." [30] Clifford and Warneke replaced men who were the victims of a profound intellectual and moral fatigue. The new Defense Secretary had the further advantage of not having been connected with the fateful decisions taken between 1961 and 1967.

The Tet offensive, spectacularly launched on January 31, had a pronounced effect on the American public, since it dramatized the continuing military capacity of Hanoi and the NLF despite the American military escalation. It also appears to have strengthened the resolve of the dissenters among the national security managers. Paradoxically, the Tet offensive also encouraged the Joint Chiefs, who apparently saw a new opportunity for pushing the Johnson administration into mobilization, insisting that a call-up of reserves must precede any new deployment of additional troops.

Two days before Clark Clifford was to be sworn in as Secretary of Defense, President Johnson asked Clifford to serve as chairman of an ad hoc task force whose assignment would be to examine the Wheeler-Westmoreland request for 206,000 more troops *and to determine the domestic implications.* Hanoi's Tet offensive had accomplished this much: this time the situation in Vietnam was to be reviewed by American officials in a context that included domestic concerns. Most of the main participants presumably viewed the assignment as being fairly narrow: namely, how to provide the troops the generals wanted while staying within the limits of "acceptable" domestic consequences, since it was well known that the question of calling up the reserves was directly related. Clifford, however, immediately broadened the inquiry by saying that he was interested in pursuing the basic question of whether the United States should continue following the course it was on in Vietnam. What was likely to happen if the United States were to put in an additional 200,000 men? Would a 700,000-man United States Army bring us any closer to our elusive objectives? Was General Westmoreland following a sensible strategic concept? [31]

After a preliminary meeting of the task force on February 28, the new Defense Secretary held day and evening sessions throughout the first week in March. McNamara attended the first meeting as Secretary of Defense; he did not participate in subsequent meetings. Clifford was joined by Paul Nitze, Paul Warneke, and

Phil Goulding from the Defense Department. (Goulding was Assistant Secretary for Public Affairs.) Dean Rusk headed the State Department delegation, which also included Undersecretary Nicholas Katzenbach, William Bundy, and Philip Habbib. General Wheeler represented the Joint Chiefs; Richard Helms, the CIA; and Walt W. Rostow, the White House. Henry Fowler, Secretary of the Treasury, and General Maxwell Taylor rounded out the group.

POLARIZATION OF ADVISERS

Clifford soon discovered that the inner circle of advisers was divided into two fairly distinct groups. Rostow, Wheeler, and Taylor saw a new opportunity in the Tet offensive since the enemy had abandoned his elusive guerrilla tactics in favor of actions that exposed his troops all over the countryside. The Vietcong in combination with the regular forces infiltrated from the North would not be able to stand up to American military might in a protracted war, according to this line of reasoning. The granting of the request for an additional 206,000 troops would provide an opportunity of decimating the enemy forces. The other group —led by Nitze, Warneke, and Katzenbach—noted the profound change in public mood at home, unfavorable to a protracted war. The American public sensed a situation in which neither side could win a military victory; hence, an approach was needed based on the kind of staying power that might lead to a compromise political settlement. In military terms, the second group argued for "no further troop increases (for the enemy could and would match them), a pullback from isolated posts like Khesanh, and a far less aggressive ground strategy designed to protect the people where they live." [32]

As the discussion developed in the several meetings of the Clifford task force, it became even clearer that most of the principals were on one side while a number of the deputies found themselves on the other. Rusk, Rostow, Wheeler, and Taylor, joined by Fowler, generally favored meeting Westmoreland's request and getting on with the war. The deputies, far more skeptical, were typically seeking an alternative approach to the escalating military stalemate. The deputies possessed one apparent slight advantage: Warneke and Goulding stayed with Clifford after every session. When the task force adjourned, Warneke and Goulding stayed on to prepare counterarguments that the chairman might use, as he saw fit, the next day. The advantage, if it was one, proved not very great, at least in the first instance. The task force drafted a set of recommendations that confirmed existing policy in Vietnam, and Clifford forwarded the report to the President. At the end of the first week in March there was little reason for the doubters to draw encouragement from the discussions. Nonetheless, the deliberations in early March had the effect of deepening Clifford's mounting doubts about the wisdom of the United States' course of action in Vietnam.[33]

Soon there were forces at work in domestic politics that helped in forcing the issue at the ultimate level of Presidential decision-making. The Presidential primary election in New Hampshire, March 12, catapulted Senator Eugene McCarthy to a position of prominence as a critic of the Johnson administration's Vietnam policy. Four days later Senator Robert Kennedy announced his candidacy for Democratic Presidential nomination. Arthur Goldberg, Ambassador to the United Nations and an old political associate of Lyndon Johnson, advised the President on March 16 to stop the bombing of North Vietnam.

The President invited a group of elder statesmen, known as the Senior Informal Advisory Group, to meet with him in Washington on March 25 and 26. The Wise Men, as the press labeled them, included Dean Acheson, George W. Ball, General of the Army Omar Bradley, McGeorge Bundy, Arthur H. Dean, Douglas Dillon, Justice Abe Fortas, Ambassador Goldberg, Henry Cabot Lodge, John J. McCloy, Robert D. Murphy, General Matthew B. Ridgeway, and Cyrus R. Vance. The members of the group, widely experienced in administering national security matters during the period of the Cold War, presumably represented establishment thinking. Indeed, as recently as November 2, 1967, virtually the same group—which then included Clark Clifford, private citizen, as a participant—had approved a further escalation of the air war. But this time the Wise Men were divided in their counsel, with an apparent majority urging the President to reverse the trend in Vietnam.[34]

The following excerpt from Townsend Hoopes's more detailed account of the President's meeting with the Wise Men suggests the nature of the discussion which took place.

> At luncheon with the President, McGeorge Bundy performed the role of *rapporteur,* summarizing with appropriate shadings what he felt to be the general view in the wake of the previous evening's briefings and discussion, and of the further debate just before lunch. The consensus, as Bundy described it, was that the present policy had reached an impasse, could not reach its objective without the application of virtually unlimited resources, was no longer being supported by a majority of the American people and therefore required significant change.[35]

Although Bradley, Murphy, and Fortas challenged Bundy's summary as not accurately reflecting the view of the full group, Dean Acheson supported Bundy's summary, saying that it clearly reflected his view and that he thought it represented the great majority present. General Taylor, who was unhappy about the advice the President received on this occasion, nevertheless later reported that the majority consensus favored some change in the course of American action. The President should not have been totally surprised to find leading members of the Cold War establishment seeking a change of course. He had consulted with Dean Acheson toward the end of February about the situation in Vietnam. It has been reported that Acheson startled the President by suggesting that the Joint Chiefs of Staff did not know what they were talking about. When the President expressed shock and asked for Acheson's independent judgment, the former Secretary of State responded by asking that he be given the resources for an independent study. Acheson spent the next two weeks in his own investigation of the United States involvement in Vietnam. The group of technicians Acheson relied upon included three men who were later to brief the Wise Men: Philip Habib of State, who was William Bundy's principal deputy on Vietnam; George Carver, a top CIA counterinsurgency specialist; and Major General William DuPuy of the Joint Chiefs of Staff organization. On March 15, having completed the examination,

Acheson offered the President his views at a luncheon meeting. According to Hoopes, who presumably learned of the meeting from Acheson, the President was told that:

> he was being led down a garden path by the JCS, that what Westmoreland was attempting in Vietnam was simply not possible—without the application of totally unlimited resources "and maybe five years." He told the President that his recent speeches were quite unrealistic and believed by no one, either at home or abroad. He added the judgment that the country was no longer supporting the war.[36]

One has to assume that such blunt talk coming from a leading architect of containment struck home. A week later the President suddenly recalled General Westmoreland, announcing that the general would be appointed Army Chief of Staff. In this fashion the signal went out on March 22 that the Johnson administration was altering its approach to the "problem" of Vietnam.

SOFTENING THE HARD LINE

The change in official policy announced by the President in his famous television address of March 31, coupled with his decision not to seek reelection, appears to have been at least partially the result of a long process of group decision-making within the inner circle of closed politics. The ultimate nature of Presidential decision-making on a matter of this extreme seriousness and complexity will perhaps remain a partial mystery indefinitely. Clark Clifford put it well with reference to the March 31 decision: "Presidents have difficult decisions to make and go about making them in mysterious ways. I know only that this decision, when finally made, was the right one." [37]

But the President's decision also was influenced by the review of policy that Clifford conducted as soon as he became Secretary of Defense. The change of leadership in the Pentagon that was effected in March 1968 coincided with the change in our course in Vietnam. The analysis in this chapter centering on the level just below the President and relying on Pentagon Papers documents shows how doubt, disenchantment, disillusionment, even despair, spread among the civilian militants throughout 1967 and on into the early months of 1968; the demoralization of the technocratic elite was influential as it affected, first, Robert McNamara and then his successor, Clark Clifford. This same growing sense of doubt had an impact on certain leading members of the foreign policy establishment. It seems fair to assume that the Bundy-Acheson relationship may have been crucial in effecting this linkage of the technocrats and establishment spokesmen.

The decisions taken by the President in March recognized what the technocrats and establishment representatives were urging: a new course of action because American military forces numbering half a million men were locked into an escalating military stalemate. The uneasiness at the top of the national security decision-making apparatus had little or nothing to do with moral revulsion over the course we were on; the difficulty was that our military escalation simply had not produced the results intended. Sustained bombing of the North had not weakened Hanoi's will, nor had it succeeded in cutting off the infiltration of men and materiel, as the Tet offensive dramatically demonstrated. This time decisions relating to Vietnam were shaped in a bureaucratic setting in which two fairly distinct groupings within the inner circle argued over quite different approaches to the Vietnam war. Equally important, the decisions in March 1968 were made in an atmosphere in which the critical state of American public opinion was consciously recognized by technicians and foreign policy establishment members as being pertinent to the decisions taken. The decision to halt the bombings and to seek negotiations with Hanoi affords an unusual opportunity to students of policy-making because the linkages between public opinion, technocratic behavior, and elite influence on a "big decision" here attain a certain visibility.

CONCLUSION

This account has stressed the connection between the disillusionment of civilian militants and the change in policy. It needs also to be recognized that the forces within the inner circle of closed politics that were resisting the change were not exactly feeble. The nature of bureaucratic politics within the inner circle of national security decision-making has seldom been examined with care; much of the process has been veiled in secrecy. In this case, one of the major participants who favored a continuation of military escalation has recorded his unhappiness with the decisions taken in March 1968 and has offered his interpretation of the events leading up to the President's dramatic announcement of March 31. General Maxwell Taylor believed at the time and still believes that it was a mistake *not* to continue applying additional elements of American military power in Vietnam. Taylor was present during the meeting of the Wise Men on March 25 and 26. He reports that the participants expressed their views to President Johnson with "the utmost candor." According to his account, Acheson, Vance, and McGeorge Bundy offered "highly pessimistic" views, while Robert Murphy, Justice Fortas, and General Taylor advocated following the course of action the administration was already on. Taylor notes that the same Wise Men, Clifford included, had met only a few short months before, in November, and had readily endorsed the President's policy, including more bombing. This time, he ruefully records, "they arrived apparently convinced in advance that the policy was a failure and must be changed." [38]

Obviously something had effected an important change in elite thinking in a short period of time. General Taylor blames "the media" and the "Pentagon doves." Whereas conventional analysis suggests that the Tet offensive produced a massive shift in public opinion, which in turn fed into a growing process of disillusionment among the civilian militants and crisis managers, General Taylor assumes that the media had a subtle effect on such leading figures as Bundy, Vance, and Acheson. It seems best to let General Taylor assess this factor in his own words:

> For what it is worth, my own explanation was based on my estimate of the effect of media reporting of the Tet offensive on many of our visitors. Most of them lived in the news enclaves dominated by the *New York Times*, and *Washington Post*, both of which were strongly anti-Administration with regard to Vietnam. It is all very well to say that intelligent sophisticates of the

Eastern Establishment would be immune to the effects of media bias, be it ever so subtle.[39]

General Taylor knew better.

General Taylor's reference to "our visitors" is to the Wise Men. (One is interested to see that the general looks upon these men as being sophisticated members of "the Eastern Establishment.") His view of the men he refers to as "Pentagon doves" also deserves some attention:

> Also I strongly suspected that the Pentagon doves with whom I had become acquainted during the recent strategy review had got to some of the visitors and had impregnated them with their doubts.[40]

General Taylor does not inquire into the manner in which the so-called "Pentagon doves" developed their doubts, nor does he identify which of the doves impregnated doubt in the minds of men such as Acheson, Bundy, and Vance. This chapter, following Hoopes's revealing account and relying heavily on the Pentagon Papers for substantiating data, has attempted to discover who some of the leading Pentagon doubters were. We also have been interested in understanding the manner in which their doubts grew. The point General Taylor misses is that the doubts were real and that they were related to the course of events in Vietnam (the Tet offensive occurred; it was not invented by the *New York Times* and the *Washington Post*) and to the impact these events were having in weakening the delicate psychic fabric that unites the American polity.

General Taylor, usually credited with being an extraordinarily sophisticated and literate representative of the professional military officer corps, derives certain lessons from the nation's tragic experience in Vietnam. The first lesson arises from "the many limitations and inhibitions placed on the use of our national power in the course of the struggle." Considering the vast resources committed to Vietnam, Taylor concludes that "the effective power generated therefrom seems to have been relatively small." The author of flexible response believes that this particular war was limited by a kind of "inefficiency in the use of national power" that is inherent in the system. (If the "defect" is "inherent," one wonders why the general advocated the doctrine in the first place.)

> There is nothing in our past history which would justify the assumption that in a crisis we will find experienced, tough-minded operators at the control points of the governmental power train, individuals capable of getting the maximum horsepower from the machine. Experience indicates the contrary to be likely [General Taylor observes].[41]

There is, in the first place, the inconvenient matter of periodic elections making it "reasonably certain" that "for one or two years out of every eight" the operators of the governmental machine will be "for the most part inexperienced newcomers." While they may be able men, they are also likely to be "neophytes in the most complex business in the world, unacquainted with the telephone numbers of their equally inexperienced colleagues." [42]

This does seem a curious argument as applied to the Kennedy-Johnson years. John F. Kennedy, son of an experienced and tough-minded operator, first came to Washington as a young congressman in 1947 after covering the Potsdam and San Francisco conferences as a correspondent. Lyndon Johnson was first elected to the House in a special election in 1938; he was a protégé of FDR, Sam Rayburn, and Richard Russell. It is doubtful that anyone in our history brought more relevant experience to the running of "the governmental power train" than Lyndon Johnson. Dean Rusk, McGeorge Bundy, Paul Nitze, and William Bundy were not neophytes in national security matters, and they knew one another's telephone numbers. They all prided themselves on being tough-minded crisis managers. And who was a more accomplished manager of complex systems than Robert McNamara?

Perhaps the problem lies elsewhere. General Taylor has still another explanation. Not only are our leaders likely to be new and untrained, they are also likely to be "timid," that is, overly cautious in the use of military power.[43] As Maxwell Taylor sees it:

> Many Americans have an inbred bias against the premeditated use of power as being an exercise in power politics which, like

secret diplomacy and clandestine intelligence, is offensive to the virtue of a respectable democracy. . . . This prejudice leads to questioning the efficacy of military force as an instrument of policy.[44]

This is where the issue should be joined. General Taylor sincerely believes that timidity and a certain moral squeamishness led to a gradualist approach in the application of our military power in Vietnam; this "weakness" in our national style was destined to lead to "failure." Other Americans saw in Vietnam the tragic misapplication of disproportionate military power in support of global containment as a substitute for a program of social reform in Southeast Asia. We persisted in following the containment dogma until finally a number of the original architects, Acheson and Clifford among them, were not able to see what or who it was we were containing in Indochina. It was in this troubled condition that we entered the 1970s.

Chapter Ten Notes

1. P.P. (Off.), Vol. 5, "U.S. Ground Strategy and Force Deployments, 1965–1967," IV Program 5, pp. 46–47.
2. Ibid.
3. Townsend Hoopes, *The Limits of Intervention* (New York: David McKay, 1969), p. 51.
4. P.P. (Off.), Vol. 5, p. 156.
5. Hoopes, *The Limits of Intervention*, pp. 199–200.
6. Ibid., p. 6.
7. Ibid.
8. Ibid., p. 9.
9. Ibid., p. 44. (Despite his concern about Vietnam policy, Hoopes accepted appointment as Undersecretary of the Air Force in 1967 and stayed on until the Nixon administration took office in January 1969.)
10. Ibid., p. 45.
11. Ibid., p. 46.
12. Ibid., p. 48.
13. Quoted in ibid., p. 87.
14. Ibid.
15. Ibid, p. 88.
16. P.P. (NYT), p. 472.
17. P.P. (NYT), p. 473.
18. P.P. (NYT), p. 484.
19. Ibid.
20. Ibid.
21. P.P. (NYT), p. 485.
22. P.P. (NYT), p. 508.
23. Ibid.
24. P.P. (NYT), p. 480.
25. P.P. (NYT), pp. 480–81.
26. Ibid.

27. P.P. (NYT), p. 517.

28. P.P. (NYT), p. 512.

29. See Richard J. Powers, "Clark Clifford, The Wisdom of Hindsight," *The New Republic*, Vol. 166, No. 14 (April 1, 1972), for a critical view of Clifford's original Cold War stance during the Truman years.

30. Hoopes, *The Limits of Intervention*, p. 165.

31. Ibid., p. 172.

32. Ibid., p. 175.

33. See Clark M. Clifford, "A Vietnam Reappraisal: The Personal History of One Man's View and How It Evolved," *Foreign Affairs*, Vol. 47, No. 4 (July 1969).

34. Maxwell Taylor, *Swords and Ploughshares* (N.Y.: W. W. Norton, 1972), p. 390.

35. Hoopes, *The Limits of Intervention*, p. 216.

36. Ibid, p. 205.

37. Ibid., p. 224.

38. Taylor, *Swords and Ploughshares*, p. 390.

39. Ibid., p. 391.

40. Ibid.

41. Ibid., p. 402.

42. Ibid.

43. Ibid. The restraint shown by our "timid" leaders is indicated in a study conducted by Professors Arthur H. Westing and E. W. Pfeiffer, which revealed that the United States forces used 26 billion pounds of explosives in Indochina between 1965 and 1971. This is twice what the U.S. used in all theaters in World War II. It has been estimated that this explosive tonnage would have the energy of 363 Hiroshima-type nuclear bombs. Of the 26 billion pounds, 21 billion were exploded in South Vietnam, the country we wish to "save." The bombs and shells are estimated to have left 21 million craters in South Vietnam, displacing 2,75 billion cubic yards of earth and spraying fragments over 26 million acres of countryside. This calculation, of course, tells us nothing about the human tragedy of Vietnam. See report by Anthony Lewis, op-ed page *New York Times*, May 8, 1972, entitled "Scorch Their Earth."

For even more horrendous facts about the U.S. bombing in

Vietnam, see Robert Kleiman's review of *The Air War in Indo-china*, revised ed., ed. Raphael Littauer and Norman Uphoff (Boston: Beacon Press, 1972) in the *New York Times Book Review*, August 13, 1972.

44.   Ibid, pp. 402–3.

11 ELITE RESPONSIBILITY

Not since we withdrew into comfortable isolation in 1920 has the prestige of the United States stood so low.

Hamilton Fish Armstrong (1972)

One of the most profound consequences of the bureaucratic revolution was the coming to power of a national security elite remarkable for its cohesiveness, consistency, and, above all persistence. . . . Never has a self-defining, self-selecting and self-perpetuating group held power so long in American politics.

Richard J. Barnet (1972)

The analysis in this book centers on the activities of a coherent elite in formulating, establishing, and administering the national security policy of the United States during the first quarter-century following the dawn of the nuclear era. Previously, academic political science has neglected the role of the strategic elite in national policy-making; the neglect is present in the conceptualization of the problem and hence in much of the empirical analysis. A further complication, noted by Daniel Ellsberg among others, is that "few analysts personally command experience or data concerning more than a few of the many dimensions" of the process in which national security decisions are made.[1] The study of national security policy has been dominated in recent years by scholars who are themselves part of the phenomenon we label "civilian militancy": that is, they are civilians who accept the premise that American military power is a benign element to be used in establishing PAX AMERICANA. Richard Barnet reminds us:

> The men in charge of those areas of the social sciences most relevant to current policy, such as "Russian studies," "Chinese

studies" or "National Security studies" were the most religious in staying within the bounds of official orthodoxy.[2]

The cases examined in this book are those that are readily available in the scholarly literature. They were prepared by participant-observers within the inner circle and by those few privileged scholars who have had access to highly classified data. For example, Hammond's study of NSC–68 and Halperin's article on the Gaither report present authoritative accounts of documents that are labeled "Top Secret." All these original studies avoid the question of elite responsibility.

The latest trend, as shown in Graham Allison's study of the Cuban missile crisis, may very well lead to a preoccupation with bureaucratic politics that may further obscure the issue of responsibility. Ronald Steel notes the danger:

> This is what is disturbing about studies such as Allison's and the impact they are having on the teaching of political science. It is not that their concern is unserious but rather that it is peripheral to the central question of political responsibility. In avoiding that question—indeed, implying that it does not exist—the architects of the study of bureaucratic politics are not, as Allison maintains, providing a "fundamental change in intellectual style" so much as they are offering a cool way out.[3]

A methodological risk is run in examining only crisis decision-making, just as we may be in danger in concentrating as much attention as we have in this book on so-called big decisions. There is the possibility that day-by-day, non-crisis decision-making may take place in a quite different mode. For this reason, we make explicit the assumption that the Pentagon Papers, selective and limited as they may be in some respects, afford a fair view of the nature of day-by-day decision-making as it takes place at a high technocratic and policy level, just below the Presidency. Our analysis is based upon the hypothesis that high-level technocrats in close association with established elite figures (they are sometimes one and the same, as in the case of the Bundy brothers) bear a major responsibility for the structuring of a series of major national security *policy-establishing* decisions. Elite leaders take the initiative in manipulating opinion and in creating the policy climate within which ultimate and formal

Presidential decision-making takes place. By foreclosing alternatives, they carry a special responsibility for the locked-in nature of national security decision-making in the recent past. The incrementalism of day-by-day decision-making, as revealed in the Pentagon Papers, took place within the conceptual framework previously established by the elite-sponsored containment doctrine.

EXTENSIONS OF CONTAINMENT

We find a direct connection between the decision to drop the A-bombs on two Japanese cities in 1945 and the series of decisions that led to the Americanization of the war in Vietnam in the 1960s. Our tragic involvement in Vietnam was not an aberration. The American role in Vietnam was not the result of historic accident. To the contrary, it was the product of a rigid adherence to, and an uncritical acceptance of, global containment, the established Cold War doctrine. The doctrine, centerpiece of the United States Cold War mosaic, was largely the creation of a small, closely knit, narrowly based policy elite, several of whose leading members influentially shaped the initial decision to drop atomic bombs on Hiroshima and Nagasaki. The initial decision was made in secret within the office of the Secretary of War by a small number of upper-class civilians months before the ultimate decision was formally made by the President. At this level, it was *assumed* that the bombs would be used. The precise decision that the first generation of civilian militants—Stimson, McCloy, Lovett, Bundy, Conant, Compton, Bush, et al.—made was simply to drop the bombs on densely populated cities. In making this decision, Stimson and his coterie were, of course, concerned to bring the war in the Pacific to a speedy conclusion; they were also profoundly influenced by their own apprehensions about the presence of Soviet power in the postwar world. The bomb was used in Japan out of a desire —which could have been felt only within the elite since no one else knew the bomb existed—to constrain Soviet behavior in Europe. The bombs were used to carry a message to Stalin as well as to the people of Japan.[4]

Having ushered in the age of atomic weapons, leading members of the elite assumed the initiative in putting together the policy of *containing* Soviet power and influence. Far from being pressured by public belligerence, the elite feared a popular mood that would limit an interventionist strategy. The first public statement of containment came in the Truman Doctrine, a deliberately contrived reaction to a specific and limited situation in the eastern Mediterranean in 1947. The doctrine was conveniently expressed in universal language, hardly a semantic disadvantage for a strategic doctrine destined to turn global less than three years later. The elitist preconceptions of Dean Acheson, principal leader of the national security elite for most of the crucial 1947–52 period, are highly visible in his own writings and have been illuminated further in Gaddis Smith's recent biography. Acheson found this meaning in the NSC–68 experience:

> If it is helpful to think of societies as entities, it is equally so to consider their direction centers as groups of cells, thinking cells, action cells, emotion cells, and so on. The society operates best, improves its chances of survival most, in which the thinking cells work out a fairly long-range course of conduct before the others take over—provided it has a little bit better than average luck. We had an excellent group of thought cells.[5]

This analysis agrees that activity within the thinking cells of society's direction centers has a vital bearing on public policy. Gaddis Smith tells us that Acheson surrounded himself to an extraordinary degree with men who agreed with him. Acheson's men seldom paused to reexamine their assumptions; his advisers either thought as he did from the beginning or quickly learned to do so, Smith reports. The thinking cells of the Achesonian elite featured the gradual elimination of Kennan's dissenting views about the nature of the Soviet threat. Acheson was willing, for his own tactical and polemical purposes, to combine Soviet ideology and the power of the Russian state into one simple, aggressive, expansionist drive. Acheson seems not to have been concerned that a Soviet policy planner using the same two factors might have offered much the same assessment of the United States drive. United States strategic doctrine underlying the whole course of the Cold War, as stated publicly in the Truman doctrine and subsequently in such secret documents as NSC–64 and NSC–68, was based upon a deliberately exaggerated version of the Soviet military threat. It was an elite assumption that the language of military power was the only language the Soviet leaders would understand, just as it was an elite notion that Stalin had placed his nation on a course of unlimited aggrandizement aimed at eventual world domination. It was an elite-initiated decision to underwrite French colonialism in Indochina and to picture Indochina as being vital to the security interests of the United States; it was a decision which ignored Lippmann's warning that a weak border state ally is likely to be a liability requiring a diversion of power, money, and prestige to support and maintain it without bringing the United States nearer to resolution of the main conflict.

Members of a small, closely knit group of civilian militants provided the essential leadership within the inner circle of closed politics in urging the development of a huge, permanent military machine featuring nuclear weaponry as a means of establishing a global order compatible with American "principles." A policy elite led the way to global containment and the new militarism. Members of the same elite continued to play a key role in recruiting the high-level technocrats who were to manage the military bureaucracies once the doctrine was established and the military machine perfected.

BOLSTERING THE COLD WAR

Pluralist-oriented political science, which tends to dominate the senior levels of the established academic order, contends that containment was a popular doctrine enjoying widespread public support. The argument is at least slightly specious, since the formulation of strategic doctrine appears to be an elite preserve. The public can at most confirm the broad outlines of a strategic doctrine; it cannot conceptualize or articulate it. In this instance, the public was conditioned to accept the premises upon which the elite built the containment doctrine. In order to obtain the "appropriate" public and congressional response, leading members of the elite exaggerated the Soviet military threat, not once but repeatedly. Fearful that the public mood would shift to one of neo-isolationism, the elite offered a view of the Soviet menace that was designed to be "clearer than the truth." The Munich syndrome was real enough; there was also a neutrality-isolationism syndrome, derived from the 1930s, that affected elite behavior. Elite leaders were profoundly apprehensive that the forces of parochialism which find a natural home in the Congress would reenforce a shift in public mood back to isolationism (that is, away from global interventionism). For this reason the public was offered a Cold War "theory" based on an official exaggeration of the Soviet military threat. As William R. Caspary has shown, the American public's attitudes toward the Soviet Union have tended to follow what the general public *has been taught* about the nature of the menace.[6] Elite leaders assumed responsibility for creating the appropriate Cold War climate in this country.

John Lewis Gaddis, who is far from being a so-called "revisionist" historian, concludes that the Truman doctrine represented a deliberate effort to "educate" the public to the necessity of "getting tough with Russia." The doctrine was, in Gaddis's words, "a form of shock therapy." While the effort succeeded in shocking Congress and the public, Gaddis notes that in the process those who were "educating" the public "trapped themselves in a new cycle of rhetoric and response which in years to come would significantly restrict the Administration's flexibility in dealing with Moscow."[7] (It is ironic that Dean Acheson was to find that the anti-Communist crusade had been joined by Senator Joseph McCarthy, who then became Acheson's chief vilifier.)

The long-range implications of the so-called "educational" campaign in behalf of the Truman Doctrine have been summarized by Gaddis:

> By presenting aid to Greece and Turkey in terms of an ideological struggle between two ways of life, Washington officials encouraged a simplistic view of the Cold War which was, in time, to imprison American diplomacy in an ideological strait jacket almost as confining as that which restricted Soviet foreign policy. Trapped in their own rhetoric, leaders of the United States found it difficult to respond to the conciliatory gestures

which emanated from the Kremlin following Stalin's death and, through their inflexibility, may well have contributed to the perpetuation of the Cold War.[8]

Pluralist scholars, accustomed to making a number of happy assumptions about their own model, tend to place an unusual burden of proof on those who would examine elite behavior in American society. Thus, Roger Hilsman, who is content with the concept "front men" in reference to the makers and shapers of national security policy, was able without apparent embarrassment to dismiss C. Wright Mills as a mere "pamphleteer." A standard pluralist contention, starting with Robert Dahl, holds that the effectiveness of elite domination of policy cannot be proved unless it can be shown that the ostensible elite held policy preferences that prevailed against the alternative views of other groups. The argument ignores the other face of power: that is, the manner in which a dominant elite forecloses alternatives by not examining them. When George Kennan offered his comparatively mild dissent from the premises of military containment, he was simply excluded from Acheson's inner circle. Pluralists have long been complacent about the difficulty weaker groups face in bringing forth alternatives in a total system that discourages the posing of alternatives. In view of this complacency, it is perhaps not surprising that academic political science has shown little curiosity about the remarkable persistence of the containment dogma for more than two decades. In domestic policy the bias of pluralism is now recognized, especially among younger scholars who see the system biased toward stability and against fundamental reform. American pluralism, examined in terms of domestic policy, describes a society in which some concerns, aspirations, and interests are privileged while others are placed at a disadvantage; among the very weak, the disadvantages are severe. At the same time, political science has largely ignored such questions as: who led the way to global containment; who encouraged and manipulated public fears of an exaggerated Soviet menace; and—perhaps the most significant question a pluralist should raise—*whose interests were served and whose were neglected* in a political system that placed the incessant demands of the new militarism *above* every other important public need?

LACK OF ELITE COMPETITION

Pluralism assumes a vigorous competition among elites over policy. In a number of leading cases, widely spaced in time, this study finds that elite competition in vital matters of national security was virtually nonexistent. Such "competition" as there was appears to have been limited to ways and means of carrying on the established doctrine while the doctrine itself remained sacrosanct. Flexible response, one of the few conceptual innovations, was brought forth in elite circles as a means of making containment more effective in the Third World. National security policy appears to be a special area in which few of the normal checks and balances apply. As Christopher Lasch has noted, "In the formulation of American policy in Southeast Asia, no conflicting claims had to be accommodated. Pluralism and countervailing power were non-existent." [9] The relative ineffectiveness of popular and legislative controls in constraining elite activity is enhanced by the now well-established (thanks to establishment sponsorship) tradition of bipartisanship, which has the effect of depoliticizing a whole range of foreign policy issues. Congressional power in national security matters is lodged in the hands of senior legislators who have dominated the armed services and appropriations committees throughout the Cold War and who are not prepared to offer a critique. The Senate Foreign Relations committee has offered the sole Congressional forum for criticism of United States Cold War activity. The committee has no direct influence on the structure of our armed forces or the military budget. This weakening of the Congressional control has been accomplished by the expedient of giving the senior Congressional barons—and their home districts and states—a sizeable stake in the new militarism. Operating in a Cold War policy climate, with a public conditioned to accept the containment dogma and a Congressional power structure set against a searching review of policy objectives, the day-by-day conduct of policy has tended to devolve upon bureaucratic managers who have felt little need for a new rationale.

The ascendancy of the policy elite, led originally by Stimson and then by Acheson during the formative years of the Cold War, carries implications for constitutionalism. The elaborate checks and balances that are assumed to apply in national decision-making have a tendency to stop at the water's edge. There is another implication: if the foreign policy–defense cluster invites exceptional influence by a few people, the ideological orientation of such an elite becomes a matter of supreme importance. Elite presuppositions may remain unexamined for long periods of time, unless challenged. It now seems clear that a small group of men in intimate contact with one another, drawn from a relatively narrow and privileged base and not representing many of the diversities of our society, came to a foreign policy ideological consensus in the postwar years. They were able to apply this consensus with few contradictions up to the late 1960s.

Members of the elite were ultimately engaged in a form of "group think" in which opposing interpretations, heretical thoughts, and even intelligence estimates were discounted, modified, and, if necessary, ignored. By the mid-1960s effective decision-making as it related to Vietnam was held within a small and shrinking circle whose members were increasingly shut off from other aspects of reality. The mode of thinking within the elite structure has been described as that which "persons engage in when *concurrence-seeking* becomes so dominant in a cohesive in-group that it tends to override realistic appraisal of alternative courses of action." [10] At the same time, those engaged most significantly in deceiving the public displayed a subtle weakness for self-deception; and, if intellectual arrogance knows no certain constitutional check, the ancient sin of pride affords a Biblical remedy. Leading members of the elite did not see themselves engaged in a plot against the public, even when they were offering official lies. They were fearful that the public could not be relied upon to support that which the elite deemed to be in the public interest: that is, a long-range program in which the United States performed the role of world policeman. They perceived their responsibility as including the task of protecting the unreflective mass citizenry from the consequences that would follow a retreat to isolation. The elite feared popular indifference toward the historic American mission whereby the United States would lead the way to the establishment of a sound, stable world order: PAX AMERICANA. Acheson and Rusk, extrapolating from the Munich experience, saw Stalin as another Hitler bent upon aggression against weaker neighboring states. George Kennan has described the viewpoint that prevailed among the military and political planners concerning the Soviet threat:

> They could not free themselves from the image of Hitler and his timetables. They viewed the Soviet leaders as absorbed with the pursuit of something called a "grand design"—a design for the early destruction of American power and for world conquest. In vain I pleaded with people to recognize that this was a chimera; that the Russians were not like that; that they were weaker than we supposed; that they had many internal problems of their own; that they had no "grand design" and did not intend, in particular, to pursue their competition with us by means of a general war.[11]

The elite soon found the difference between their own vision of a world order and their perception of the Kremlin's "grand design" irreconcilable. Despite his own doubts, George Kennan's Mr. X article remains an authoritative statement of the historical and philosophical grounds upon which containment was originally based.

CIVILIAN MILITANCY

With few exceptions, the members of the national security policy elite were civilians who characteristically urged reliance upon superior military power rather than upon negotiation with the Soviets.[12] The same group of men provided much of the leadership in maintaining the new permanent military establishment. Barnet calls attention to the fact that seventy of the ninety-one people who held the very top jobs between 1940 and 1967 —Secretaries of Defense and State, Secretaries of the three services, the Chairman of the Atomic Energy Commission, and the Director of the CIA—have been businessmen, lawyers for businessmen, and investment bankers:

> Between 1940 and 1967, when I stopped counting, all the first and second-level posts in the huge national security bureaucracy were held by fewer than four hundred individuals who rotate

through a variety of key posts. The temporary civilian managers who come to Washington to run America's wars and preparations for war, the national security managers, were so like one another in occupation, religion, style and social status that, apart from a few Washington lawyers, Texans, and mavericks, it was possible to locate the offices of all of them within fifteen city blocks in New York, Boston and Detroit.[13]

The essential limitations of such a group have been noted by Henry A. Kissinger:

the typical Cabinet or sub-Cabinet officer in America comes either from business or from the legal profession. But very little in the experience that forms these men produces the combination of political acumen, conceptual skill, persuasive power, and substantive knowledge required for the highest positions of government.[14]

The elite did not simply articulate the doctrine but was also largely responsible for recruiting the top management of the national security bureaucracies. In doing so, the national security area was sufficiently closed to pluralist forces so as to shut off any very effective challenge to the established doctrine. Regardless of the assessment one makes of Soviet intentions—the point of Kennan's dissent from the Acheson-Nitze line—the disadvantages that accrue in a situation when one ideological mind-set goes virtually unchallenged for an extended period appear obvious. Kennan has said this as well as anyone: the containment doctrine lost much of its rationale with the death of Stalin and with the development of the Soviet-Chinese conflict. But the doctrine had turned dogma, and it persisted. The doctrine remained unexamined for so long that men who evidently did not accept its premise continued to act officially as if they were ideologues.

Kissinger has offered a partial explanation for the seeming rigidity of elite behavior:

The rigidity of American policy is therefore often a symptom of the psychological burden placed on our policymakers. Policies developed with great inner doubt become almost sacrosanct as soon as they are finally adopted. The reason is psychological. The *status quo* has at least the advantage of familiarity. An attempt to change course involves the prospect that the whole searing process of arriving at a decision will have to be repeated.[15]

Observers as diverse in background, interest, and bias as Hannah Arendt, Graham Allison, Richard Barnet, William Domhoff, John K. Galbraith, David Halberstam, Godfrey Hodgson, Christopher Lasch, and Maxwell Taylor have made reference in recent writings either to the elite or to the foreign policy "establishment." Barnet's study examines in depth the background, education, techniques, and ideas of this "small, durable and exclusive club." Christopher Lasch finds essentially the same elite emerging after a long struggle to gain ascendancy against the forces of parochialism:

> Precisely because it had to contend against provincial conservatives in both parties, the foreign policy establishment has needed all the more urgently to develop an elan of its own, to make itself indispensable at the middle and upper levels of the administrative hierarchy, and thus to achieve immunity from the shifts of partisan politics.[16]

ELITE WORLD VIEW

The national security elite's view of the world was shaped by the experiences surrounding our entry into World War I, the rejection of the Wilsonian vision of collective security, the retreat to normalcy, the Nye committee investigations, the long isolationist slumber and the neutrality experiment of the 1930s, the reluctance of many Americans to recognize the Hitler menace, and the painful struggle to gain public support for aid to Britain and France in 1939–40. Out of this set of experiences was formed "the war class," as Lasch labels this elite, a small group of upperclass gentlemen, Wilsonians all, who were principally devoted to making the United States the "responsible" leader of a "sound" world order based upon "freedom." As the end of the Second World War approached, a few leading members of the elite found themselves uniquely situated in positions to assist in making American technological-military power the dominant force in world politics. This time there must be no retreat to isolationism, no rejection of United States responsibility. The power was at hand in unprecedented form, nuclear power, to shape the order of the world. (Acheson was to write later about having been "present at the creation.") Leaders of the elite willingly took this responsibility upon themselves. At times the deeper psychic urge seemed to be to make over the entire world in the American image—"the arrogance of power." Thus, Henry L. Stimson entertained a fleeting hope that somehow the United States should find a way to convince Stalin that his 1936 Soviet Constitution meant what it said about "freedom," or, more accurately, that it meant what Stimson thought it meant.

The power or ruling elite concept assumes the presence of a small group in control of decision-making with a common interest in the maintenance of capitalism. The national security elite that Stimson first brought together—and that Acheson later led with distinction during the period when containment became the established doctrine—had an interest in the maintenance of the *total* system, of which the American version of capitalism is one part. The Stimson-Acheson elite was comprised of men who saw themselves as the sophisticated, cosmopolitan spokesmen for the established order, not as the defenders of capitalism, per se. And they were actively involved in promoting a world role for this total American system. The policy of intervention against revolutionary change around the globe was not based solely on the need for markets and raw materials. Lasch and Alperovitz are closer to reality in noting that what may have begun as "dollar diplomacy" in an earlier period "soon achieved the status of a 'moral mission' to stamp out political heresy. In other words, it assumed the form of a messianic ideology that acquired a force and persuasiveness of its own, quite independent of the political and economic interests underlying it." [17] The analysis in this book tends to support Hannah Arendt's view that elite behavior during the Cold War does not reveal "a grand imperialist strategy" or a "will to world conquest" in the sense that a neo-Marxist interpretation might suggest. In an age of frightful new weaponry, facing tides of social upheaval that they did not understand and an enigmatic, perverse, suspicious adversary, these elite leaders wished to see established a world order based upon their principles (about which they were often exceedingly vague). They soon came to believe that only a preponderance of United States military power would make this kind of world order tenable. Walter Lafeber has shown how this obsession with armed strength has tended to divert attention from the *purposes* and *objectives* of American policy: "The question was not whether the United States had greater power or whether American officials were willing to apply enough power in various situations. The crux of the problem was the ends for which that power could most profitably be used." [18]

There was an ominous implication in the elite's failure to examine the objectives of containment. Lafeber continues: "This dominance of power was leading American leaders and public opinion to believe in a military solution for the primary, unsolvable problems." [19]

CONTAINMENT AS JUSTIFYING IDEOLOGY

The bulk of the evidence concerning the official behavior of leading members of the Cold War elite indicates that their driving motivation was political, even when they succumbed to the allure of military technology. In the process, elite leaders were soon entangled in the thicket of their own ideological presumption. Containment was not merely an official doctrine useful in preparing NSC position papers and in making annual budgetary allocations to the armed forces, it also rapidly took on the characteristics of a "justifying" ideology.[20] A justifying ideology tends to make optimistic assumptions about its own efficacy while ignoring empirical data that does not support these assumptions. In any event, we know that the containment doctrine was formulated with an eye to the "educational" effect it might have on the general public as well as to gain the support of Congressional oligarchs whose parochial bases made them rather suspect in the eyes of the cosmopolitan elite. In writing about NSC–68 in his memoirs, Acheson was frank to say that his purpose was to bludgeon the mass mind of top government so that the President would make the decision the elite desired and so that the decision could be carried out. The decision Acheson sought, of course, was a massive increase in American military power. The object in view was Europe, and Germany was the key, although Korea provided the opportunity.[21] NSC–68 exaggerated the Soviet military threat. Once the exaggeration was built into the inexorable process of the military bureaucracies, once it was taken over as part of "standard operating procedure," the nation was headed for the kind of tragic involvement that finally occurred in Indochina, of all places. As Lasch observed, the *logic* of containment demanded in the long run "an increasing commitment of American money, military advice, air power, and, finally, troops to anti-Communist regimes which could not survive without them." [22]

As containment persisted, unchallenged within the inner circle, it was probably inevitable that corollary doctrines would develop; the domino theory as applied in Southeast Asia and the doctrine of flexible response, which called for an American military capacity to carry on the role of counterinsurgent in the Third World, are prime examples. The Pentagon Papers indicate that there were few men within the inner circle during the period of escalation who accepted the domino theory in any literal sense, and yet United States policy was conducted *as if* the domino theory were valid. Whatever the degree of private skepticism may have been, leading civilian militants continued using the domino theory, as Miss Arendt has noted, "not merely for public statements, but as part of their own premises as well." [23] This is another aspect of the interrelationships between deception and self-deception. An uncritical acceptance of containment's premises, once the doctrine took on the garb of justifying ideology, subtly affected elite behavior:

> This ideology was at the root of all "theories" in Washington since the end of World War II. I have mentioned the extent to which sheer ignorance of all pertinent facts and deliberate neglect of postwar developments became the hallmark of established doctrine within the establishment. They needed no facts, no information; they had a "theory," and all data that did not fit were denied or ignored.[24]

The new ideology embodied a more doctrinaire anti-Communism than that usually reflected in the old-fashioned American hostility toward Marxist ideas. (An extreme form of the new anti-

Communism appears to have functioned as an obsessive force in the final, tragic months of James Forrestal's life.[25]) There was a kind of anti-Communist reflex at work in the official activities of the national security policy elite.

MANIPULATING OPINION

Pluralists contend that elite leaders have been effective in influencing postwar national security policy because they were simply *reflecting* a broader consensus that was also anti-Communist, and yet Barnet has shown in chilling detail how energetically and persistently civilian militants were engaged in *manipulating* public opinion to an acceptance of the policy consensus that had previously been arrived at within elite circles.[26] Thus, as we have seen, the X article, originally prepared very much as an insider's document, was shared by Secretary Forrestal with Arthur Krock of the *Times,* a friend and influential moulder of opinion. After Kennan had had an opportunity to explain his thesis at a meeting of the Council on Foreign Relations, the article found its way to speedy publication in *Foreign Affairs,* where it was certain to gain the attention of the attentive public. When it was deemed important in elite circles that the public have the "facts" about United States military "weakness," the Gaither report, highly secret and prepared only for Presidential eyes, was systematically leaked to the press against the President's wishes. At other crucial moments, facts that might have impeded elite activity were conveniently hidden from public view or were lied about publicly, as was so often the case in Vietnam decision-making. Crises were exaggerated. Stalin was not about to take over Greece in 1947. At least one "crisis" was stage-managed in order to elicit the appropriate public and Congressional response, as the Tonkin Gulf episode attests. In time scenario-writing was to become a specialized Washington art form.

There appears to be a high degree of sensitivity in elite circles, at least during crucial moments, to the possibility that the public mood may shift away from the normal uncritical acceptance of established dogma. Elite behavior appears to have been profoundly affected by the widespread display of public disenchantment following the Tet offensive in 1968. Early in the Cold War, Gabriel Almond found the American foreign policy mood "permissive," with the general public predisposed to follow the lead of a unified and resolute elite; elite nervousness may stem from deeper psychic insecurities, as presumably was the case with Secretary Forrestal. In any event, the relationships between elites and non-elites in policy-making are far from being established in the scholarly literature. As Barnet observes: "Nowhere is the mysterious interaction between leaders and led more elusive than in the area of foreign policy." [27]

THE NEED-NOT-TO-KNOW

In the case of Vietnam it was thought necessary to feed the gullible public a steady diet of optimistic statements about the course of the war. A system of reporting—body counts, et al —was superimposed from the Secretary of Defense upon the field; the field fed back an unending stream of "optimistic facts" that were then computerized and aggregated for public consumption. It is a nice question who was fooled more profoundly, the general public or Secretary McNamara, whose whole managerial system depended upon quantifiable facts.[28] Apparently many months went by while McNamara remained supremely confident that his system was reporting "reality." Political analysis, enriched by work in the other social sciences, is slowly beginning to understand the selective ways in which various political actors tend to *perceive* reality. "Facts" are observed and recognized when they fit general operating "theories": facts that do not "fit" are often ignored. This is related to the "need-not-to-know" syndrome. Daniel Ellsberg, who served as a Cold War technocrat with direct experience in Vietnam and as John McNaughton's special assistant, has subsequently revealed that he remained unfamiliar with the earlier history of the French struggle against Ho Chi Minh until 1969. There is little reason to suppose that Ellsberg differed from his superiors in this respect.

The "need-not-to-know" occasionally included appalling ignorance of basic matters when specialized information should have been readily available. Michael Forrestal, who served as a member of the White House national security staff and who enjoyed a warm personal relationship with the Kennedys, has admitted that in 1963—thirteen years after containment was extended to Indochina—he experienced great difficulty in finding anyone within the bureaucracy with knowledge of the Buddhists in Indochina. Speaking of the outrages perpetrated against the Buddhists by the Diem regime in the summer of 1963, Forrestal later recalled:

> This is hard to believe in hindsight, but my strong recollection is they came as a complete surprise. In fact, I recall that it was very difficult to find anyone in our government who knew anything about Buddhism in South Vietnam.[29]

The human behavior remains puzzling until one recognizes, along with Hannah Arendt, that those responsible for the conduct of our policy in Southeast Asia felt no special urge to understand the history and culture of the country being manipulated because Vietnam was officially perceived *as an object* within the containment pattern.

There obviously are psychological aspects of the Vietnam experience that reach beyond the limits of this study. "Selective inattention," "perceptual defense," or just "not paying attention" are ways of labeling the behavior of policy-makers who disregard inconvenient facts.[30]

McNamara, the compulsive seeker and compiler of facts, failed to examine the nature of the Asian society we were "helping." Kissinger, in an essay written *before* the McNamara era offers a psychological insight that appears to fit the special con tours of the McNamara experience:

> The more intense the effort to substitute administration for conception, the greater is the inner insecurity of the participants. The more they seek "objectivity," the more diffuse their efforts become. The insecurity of many of our policymakers sometimes leads to almost compulsive traits. Because of the lack of criteria on which to base judgements, work almost becomes an end in itself.[31]

INCREMENTALISM

Conventional political analysis, including aspects of my own earlier work, tends to focus on the incremental nature of public policy-making in the American polity. There is no doubt that a portion of the process moves bit-by-bit, committee-by-committee, budget-by-budget, and the strain toward agreement is felt by the bargainers. Incrementalism is useful in describing the way in which the process moves as seen, for example, within the framework of a "bureaucratic politics" model. Bureaucratic politics exists—of this we may be sure—and there is enough there to keep a generation of empiricists busily engaged. Unfortunately, incrementalism may reveal little about the purposes and objectives toward which the process moves—or about the purposes and objectives whose accomplishment the process impedes and obstructs. A preoccupation with incrementalism, as previously noted, may preclude asking *whose interests* are being served, and the bureaucratic politics model may evade the issue of power and responsibility. In any event, political analysis has remained comfortable with the strain for agreement that helped lock the nation into containment for a quarter-century while holding off fundamental social reform. Mills would suggest that incrementalism describes the middle level of politics, where bureaucratic politics flourishes. But the overreliance on military power that has characterized the response to the Sino-Soviet presence and the counterrevolutionary posture the United States has adopted in the face of the incessant pressures for social change in the Third World did not originate in the middle levels of technocratic society.

This assessment of elite responsibility would not be complete unless it were to ask how seriously leading figures took the general operating theory that they had inherited from an earlier phase in the Cold War, based as it was on the comprehensive anti-Communist ideology. Although containment was not effectively challenged, apparently there were relatively few Cold War ideologues within the inner circle during the Kennedy–Johnson era. Rusk, Rostow, and Taylor seem to qualify; but the civilian militants, as a group, were sufficiently sophisticated to reject global containment, at least in its vulgar bureaucratized

version. And yet no challenge to containment was presented.
George Ball stood almost alone in questioning the political premises undergirding our involvement in Vietnam. Honorable men,
including establishment intellectuals, offered no moral doubts
about a national course of action that violated elemental stand-
ards of human decency. As the Vietnam ship slowly sank, leading
members of the inner circle left, one by one, to accept honored
positions within the established order, with the World Bank, the
Ford Foundation, Harvard, Princeton, and MIT offering the
choicest locations. By way of contrast, the ideologically committed who stayed on board were fortunate to find havens of
refuge in Georgia and Texas. It is difficult to imagine McGeorge
or William Bundy being quite so deeply affected by the Munich
syndrome as their father's generation was. The unwillingness
of intelligent and sophisticated members of a privileged elite
to question official, bureaucratic dogma frozen in its own vacuity
would be troublesome enough, but what is to be said when elite
leaders continue *to act* as if they were ideologues? In a huge
technocratic society that appears to be orchestrated to an established doctrine, who is to challenge the doctrine? [30] The gigantic
bureaucratic structures of the postindustrial era will not be
wished away, nor are they likely to be overthrown by itinerant
bands of basket-weavers cheered on by professors of constitutional law. But is it unreasonable to expect that the leading
members of one of the world's most privileged elites might refrain
from acting as if the force of bureaucratic momentum had behind it some divine imperative?

BIPARTISANSHIP: FORECLOSING THE ALTERNATIVES

The Cold War experience highlights the difficulty this nation
faces in developing policy alternatives on the most vital issues.
The national security elite foreclosed alternatives rather than
opening them. It is a tragic mistake to remove national security
issues from politics, especially in a political system as sluggish
as ours. The function of bipartisanship is to remove the most
important issues, both foreign and domestic, from meaningful
public debate. Established doctrine should be continuously re-

viewed, questioned, and criticized by groups enjoying prestige and the capacity to change the policy climate. An establishment needs a counterestablishment; this is the minimum precondition of pluralism-in-miniature. No influential elite should be drawn from such narrow and limited sources as the Cold War elite was. A national security elite drawn from the upper class, with little or no interest in domestic reform, cut off from the existential experiences of electoral politics, is not likely to show a high degree of sensitivity to the forces of social change in the rest of the world. The Cold War elite featured a group of men who prospered economically during a period when their own generation was suffering the traumas associated with the Great Depression. Gaddis Smith is one of the few to comment even obliquely on this aspect:

> Acheson might on occasion make lugubrious comparisons between present and past, but the present served him well. His life to date had been full and placid, with no touch of tragedy. . . . There was the house in Georgetown and the farm in Sandy Spring, Maryland, twenty miles north of Washington. . . . Talented and witty friends were at hand. There had been time to read—mostly English literature and modern history—and to travel to Europe. *The depression had scarred and scared the nation but had not threatened the security of Acheson and the security of his family.* The year 1939 was good from a personal point of view. [Italics mine.] [33]

Acheson, whose life in the 1930s was "full and placid," headed an elite preoccupied with United States responsibilities abroad. Fearful of the general public's tendency to withdraw from this role, the elite sponsored "bipartisanship" to persuade the country that foreign affairs should be kept out of politics; it thus insured that the elite's policies would prevail, at least in the area of national security. But there is another side to bipartisanship that the Cold War elite accepted with apparent equanimity. The bipartisan coalition that has been in effective control of the Congress most of the time since 1938 has no difficulty in supporting a "tradition" that keeps vital issues of foreign and defense policy from receiving the critique they should have in the legislative arena. The same bipartisan coalition—this is the other side of power—opposes domestic reform programs, including any real reform of the Congress that might make it possible for the national legislature to function as a check on the new militarism.

The problem is political in the deepest, most profound sense. All Presidents throughout the Cold War have been able to win Congressional support for military spending to support global containment. The Congressional committees responsible for national security policy are part of the new militarism. The Appropriations committee and the Armed Services committee are not prepared to undertake a searching reappraisal of that which they underwrite. These committees are presided over by senior men wholly committed to the new militarism. Even death apparently brings no change as Richard Russell is succeeded by John Stennis and Mendel Rivers by F. Edward Hebert. The literature of political science notes the presence of two Presidencies, one for foreign affairs, the other for domestic affairs.[34] A President wholly committed to containment and the new militarism may look forward with confidence to the full support of the bipartisan Congressional coalition composed of Southern Democrats and most of the Republicans. A President intent upon a program of domestic reform, even mild reform, invites the stubborn resistance of the same coalition. Whose interests are served by this kind of bipartisanship?[35]

REEXAMINING AMERICAN SOCIETY

Richard Barnet has written:

The disastrous adventure in Indochina has compelled the most searching reexamination of America's role in the world since the eve of World War II. Henry Stimson's recruits and their disciples, relatives and business associates, men schooled in the war against Hitler who promoted the extravagant imperial creed of global responsibility and perfected the techniques of expansionism, are leaving the stage at the very moment the foreign policy consensus they labored so long to create is cracking. The remarkably consistent policies they pursued for a generation no longer seem to most Americans quite so noble or inevitable as at the height of the Cold War.[36]

Perhaps so, although it is far from clear that the searching reexamination may be expected to alter "the extravagant imperial creed" in the absence of fundamental reform within the American society. If one accepts Barnet's thesis that war is the inevitable by-product of a set of United States social and economic institutions, something more than minimal change in the system would seem to be a prerequisite to effect the change in policies Barnet has in mind. How does a society that has been organized for war reorganize itself away from war? How is the much-needed politicization of foreign policy issues, which Barnet calls for, to be achieved in a political process that tends to blur *any* major issue? Although it is true that the Cold War policy elite is leaving the stage as the policy consensus shows signs of cracking, it is not evident who is prepared to offer fresh alternatives or what these alternatives are.

The reordering and rearranging of priorities and decisions in our technocratic society proves to be extraordinarily difficult. Lasch warns that "the policy of interventionism has acquired a momentum of its own, not only ideological but institutional as well." [37] There appears to be no sure prescription for resisting the momentum of events (and bureaucratic momentum) so as to break out of the "locked-in" quality of men and institutions, as noted by Alperovitz. [38] Although the establishment orchestration model assumes a latent power among non-elites to alter the direction of public policy, this power depends very much on special circumstances and is likely to be checked by elite forces once modest change has been effected. Dolbeare and Edelman in constructing their model assume "incomplete domination of government" by elites, as well as a need for its legitimating power; this, they believe, "opens an aperture for non-elite penetration." As they see it, non-elite segments of society "may succeed in short-circuiting accepted practices or even in introducing new priorities." Still the capacity of non-elites to alter conditions is limited. Dolbeare and Edelman warn that non-elite penetration requires "a special convergence of people, events and conditions, and even then is likely to proceed only to modest lengths before enough popular demands are satisfied to reduce the situation to a manageable level again." [39]

The precise manner in which a powerful and prestigious elite reacts in time of supreme crisis when its own position within the system may be threatened is not easily ascertained empirically.

When high-level technocrats, such as John McNaughton, grew to fear the possibility that "the Establishment is out of its mind," one finds it reasonable to assume that elite leaders felt *some* effect. McNaughton was intimately associated within the inner circle with McNamara, the Bundy brothers, and others having close ties to the foreign policy establishment. Although one cannot be sure what factors influenced Acheson and a majority of the so-called Wise Men in speaking as they did in their meeting with President Johnson late in March 1968, the establishment orchestration model offers a plausible hypothesis:

> The establishment recognizes that it must at least appear to satisfy changing demands among the major segments of the population, and may even be led to new policies by such changes. But changes in values and ideology require long periods of education, among the principal devices for which is the behavior of leading establishment figures themselves.[40]

POLITICAL STALEMATE

The public silence of men such as McGeorge Bundy and Robert McNamara on the obvious questions raised by the Vietnam tragedy, the inability of men such as Rostow and Taylor to doubt their own certitudes, the ease with which honorific positions in the best universities, foundations, and the higher corporate structures opened up to the civilian militants, make it improbable that the elite we have met in the course of this study will lead the way in reforming American society.[41] The searching reappraisal that Barnet, Alperovitz, and others seek also encounters the reality of political stalemate at the middle level of politics. The public priorities prevailing in the United States have been dictated by our Cold War stance.

In the meantime, we live with the reality that the American political system simply does not deal adequately with that which the Cold War reflects: the continuing United States involvement in world affairs as a major power and a massive, permanent military establishment.

An exchange between Representative George Mahon, Democrat of Lubbock, Texas, who served as chairman of the powerful House Appropriations committee, and Sargent Shriver, who was heading up the so-called "war on poverty" illustrates how the balance of priorities stood in the midst of Vietnam escalation. Representative Mahon, it should be noted, had served for years as chairman of the Appropriations subcommittee, which handles the annual military spending budget. The Mahon-Shriver exchange, excerpted below, took place in October 1966. The Johnson administration earlier in the same year had cut Shriver's budget request virtually in half, and he was fighting in October to retain even that sharply reduced figure:

> Mr. Mahon: . . . you and I know that there is no magic in figures, there is no magic in the budget as far as that is concerned. . . . But you made reference in your statement to this being a budget for troubled times. And of course there are certain priorities which have to be taken into consideration. . . .
>
> Mr. Shriver: . . . It is a little bit like the priority if you are fighting a war. In the war, you do send, as the President frequently says to General Westmoreland, what he needs to win the war. It is not that he could not do a good job with half the number of bullets. We will do what we can with half the bullets. But this is not, on the other hand, to say that we can do what needs to be done in this war with half the ammunition.
>
> Mr. Mahon: . . . Yes, but you do not think you can do it with $1,750 million. You think you need $3.2 billion. So you do not have all you originally asked for—you cannot do the whole war. You are not going to have but half the bullets according to your earlier estimate, here.
>
> *The question is, which war is more important at this particular time? We have had poverty always. We will always have it.* [Italics mine.] [42]

The undeclared war in Vietnam held a far higher priority than the attack on poverty at home. There is no evidence that any consideration was given within the inner circle to the domestic implications when the decisions to Americanize the Vietnam war were taken. Indeed, Eidenberg has established that the decisions were made *without regard to cost.*[43] Chairman Mahon' committee experienced no difficulty in holding the OEO budget figure in 1966 to $1.6 billion at a time when military spending approached $75 billion annually, with Vietnam soon to require $25 to $30 billion each year. In the Johnson years alone, Representative Mahon presided over a process that fed $100 billion into the Vietnam quagmire while holding total Economic Opportunity Act expenditures to less than $10 billion. The latter figure would have funded our Vietnam adventure at its peak for four or five months.[44]

The Congress does not lack inherent power to exert some control over the foreign policy of the Presidency and the new militarism, if there were an effective desire within the Congress to do so. Mahon's committee does not lack the power to control executive action. Schlesinger, noting that the Congress has done little to correct the situation, observes:

> Its problem has been less lack of power than lack of will to use the powers it has—the power of appropriation, the power to regulate the size of the armed forces, the power through joint resolution to shape foreign policy, the power to inform, investigate and censure.[45]

Congress lacks the will to reform itself, so as to carry out its constitutional responsibilities, because it is effectively controlled by a senior bipartisan coalition committed to the new militarism and opposed to social reform at home. Once again, the problem is political in the most profound sense, and the responsibility of the Cold War elite in sponsoring "bipartisanship" as a means of depoliticizing issues that go to the very vitals of American society is a large one. The failure of the nation to find the way to reorder its priorities, to engage in fundamental social reform, and to perform a role in the world worthy of its own inherited values is a failure of intellectual and moral leadership, political action, and national will—three areas in which elite leadership bears prime responsibility.

CONCLUSION

The Cold War national security policy elite did not just "happen." Its members were drawn from the upper levels of the established order, the leading financial houses, the prestigious law firms of New York and Washington, the major corporations, and the best universities. The business-financial-legal circles possess a large reservoir of talent as well as enormous material resources, and their interests have predominated in American society throughout the twentieth century.[46] As we have seen, the values and attitudes of this policy elite have shaped the parameters of our national security policy during the past thirty years.

The elite mind-set (and it was set) with its obsessive fear of Communist expansion, its voracious hunger for foreign markets (but not until recently in the so-called Communist world), its limited perceptions of the social revolution in the Third World (combined with a blindness or indifference to social pathologies at home), and its predisposition to rely upon military technology in shaping a global order conceived in terms of lessons derived from experience with Hitler's aggression, established the framework of United States strategic thinking during the formative stages of the Cold War. The coherence (based upon social and class ties) and the persistence of the elite and the success achieved in closing off policy alternatives by depoliticizing the substance of foreign policy meant that the official strategic doctrine of the 1940s and 1950s, grounded as it was in an exaggerated view of the Soviet "menace," soon became the rigid conceptual strait jacket of the 1960s. In time, leading members of the elite seemed incapable of accepting the invalidity of globalized containment once the world had been transformed beyond the simplistic bipolarity of the Truman-Acheson era. Even if one were to accept the hypothesis of an inherent capitalist expansionist drive at work in our foreign policy, there is no obvious reason to assume that the national security elite would have found the interests of the "capitalist system" well served by the course that led to Vietnam. Perhaps we shall understand better the higher irrationality of recent American experience in the Cold War when we see more clearly how the structures of the contemporary econopolity are related to the enduring reality of human arrogance and perversity.

Chapter Eleven Notes

1. Daniel Ellsberg, *Papers on the War* (New York: Simon and Schuster, 1972), p. 12.

2. Richard J. Barnet, *Roots of War* (New York: Atheneum, 1972), p. 303.

3. Ronald Steel, "Cooling It," *New York Review of Books*, October 18, 1972, pp. 43–46.

4. Herbert Feis, the quasi-official American historian of the Cold War, continued to the end to deny this fundamental point. See his *From Trust to Terror, The Onset of the Cold War, 1945–1950* (New York: W. W. Norton, 1970). Feis, a trained economist whose first book, *The Settlement of Wage Disputes*, was published in 1921, served as Economic Advisor to Secretary of State Henry Stimson in the early 1930s, remaining in the State Department in various capacities until 1943. Feis next served as special consultant to Secretary of War Stimson from 1944 to 1947. He was a member of the State Department's policy planning staff during 1950–51. In a very real sense, the national security elite had its own historian.

5. Dean Acheson, *Present at the Creation* (New York: W. W. Norton, 1969), pp. 374–75.

6. See William R. Caspary, "United States Public Opinion During the Onset of the Cold War," Peace Research Society, Papers IX, Cambridge Conference, 1968, pp. 25–46. Barnet, *Roots of War*, chapter 9, has a novel interpretation of the relationship between isolationism and interventionism. Isolationist thought in the 1930s contained a distinctly nationalist flavor. See my "Congressional Isolationists and the Roosevelt Foreign Policy," *World Politics*, Vol. 3, No. 3 (April 1951), 299–316.

7. John Lewis Gaddis, *The United States and the Origins of the Cold War* (New York: Columbia University Press, 1972), pp. 317–18, 350–51.

8. Ibid., p. 352.

9. Christopher Lasch, "The Making of the War Class," *The Columbia Forum*, Winter 1971, p. 2.

10. Irving L. Janis, "Groupthink," *Psychology Today*, Vol. 5, No. 6 (November 1971), 43–46, 74–76. For a more detailed analysis applied to several major decisions, including Vietnam escalation in the Johnson years, see Professor Janis's *Victims of Groupthink* (Boston: Houghton Mifflin, 1972).

11. George Kennan, *Memoirs, 1950–1963* (Boston: Little, Brown–Atlantic Press, 1972), p. 92.

12. See Charles E. Bohlen, *The Transformation of American Foreign Policy* (New York: W. W. Norton, 1970). This brief survey of American policy toward the Soviet Union written by Kennan's former colleague shows clearly how official thinking has been limited throughout the Cold War by the basic assumption that the Soviet Union can only be dealt with effectively by ever increasing our military power.

13. Barnet, *Roots of War*, pp. 48–49.

14. Henry A. Kissinger, *The Necessity for Choice* (New York: Harper, 1960), p. 341.

15. Ibid., p. 347.

16. Lasch, "The Making of the War Class," p. 4. A recent essay by Godfrey Hodgson, "The Establishment," *Foreign Policy*, No. 10 (Spring 1973), pp. 3–40 tends to confirm the thesis of this book.

17. Christopher Lasch, Introduction to *Cold War Essays*, by Gar Alperovitz (New York: Doubleday-Anchor, 1970), p. 15.

    It should be noted that revisionist historians, most notably William Appleman Williams and Gabriel Kolko, argue that the Cold War, defined in this book in relation to nuclear weapons and the politico-military struggles following the close of World War II, must be seen in the larger context of a process of American intervention dating back, at least, to Wilson. The deeper roots of American interventionism remain largely unexplored and seem likely to prove to be more complex than the revisionists have yet revealed. The isolationism of the interwar years offers an obvious problem to those who would tie the Cold War directly to the Wilsonian era.

18. Walter Lafeber, *America, Russia and the Cold War* (New York: John Wiley and Sons, 1967), pp. 258–59.

19. Ibid., p. 259.

20. See William Connolly, ed., *The Bias of Pluralism* (New York: Atherton, 1969), examines pluralism as justifying ideology, p. 33.

21. Smith, *Dean Acheson*, pp. 315–16. Cf. Barnet, *Roots of War*, pp. 274–75.

22. Lasch, "The Making of the War Class," p. 6.

23. Hannah Arendt, *Crises of the Republic* (New York: Harcourt Brace Jovanovich), pp. 17–18.

24. Ibid., p. 39.

25. See Arnold A. Rogow, *James Forrestal, A Study of Personality, Politics and Policy* (New York: Macmillan, 1963).

26. See especially chapter 10, Barnet, *Roots of War*.

27. Barnet, *Roots of War*, p. 242.

28. David Halberstam, "The Programming of Robert McNamara," *Harper's Magazine,* February 1971, p. 60.

29. NBC News White Paper, "Vietnam Hindsight," August 25, 1972, produced and written by Fred Freed, Act V, p. 5 of the script.

30. See Ralph K. White, "Selective Inattention," *Psychology Today,* Vol. 5, No. 6 (November 1971), 47–50, 78–84.

31. Kissinger, *Necessity for Choice,* p. 345.

32. In examining the ideological roots of "the pragmatic, experiential character of American politics," Everett Ladd, Jr., concludes: "Basic ends have rarely been questioned. Who was there to question them?" See Everett Carll Ladd, Jr., "Ideology and Belief Systems in the United States" mimeographed essay, 1973.

33. Gaddis Smith, *Dean Acheson* (N.Y.: Cooper Square, 1972), p. 12.

34. See Aaron Wildavsky, "The Two Presidencies," *Trans-Action,* Dec. 1966.

35. See John C. Donovan, *The Policy Makers* (N.Y.: Pegasus, 1970).

36. Barnet, *Roots of War,* p. 333.

37. Lasch, Introduction to *Cold War Essays,* p. 20.

38. Alperovitz, *Cold War Essays,* p. 2.

39. Kenneth M. Dolbeare and Murray J. Edelman, *American Politics: Policies, Power and Change,* 2nd ed. (Lexington, Mass.: D. C. Heath, 1974), p. 476.

40. Ibid.

41. The rigidity of Rostow's stance as Cold War ideologue is revealed in his own *The Diffusion of Power* (New York: Macmillan, 1972) and is further illuminated by David Halberstam in *The Best and the Brightest* (New York: Random House, 1972). Halberstam's portraits of Rusk and Taylor confirm the interpretations offered in our analysis, as do his profiles of Bundy and McNamara, which originally appeared in *Harper's Magazine.*

42. Hearings, Subcommittee of the Committee on Appropriations, Supplemental Appropriation Bill, 1967, House of Representatives, 89th Congress, 2nd Session, p. 267.

43. Eugene Eidenberg, "The Presidency," in *American Political Institutions and Public Policy,* ed. Allan P. Sindler (Boston: Little, Brown, 1969).

44. For a further discussion see my *The Politics of Poverty.*

45. A. M. Schlesinger, Jr., "Congress and the Making of American Foreign Policy," *Foreign Affairs,* Vol. 51, No. 1 (Oct. 1972), 104.

46. See Gabriel Kolko, *The Triumph of Conservatism* (New York: Free Press, 1963), an interpretation that sees business control over politics as the significant phenomenon of the Progressive era.

INDEX

Containment policy (*Cont.*)
  as justifying ideology, 272–74
  and policy elite, 268–70
  for Vietnam, 107–27
Cooper, Chester, 107, 108
Corson, John J., 132
Council on Foreign Relations (CFR), 11, 19, 126
Cuban missile crisis, 15, 50
Cutler, Robert, 131

Dahl, Robert, 17–18, 265
Dean, Arthur H., 248
Decision-making, theory of incremental, 227–28
Diem, 180, 185–86, 192, 197
Dien Bien Phu, 121
Dillon, Douglas, 248
Dolbeare, Kenneth, 22–25, 281
Domhoff, G. William, 11, 126, 132, 270
Domino theory, 115, 118–20, 224–26, 227, 273
Douglas, William O., 180
Du!les, Alan, 50
Dulles, John Foster, 50, 120–21, 126, 138, 143, 146
DuPuy, William, 249

Edelman, Murray, 22–25, 281
Eden, Anthony, 113
Eidenberg, Eugene, 205–206, 207–208, 209, 211, 227, 283
Eisenhower, Dwight D.,
  and fixed defense expenditures, 136–38, 141, 143, 156–57
  and Gaither report, 132, 134, 141–43
  and global containment policy, 124
Ellsberg, Daniel, 166–69, 176, 182–83, 259, 275
Enthoven, Alain C., 152–53, 155–56, 157, 158, 164–67

Essence of Security, The (McNamara), 172
Establishment orchestration model of foreign policy, 22–25
ExCOM: *see* National Security Council, Executive Committee of

FCDA: *see* Federal Civilian Defense Administration
Federal Civilian Defense Administration (FCDA), 131
Feis, Herbert, 32, 35
Flexible response, doctrine of, 266, 273
Foreign Affairs, 4–5, 65, 68, 159, 274
Forrestal, James, 38–39, 60, 67, 76
Forrestal, Michael, 192, 233, 276
Fortas, Abe, 248, 249, 252
Foster, William C., 50, 132, 133, 139–40, 144, 177
Fowler, Henry, 247
France
  colonial control of Indochina by, 107, 110
  U.S. military aid to, 113, 116
Fulbright, J. William, 203

Gaddis, John Lewis, 264–65
Gaither, H. Rowan, 131–32
Gaither report, 27, 274
  as civil defense study, 130, 135
  and global containment, 154, 158
  and Kennedy administration, 175
  preparation of, 130–47
  resemblance of, to NSC–68, 131, 137, 146
  secrecy of, 141–43
  and Soviet military power, 131, 134–36, 138
Galbraith, John K., 49–50, 270
Gelb, Leslie H., 107, 168, 176